More Toddlers Together

More Toddlers Together

The Complete Planning Guide for a Toddler Curriculum, Volume II

by Cynthia Catlin

Illustrations by Joan Waites

gryphon house

Beltsville, Maryland

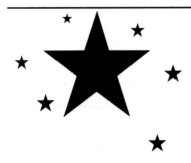

In celebration of

beginnings and endings

with living and learning in between,

from Aaron Ray

to Marcus Kent

Copyright © 1996 Cynthia Catlin

Published by Gryphon House, Inc.
10726 Tucker Street, Beltsville, MD 20705

World Wide Web: http://www.ghbooks.com

Printed in the United States of America.

Cover Design: Lightbourne Images
Text Illustrations: Joan Waites

Library of Congress Cataloging-in-Publication Data

Catlin, Cynthia. 1962-
    More toddlers together : the complete planning guide for a toddler
curriculum, volume II / by Cynthia Catlin ; illustrations by Joan Waites.
      p. cm.
    Continues the author's Toddlers together.
    Includes bibliographical references and index.
    ISBN 0-87659-179-9 (pbk.)
    1. Education, Preschool--Activity programs. 2. Education,
Preschool--Curricula. I. Catlin, Cynthia. 1962- Toddlers together.
II. Title.
LB1140.35.C74C378 1996
372.21--dc20   96-26582
                                                         CIP

Table of Contents

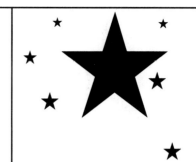

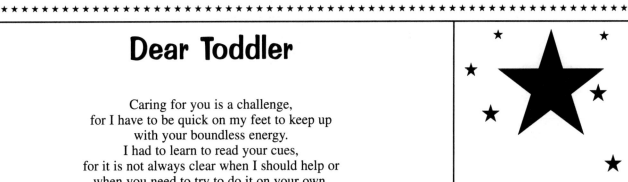

Dear Toddler

Caring for you is a challenge,
for I have to be quick on my feet to keep up
with your boundless energy.
I had to learn to read your cues,
for it is not always clear when I should help or
when you need to try to do it on your own.

I have to be readily available always,
to snuggle,
sometimes just to nod
and other times to be a secure base,
from which you leave to explore
but to come back to
when you need.

Together, we are finding that sensitive balance and
understanding of each other.

Caring for you is rewarding,
a worthwhile challenge,
filled with growth and development of you,
and of me as I, too, uncovered,
through your discoveries,
the simple joys and the excitement
of the newness of it all
that I had forgotten
so long ago.

Together, we shared our excitement about the magical
wonder of life.

Caring for you is my gift to you,
for I understand
you will not remember much about me,
what we did together,
what we explored together,
what we learned together,
but from me
I pray you will get
a love of learning and discovering
a sense of trust and worthiness,
that you will take with you
into your future
learning experiences and relationships.

Together, dear toddler, we have laid the foundation for a
lifetime.

Your teacher

Introduction

When an activity works with toddlers, they ask for more. They want to do it again, and again and again. Children under three can have long attention spans, if they are doing something that interests them. Like toddlers, teachers also ask for more when the ideas work with children. Therefore, it seemed only natural to write *More Toddlers Together* after hearing from so many teachers that the activities and ideas in *Toddlers Together* captured the attention of this unique age and really worked.

More Toddlers Together would not have been possible without many individuals providing some behind-the-scenes support. Many thanks to Shirley and Marc for the foundations in language; Aaron and Alan for the inspiration for new ideas; Ron for picking up the missing pieces and files; Rose Ann for planting the seed for a toddler book when she said many years ago, "Someday you'll write a book;" and to Kathy Charner at Gryphon House for the wonderful opportunity to share my ideas with others. Many thanks to the families and the staff of University Presbyterian Children's Center. The children and teachers have "field-tested" the activities for over fourteen years and generated new variations. *More Toddlers Together* would not have been completed without the support of Mamie, Ellen, Angela, Blanche, Carrie, Cindy, Diane, Eunice, Janet, Jennifer, Norma, Oralia, Rose Ann, Rosie, Sonia, Terry and Thelma. You each in your own way have provided top-notch, dedicated care to the families and children, especially my two sons, while I re-created the toddler classroom through the computer screen. Thanks one and all.

Unfortunately, one and two year olds are often misunderstood in terms of their unique characteristics and needs. Environments and activities for toddlers have often been geared more towards infants or resemble a "push down" of a preschool class. Expecting toddlers to stay involved in activities not stimulating enough or, conversely, too advanced for their developmental abilities tends to lead to frustration for both the child and the caregiver. Toddlers have specific needs and characteristics unique to their stage of development that must be taken into consideration when planning for children under three.

The ideas in this book come from ten years of experience teaching toddlers, providing first hand knowledge of the characteristics of the age and a belief in the special nature of teachers who choose to teach

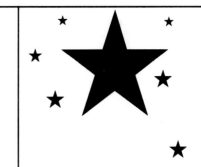

one and two year olds. The underlying premise emphasizes teacher involvement and what is appropriate for children from one to three years of age. Many of the activities have suggestions for modifying the activity for younger toddlers, for older toddlers or for differing developmental levels within a group. The references to ages are guidelines only, not rigid classifications. Each teacher knows the children, their capabilities and what will work with them better than any outsider.

The activities in *More Toddlers Together* are a combination of new themes and extensions of topics in *Toddlers Together*. The book continues with a seasonal approach along with some activities that work well at any time of the year. Use the seasons only as a guideline since planning must allow flexibility to follow the interests and needs of the toddlers. Strive to develop themes based on what is happening in the lives of the children. For example, if the circus comes to town during the summer and the toddlers are talking about it, focus on this topic then rather than in the fall when it is included in the book. Let the curriculum reflect the lives of the toddlers as much as possible rather than "inventing" topics for them.

Throughout the book the emphasis is on the child's choice of activities and on teachers interacting with the toddlers one-on-one and in small groups. This is based on the social-emotional needs of children under three. The most crucial elements of the toddler classroom are the teachers. They must be wholly available and responsive to the individual needs of the children. Ideal teaching situations for toddlers are caregiving routines of diapering, toileting, dressing, handwashing, mealtimes as these are the times that toddlers and their teachers can interact individually and learn together. Thus, many of the ideas in the book can be implemented while involved in necessary routines, such as changing a diaper or eating snack with the children.

Since there is so much growth from one to three years of age, many of the activities suggest how to adjust the idea from younger to older toddlers and among the various developmental levels within a group. Also included are suggestions for extending the activities to provide additional explorations of the original idea since toddlers enjoy doing "Again!" and benefit from the familiarity of repetition. Each idea includes sample words and phrases to emphasize when talking with toddlers due to the tremendous language growth during the toddler years.

Language development also involves written language so many of the activities suggest books and ways to let the toddlers scribble or make their "most important marks," referred to as MIMs in the book.

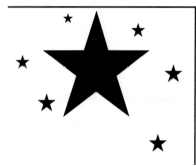

Reading to toddlers and providing opportunities to make MIMs are both crucial for future literacy development. Before children can learn to read they must be exposed to the world of books, even very young toddlers. Likewise, before children can learn to print, they must scribble and make the "babbles" of later writing efforts.

The activities in *Toddlers Together* and *More Toddlers Together* are not limited to the toddler classroom, offering many ideas that can be used by home care providers, special education teachers, play groups and with young children at home. Parenting tips related to the ideas have been added to many of the ideas to help parents understand and plan fun activities for their toddlers. Teachers can share these suggestions with parents through newsletters or simple "Home Connections" blurbs. Since parent communication is another crucial element of working with toddlers and their families, sample newsletters and daily reports have been included to help teachers develop effective communication.

Teaching hints are provided with many of the activities; these hints are for both teachers and parents. Guidelines for setting up the activity areas, suggestions for supplies, sample schedules and lesson plans have been included to assist teachers with the "nuts and bolts" of caring for toddlers. These are to be used as guidelines only since each toddler group and program has its own unique needs and characteristics, just like toddlers. The goal throughout *More Toddlers Together* is to provide teachers, caregivers and parents of toddlers ideas that will promote the optimal development of each child and that both child and adult will want to do "Again!"

For Teachers of Toddlers

Guidelines for the Toddler Environment

Setting up the Classroom

When setting up the environment for toddlers, consider the height of toddlers and what they see. Get down on your knees to determine whether pictures and mirrors are at toddlers' eye level and if toys are within their reach. Shelves and furniture should be at the following height appropriate for toddlers: child-size chairs at 8"; toilets at 11"; tables and play sinks at 16"-18". All toys and materials for children under three must pass the choke test (larger than approximately 2 1/2" with a diameter of 1 1/4," or not small enough to fit inside a 35mm film canister) to prevent a choking hazard. Make toys available for toddlers' independent use on shelves, the floor and tables rather than in toy boxes. It is vital to have duplicate or fairly similar toys so toddlers can be redirected to another object rather than sharing and taking turns.

Items not intended for toddlers must be out of reach and out of sight if possible, for toddlers will find a way to get to the items if they see something enticing. Thus, provisions must be made to store the teachers' and classroom supplies safely. In addition, each child must have space for storage of personal items, such as diapers, extra clothing, blankets, food and notes home.

A "Parent Board" with class information, reminders, sign in/sign out sheets, menus of snacks and meals, and other pertinent information is also helpful to have near the classroom entrance for parents to check regularly.

Toys for toddlers are usually brightly colored. Combine this with the busy nature of toddlers and the classroom environment can easily become overstimulating. Try to use wood tones and natural colors whenever possible. Also, provide for "blank space" in the toddler classroom. Leave some wall space empty to help toddlers develop their perceptual skills and reduce the clutter in the classroom. Arrange the room so it has a peaceful, soothing feeling to counteract toddlers' busy nature.

To help the environment be more of an extension of home, the classroom for toddlers should have a cozy quality, filled with softness, familiar objects and spaces for the toddlers to get away from all the activity. Introduce soft textures with pillows, stuffed animals, puppets, cushions, rugs, curtains and soft toys. Although these items are harder to clean, the soft element of the classroom helps reduce the noise level and promotes relaxation during the day. Include familiar home items such as pictures, unbreakable mirrors, nonpoisonous plants, homeliving furniture (sink, dishes, foods), simple dress-up clothing, hats, dolls, stuffed pets, baskets and boxes. Pictures of real children, families and animals should be used rather than cartoon depictions. Photos of the children in the

class, their scribbles (MIMs) and paintings also make nice displays. Supervision is of primary importance when arranging the furniture and spaces in the room. The teacher should be able to see all areas of the room, ideally while sitting down on the floor. Keep in mind that small spaces can lead to aggression while wide open spaces can result in random behaviors and running.

Toddler Activity Areas

The toddler classroom should be divided into four or five distinct activity areas or zones: Sensory—Art—Messy Play, Large Motor—Active Play, Dramatic Play—Homeliving, Cozy—Quiet—Library and Discovery—Fine Motor Play (sometimes combined in sensory or the quiet area). Each area is defined by the materials, the presence or absence of carpet, the furniture, shelves and other dividers as needed. Although the playground is not in the classroom, it should be considered an extension of the learning environment. The following are suggested arrangements, toys and materials for each learning center or classroom activity space.

Sensory—Art—Messy Play Area

This area should be close to a sink and have an easily cleaned floor (no carpets). Suggestions for The Sensory—Art—Messy area include:

Equipment
> sensory table, dish tub or baby bath tub
> easel
> table (chairs not needed)
> newspaper, shower curtain, plastic tablecloth for floor covering
> smocks, old shirts
> storage for supplies
> plastic cups, containers and items for sensory and water play
> clothespins on a string or way to hang pictures to dry

Toys and materials
> paper
> markers
> crayons
> chalk
> paints
> paintbrushes
> fingerpaint
> playdough
> cookie cutters, playdough hammers
> bubbles
> plastic bottles filled with items
> sand with shovels and containers
> fabrics and textures

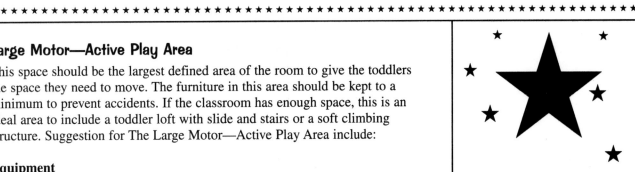

Large Motor—Active Play Area

This space should be the largest defined area of the room to give the toddlers the space they need to move. The furniture in this area should be kept to a minimum to prevent accidents. If the classroom has enough space, this is an ideal area to include a toddler loft with slide and stairs or a soft climbing structure. Suggestion for The Large Motor—Active Play Area include:

Equipment
>large boxes
>tunnel
>small slide
>small climbing structure
>"sit and spin" for older toddlers
>pounding bench
>large cardboard building blocks
>blocks

Toys and materials
>balls
>push toys, pull toys
>bells, children's instruments
>wheel and riding toys
>wagons, large dump trucks
>shakers
>cars, trucks, trains and other vehicles
>scarves and ribbons for dancing

Dramatic Play—Homeliving Area

This area works well next to the large motor area since both tend to be loud areas and play items easily overlap. The Dramatic Play—Homeliving Area should have several unbreakable mirrors and some of the following items:

Equipment
>dolls and stuffed animals
>doll bed, preferably large enough for toddlers to sit on
>small rocking chair
>doll stroller, doll high chair
>dress-up clothes, hats, purses
>toddler-size sink and stove
>play table, small chairs
>toddler play refrigerator

Toys and materials
>food packages, plastic fruits and vegetables
>plastic dishes
>old cameras, play telephone
>tote bags, back packs, purses
>small blankets
>puppets
>simple doll clothing or newborn size outfits
>hats
>simple dress-up items

For dramatic play with older toddlers, this area could also include
> play farm and farm animals
> zoo animals
> stuffed animals
> cars and trucks
> wading pool (without water)
> boxes

Cozy—Library—Quiet Play Area

This area should be in a quiet, carpeted area of the room away from the traffic flow and the active play of the large motor area. It can be near the homeliving area as some of the dolls and stuffed animals can be incorporated into this space. Ideally, the toddler classroom should have more than one place for the toddlers to "get away" and relax. A large box or small wading pool can be used for an additional "cozy space" in another area of the room. The Cozy—Library—Quiet Play Area should include some of the following items:

Equipment
> pillows and cushions, large and small
> soft throw rug, fuzzy bath mat
> stuffed animals
> pictures of real people or animals on the wall
> overstuffed chair or child-size sofa

Toys and materials
> puppets
> dolls
> books
> magazines
> large, simple pictures
> tapes and records

Discovery—Fine Motor Play Area

This space can be combined into the sensory or quiet area or have its own separate space. The Discovery— Fine Motor Play Area should have the following items:

Equipment
> manipulatives
> interlocking blocks, such as Duplo
> boxes, gift bags, tote bags and baskets for dump and fill
> wooden (older) and/or plastic blocks
> large beads or spools for stringing

Toys and materials
> textures to feel
> shape sorters
> nesting toys
> action/reaction toys
> puzzles, matching games

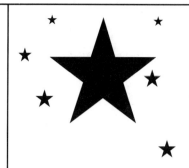

items to sort
dump and fill containers
shakers
children's musical instruments
nature items

Playground

The playground is not just a place to let the toddlers go and play. It is an integral part of the toddler environment. The toddler playground should include any of the following:

Equipment
    shade trees or shade cover
    structures safe for toddlers to climb/slide
    toddler swings
    wheel toys
    sensory tub and items for sand, water and sensory play
    toddler-size picnic table
    playhouse
    boxes
    milk crates
    area for quiet play, such as blanket or empty wading pool with
    books, puppets in shady area

Toys and materials
    balls
    push/pull toys
    large dump trucks

Suggestions of items to have in all areas
    all sizes and kinds of boxes
    plastic bowls, cups and containers
    empty food packages
    diaper wipe containers

An Available and Responsive Teacher

Overall, the most crucial element of the toddler environment is an available and responsive teacher. Teachers of toddlers must be physically and emotionally accessible to each child, giving each one undivided attention throughout the day. They should interact with the children individually and in small groups, using caregiving routines as optimal teaching opportunities and following the interests of the toddlers. Those who care for toddlers must understand this challenging age group and be responsive to their unique needs. The adults set the overall tone in terms of the socio-emotional quality of the environment while furniture, toys and supplies determine the aesthetics of the physical environment. State of the art equipment is an ideal and definitely good to have, but its importance is minimal compared to the role of the caregivers in the classroom.

Sample Daily Schedule

Schedules for toddlers must have flexibility to follow toddlers' interests and needs as much as possible. Rather than locking into set times for each activity, a daily schedule with predictable patterns and routines works best. Toddlers thrive on routine; it gives them a sense of security knowing what comes next. Keeping in mind that all programs have their unique characteristics, the following is a sample schedule with suggested sequence of events and time frames to use as a guide.

Arrival and Play Areas (at least an hour)

✓ Toddlers explore choice of activities in each of the four to five centers.

✓ Teachers available and interacting with toddlers individually and in small groups; greet toddlers and parent upon arrival.

✓ "Wow" activity where the teacher introduces special activity when most of the children have arrived. Toddlers free to join in or may choose to play elsewhere. Some activities may require more teacher supervision or involvement than others (playdough, painting, reading books).

✓ Diapering and toileting as needed.

Circle Time for Older Toddlers (optional: not more than 10 minutes)

✓ Singing songs, reading short books or movement songs introduced casually as an activity choice; toddlers are not required to sit as one large group. They are allowed to watch from a distance or be in one of specified activity areas if they prefer. Most toddlers will choose to join in with circle time books and songs if they are on a toddler's developmental level.

Handwashing and Snack

✓ Emphasize toddlers' independence

✓ Teachers sit with toddlers; optional time to interact with toddlers

Diapering and Toileting

✓ Toddlers explore play areas while teacher is changing diapers or helping with toileting

✓ Crucial time for one-on-one interaction

Outside Play (at least an hour as weather permits)

✓ Toddlers exploring outdoor environment

✓ Teachers supervising, interacting and introducing simple "Wow" activities when possible

Relaxing Songs or Story

✓ Transition to indoors if needed

Handwashing and Lunch
(See Handwashing and Snack)

Diapering and Toileting
(See above)

Rest Time

✓ Quiet music

✓ "Snugglies" available

Diapering and Toileting
(See above)

Choice of Quiet Play Areas as Toddlers Awaken

Handwashing and Snack

Afternoon Outside Play (at least 45 minutes if possible)

✓ Same routines as the morning with teacher(s) available and toddlers exploring outdoor environment

Inside with Choice of Play Areas and Departure

✓ Toddlers exploring materials and teachers interacting with toddlers, reading books, doing simple activities

✓ This is also a crucial time for parent communication.

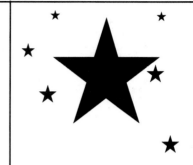

Sample Lesson Plan for Toddlers

Lesson plans for toddlers must remain flexible to be able to adapt and follow the needs and interests of one and two year olds. Topics or themes developed over two weeks tend to work best for most toddler groups. The first week they are exploring and the second week they start to integrate the ideas. Days can be specified for some of the "Wow" or special activities if needed for the planning and gathering of materials. The following is a sample of things to include in a toddler lesson plan.

Concepts—objectives and ways the topic will be emphasized at the toddlers' level

Language to use—vocabulary, phrases

Songs, chants, fingerplays

Books—to read, have out and make

Sensory exploration

Gross motor activities, creative movement

Fine motor activities

Games—matching, sorting, hide and seek

"Wow" activities—special activities that require closer supervision or one-on-one interaction, such as painting, drawing, cooking

Pretend play—homeliving and dramatic play

Outdoor play—simple activities for the playground or walks

Health, safety—ways to emphasize staying healthy or safe

Anti-bias—ways to develop an understanding and appreciation of diversity.

Plans for individual children—specific activities or work with specific children, such as separation from parents, behavioral issues, developmental changes, toileting should be kept separate from posted lesson plans to remain confidential

Other—reminders, things to do

Dates:	**Topic:**

Concepts : A B C Language:	Sensory:	WOW Activites:
Songs/Chants:	Fine Motor:	Gross Motor:
Books:	Games:	Outdoor Play:
Pretend Play:	Health/Safety Anti-bias	Other/To do: Individual Plans: (on back)

Dates: 12-23   Topic: Hands and Feet

Concepts: A
I have 2 hands, I have 2 feet.
Washing hands is important.
I can do _____ with my hands
and feet. B

Language: C
hands, feet, fingers, toes, feel,
touch, texture vocabulary
clap, stamp, wiggle
clean, dirty

Sensory:
Feely box with fabrics, fur,
sandpaper

Various textures bags with
shaving cream, fingerpaint

hand and foot massage

washing dolls

WOW Activities:
M, 12: Fingerpaint and make handprints

T, 13: Fingerpaint with sand added

W, 14: } make footprints and soak
Th, 15: } feet

F, 16: use paper from paper tearing
for collage

T, 20: print with hand and foot
shaped sponges

W, 21: Thumbprint cookies
open times: Shaving cream, draw with
markers and crayons; trace toddlers'
hands

Songs/Chants:
"Ten Little Fingers and Toes"
"Two Friends"
"My Body"
"Skip to My Lou" using hand and
foot actions
"This Little Piggy" nursery rhyme
"Wash Hands"

Fine Motor:
pinching playdough

tearing paper from old phone book

threading spools

popping packing bubbles
with hands and feet

action tops -- explore pump,
spray, pop up tops to
containers

Gross Motor:
actions with feet
(stamp, march, tiptoe,)
jump

actions with hands
(clap, roll, rub, wiggle)

Foot Dance - hands behind
back

Hand Dance - move only hands
to music

Books:
"Ten Little Piggies" by Wood
"Hand Hand Fingers Thumb"
by Perkins
"Ten Nine Eight" by Bang
"Shoes" by Bailey
other books about hands and feet
in cozy corner -- trace hands
using "Hand Book"

Games:
Sorting socks by color

Sorting baby, child, adult
shoes by size into boxes.

Counting fingers and toes

Outdoor Play:
spray bottles with
water to mist on
trees, grass

picking up and tearing
leaves

looking at shoe prints on
damp sand

running

Pretend Play:
dolls -- Count fingers and toes on dolls,
put on baby booties

dress-up -- try on slippers and
mittens, different kinds
of shoes

home living -- hot pad
holders for hands

Health/Safety
Anti-bias:
"Washing Hands keeps us from
getting sick."

Sorting baby, child, adult shoes
by size into boxes.

Counting fingers and toes

Other/To do:
plans for individual
children

Individual Plans:
(on back)

The Bridge Between Home and School

Parent Communication

Communication with parents is an integral component of a successful toddler program. All too often, communication is limited, with specifics about a child shared only at conference time or when an issue arises. Parents must be given details about their child's time away from home beyond the stock phrase of "He had a good day" or "She's doing fine." Every day tell each parent something his or her child enjoyed, did, said or played. Daily Reports (see sample) covering routines (meals, naps, toileting) and activities help with sharing this information, especially when verbal contact is limited or difficult to do without interruptions. Newsletters (see sample) keep parents informed of the activities, dates, reminders, themes for the entire class. The addition of ideas to do at home provides simple parenting tips and helps parents understand toddler development. Use daily verbal contact, Daily Reports, newsletters, notes and phone calls to establish an effective line of communication with parents and bridge the gap between school and home.

Child _____ Date _____

At Lunch I
Wasn't Hungry
Ate Some
Ate Everything

I had a bowel movement at _____

I took a nap at _____

Today I was:

___ Cheerful   ___ More Easily Upset Than Usual
___ Needed Extra Adult Attention   ___ Happy
___ Quieter Than Usual   ___ Tired
___ Content

Today I enjoyed:

___ Blocks   ___ Art
___ Cars & Trucks   ___ Dress Up
___ Dolls/Stuffed Animals   ___ Clean Up
___ Puzzles   ___ Snack
___ Stacking Toys/Shaper Sorters   ___ Songs
___ Looking at Books   ___ Listening to Stories

___ Boat/Rocking Horse
___ Climbing
___ Outside Play
___ Sandplay
___ Swings
___ Trikes/Push Toys

Other Information:

Suggestions for topics to include in a class newsletter

Title

Terrific Toddlers (or class name)

Mark Your Calendar

List any special activities and holidays

Friends and Family

List any birthdays for the month, new children to the classroom, new siblings

Looking Back

Highlight activities from the previous month that the children really enjoyed or that worked out especially well.

Looking Ahead

Highlight upcoming activities planned for the month, emphasizing how the topic will be introduced into the various classroom activities. This section can be divided into skills or sections to make it easier to read, such as:

✓ Sensory Activities—sensory tub play, water play, playdough
✓ Movement Activities—gross motor, dancing, creative movement
✓ Small Motor Activities—drawing, painting, games
✓ Pretend Play Activities—dramatic play
✓ Language Activities—books, songs, chants. Include words to a few of the songs and chants.
✓ Special Activities—highlight cooking, parades, special days

Save and Send

List any items the parents can help provide for the month and upcoming in future months.

Reminders

Home Connections

Suggestions of things parents can do at home related to the class activities.

Here's a Sample Newsletter based on apples and red theme

Terrific Toddlers

Mark Your Calendar

2nd—Cooking Activity: applesauce and apple sandwiches. Please bring a red apple to school.
25th—Red Day: wear red to school.

Friends and Family

Happy Birthday to:
1st—AARON
14th—ALAN
Welcome to our new friend ALEXANDRA. Her parents are Marc and Shirley.

Looking Back

Last month, the toddlers really enjoyed our movement songs about all their bodies can do. Jumping and spinning were the favorite actions. So that we didn't spend the whole day doing jumps and spins repeatedly, we discovered new ways we could do those actions with our bodies, such as jumping our shoulders, jumping with our knees so our feet didn't come off the floor, spinning our hands and even spinning while sitting down. The toddlers also had lots of fun washing the baby dolls. They were very careful not to get any soap in the babies' eyes. A Class Handbook made with each child's hand print and picture has been a special addition to our cozy space. We invite you to take a few minutes to look at this book with your child one day.

Looking Ahead

We'll focus on Apples and Red this month. Some of our activities will include:

Sensory activities—washing and polishing apples, using shakers filled with red poker chips and exploring all sorts of red things in a big red basket.

Movement activities—marching and dancing with red ribbons and scarves, doing an Apple Dance and stretching up high as we pretend to pick apples from a tree.

Fine motor activities—making important marks with red markers and crayons, using red playdough, painting with shades of red and making a collage with red scraps.

Pretend play—making apple juice for each other, using red bandannas for dress-up fun and building tall red houses with our cardboard brick blocks.

Language activities—reading *Apples and Pumpkins* by Anne Harlow and *Mary Wore Her Red Dress* by Merle Peek, looking at pictures of red things and singing about our red clothes with "Mary Wore Her Red Dress."

> *Mary wore her red dress, red dress, red dress*
> *Mary wore her red dress all day long.* (substitute child's name and specific item of red clothing)

Also, chanting about apples with:

> *Way up high in the apple tree* (point up)
> *Two red apples smiled at me.* (point to cheeks)
> *I shook that tree as hard as I could.* (shake fists)
> *Down came the apples* (pound floor)
> *Mmm, they were good.* (rub tummy)

Special Apple and Red Activities

Please send a picture of your child with his favorite toy, person or favorite activity for our "You're the Apple of My Eye" bulletin board.

We'll taste different kinds and colors of apples at an apple tasting party.

Send an apple with your child on the 2nd so we can make applesauce and apple sandwiches from apple slices and peanut butter.

Wear red on the 25th for our "Red Day." We'll have a red parade, use red fingerpaint and eat a "red snack" with strawberries, apples and cranapple juice.

Save and Send

Red bandannas, red baseball hats and any scraps of red fabric or ribbons. We'll also need all kinds of boxes for next month.

Home Connections

Point out the color red on a variety of things including clothing.
Make spaghetti after our red day.
Visit an orchard to pick apples with your child.
Take a walk to look for red cars in the neighborhood.

Books For Toddlers

12 months and older

Arma, Tony. (1995). *Dress-up Time*. New York: Grosset and Dunlap.

Arma, Tony. (1995). *Little Grown Ups*. New York: Grosset and Dunlap.

Beylon, Cathy. (1992). *Hush Little Baby*. New York: Checkerboard Press.

Breeze, Lynn. (1990). *This Little Baby Goes Out*. Great Britian: Orchard Books.

Carle, Eric. (1984). *The Very Busy Spider*. New York: Putnam and Grosset Group.

Ericksen, Amy. (1995). *Jungle Animals*. San Francisco: Chronicle Books.

Ericksen, Amy. (1995). *Sea Animals*. San Francisco: Chronicle Books.

Hague, Michael. (1993). *Teddy Bear, Teddy Bear*. New York: Morrow Junior Books.

Hennessy, B.G. (1989). *A,B,C,D, Tummy, Toes, Hands and Knees*. New York: Penguin Group.

Hoban, Tana. (1985). *A Children's Zoo*. New York: Mulberry Books.

Lear, Edward (1991). *The Owl and the Pussy Cat*. New York: Putnam and Grosset.

Martin, Bill (1983). *Brown Bear, Brown Bear, What Do You See?* New York: Henry Holt and Company.

Martin, Bill (1991). *Polar Bear, Polar Bear, What Do You Hear?* New York: Henry Holt and Company.

Melmed, Laura Krauss. (1993). *I Love You As Much*. New York: Lothrop, Lee and Shepard.

Moroney, Tracey. (1994). *Humpty Dumpty*. Wilton, CT: Wishing Well Books. Additional titles by this author: *Three Little Kittens* and *Old Mother Hubbard*.

Porter, Gaylord. (1991). *I Love My Daddy Because...* New York: Dutton Children's Books.

Porter, Gaylord. (1991). *I Love My Mommy Because...* New York: Dutton Children's Books.

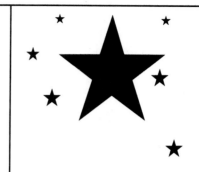

Reasoner, Charles. (1995). *Who's In the Sea*. New York: Price Stern and Sloan.

Ricklen, Neil. (1992). *Grandpa and Me*. New York: Simon and Schuster. Additional titiles by this author: *Mommy and Me, Daddy and Me, Grandma and Me, Baby's Zoo, Baby's Bithday, Baby's School* and others.

Trapani, Iza. (1993). *The Itsy Bitsy Spider*. New York: Scholastic.

Wolf, Ashley. (1980). *Baby Beluga*. New York: Crown Publishing.

18 months and older

Benjamin, Cynthia. (1994). *I Am A Doctor*. New York: Barrons Educational Series.

Brown, Margaret Wise. (1961). *Home for a Bunny*. New York: Golden Press.

Brown, Margaret Wise. (1942). *The Runaway Bunny*. New York: Harper and Row.

Guarino, Deborah. (1989). *Is Your Mama a Llama?* New York: Scholastic.

Jonas, Ann. (1995). *Splash*. New York: Greenwillow Books.

Krauss, Ruth. (1945). *The Carrot Seed*. New York: Harper and Row.

Ray, Karen. (1995). *Sleep Song*. New York: Orchard Books.

Williams, Vera. (1990). *More, More, More Said the Baby*. New York: Scholastic.

Wood, Audrey. (1984). *The Napping House*. San Diego: Harcourt Brace Jovanovich.

Wood, Audrey and Wood, Don. (1991). *Piggies*. San Diego: Harcourt Brace Jovanovich.

24 months and older

Barton, Byron. (1990). *Bones, Bones, Dinosaur Bones*. New York: Thomas Crowell.

Barton, Byron. (1989). *Dinosaurs, Dinosaurs*. New York: Thomas Crowell.

Crebbin, June. (1995). *The Train Ride*. Cambridge: Candlewick Press.

Crews, Donald. (1995). *Sail Away*. New York: Greenwillow Books.

Crimi, Carolyn. (1995). *Outside, Inside*. New York: Simon and Schuster.

Garland, Michael. (1993). *Circus Girl*. New York: Dutton Children's Books.

Rockwell, Anne. (1989). *Apples and Pumpkins*. New York: Macmillian.

For Toddlers Anytime:
Basics and Boxes

May I?

Involving toddlers in caregiving tasks helps them feel respected and increases their cooperation.

Skills encouraged

self-esteem

Language to use with toddlers

I need
wash face
wipe nose
check diaper
May I?
in five minutes
soon

Materials

none needed

To do

1. Identify the situation for the toddlers and tell the toddler what you need to do before starting the caregiving task.

> *Oh, you have spaghetti on you cheek. I need to clean it off with this wet washcloth. (Then wipe child's face.) Thank you. Now it's all gone.*

> *I see your nose has mucous. I need to wipe it with this tissue. (Then wipe child's nose.) Thank you. Now it is all clean.*

> *I may need to change your diaper before we go outside. Let me check to see if it is dry. (Then check child's diaper.) Thank you. You are wet. Now let's get a dry diaper.*

2. Do the same respectful caregiving with other routine tasks.

3. Let the toddler also have a turn at wiping his face and using a tissue. Encourage them to help with caregiving tasks as often as possible.

To do again

Let toddlers know when a change is coming so they are not caught off guard, such as forewarn them of the upcoming time to go inside, clean up, take a nap.

Teaching hints

Toddlers' tantrums and seemingly negative behavior often stem from a need to assert their emerging autonomy. Even adults would resist someone coming up from behind, putting a hand over their mouth and wiping their face with a cold, wet rag without knowing it was going to happen. With the caregiver in a sense asking, "May I?" toddlers have an idea what will be happening to them and more of a say in the matter. This type of respectful care will lessen tantrums and toddlers' resistance to many caregiving tasks.

Home connections

Establish routines with your toddler throughout the day, not just at bedtime. Let your child know in advance when it will be time to leave, put on shoes, get in the car, eat dinner, rather than announcing "It is time, now." Also, whenever possible, provide real choices, "Would you like to wear the red or the white shirt tomorrow?" Give your toddler a way to express his autonomy in positive ways.

Chapter Two

Toddler Gallery

Help build toddlers' sense of self-worth by prominently displaying the toddlers' most important marks (MIMs) along with other artwork and photos in a Toddler Gallery.

To do

1. Display the toddlers MIMs (most important marks, also known as scribbles), paintings and other artwork prominently around the room. Photographs of the children at school and at home should also be displayed on the walls and in simple photo albums.

2. Provide a specific place on the wall that is set aside for each child's own space to display her pictures and creations. Identify the area with her name and photo. A bulletin board border can be used to define a boundary.

3. Place a picture of the child's family in the area as well.

4. Look at the child's pictures and photos with her.

5. Point out the area to the child's parents as well. Emphasize to the parents the importance of the child's early scribbles as the most important marks for future writing.

6. Change the display often to maintain interest.

7. Display photos of the children at school around the room. Make a class photo album with pictures of the children at school for the book or cozy area. Encourage parents to look at the book occasionally as well.

To do again

Save samples of each child's MIMs, paintings, photos at school and other artwork from throughout the year to help record the growth and development of each child. Fold poster board in half and staple or tape the ends to make a folder to store the items. Send the special collection home at the end of the year.

Teaching hints

Saving and displaying the children's MIMs helps parents see the value of these early marks, especially when there is a display area near the cubbies, door or central location that they will see often. Having a set location helps each child know her space and feel a sense of pride.

Home connections

Display some of your child's MIMs, paintings or drawings at home in places other than just the refrigerator, such as your child's room, bathroom mirror and the front door to show that you value her work.

Skills encouraged

self-esteem

Language to use with toddlers

mine
picture
drawing
family
wall
see
look at

Materials

bulletin board border
toddlers' artwork
photographs of the children

Toddler Decorating

Give the toddlers a role in decorating and redoing the room with pictures attached to the wall with pieces of velcro.

Skills encouraged

fine motor, self-esteem

Language to use with toddlers

pictures
see
What is it?
put up
take down
another one

Materials

pictures
poster board or tagboard
clear self-adhesive paper
velcro pieces
stapler

To do

1. Gather large, simple pictures. Mount the pictures to poster board or tag board. Laminate or cover with clear self-adhesive paper for durability.

2. Attach a 3"-4" strip of the fuzzy side of velcro to the top-center of each picture.

3. Staple 3"-4" hook side strips of velcro to the wall around the room at the toddlers' level.

4. Encourage the toddlers to decorate the wall with their choice of pictures.

5. Talk with the toddlers about the pictures they put up on the wall all by themselves.

6. Leave out a basket of more pictures for the toddlers to redecorate as they desire.

To do again

Create matching games for older toddlers. They use the velcro pieces to stick the same colored items or pieces together, or attach the hook side of velcro to felt pieces to help them stick to the flannel board.

Teaching hints

Uncluttered, single subject pictures at least 8 1/2" x 11" work best for toddlers. Toddlers especially enjoy pictures of babies, children, people and animals. Use pictures of real things. If toddlers try to take down pictures on the wall redirect them. Let them take off the velcro pictures or put masking tape on the table or floor so they can practice their fine motor skills.

Wash, Hands, Wash

Washing hands can be enjoyable, especially with simple songs and chants to encourage proper hand washing.

To do

1. Chant the following while washing hands with toddlers:

> *This hand is the baby hand.*
> *This hand is the mother.*
> *Together they rub and they rub together,*
> *One hand scrubs the other.*

2. Another chant to try with older toddlers:

> *Wash, hands, wash do you know how?*
> *Soap and water and scrub and scrub.*
> *That is how.*

To do again

Sing about washing hands to the tune of "Mulberry Bush."

> *This is the way we wash our hands, wash our hands, wash our hands.*
> *This is the way we wash our hands to get them clean.*

Teaching hints

It's a fact—the primary way to prevent the spread of diseases is by proper and frequent hand washing by both the teachers and children. Encourage the toddlers to rub their hands together until they make bubbles to help get them to thoroughly wash their hands.

Home connections

Make hand washing part of the routine at home to establish an effective hand washing habit.

Skills encouraged

self-help

Language to use with toddlers

wash hands
clean
dirty
scrub
rub
bubbles
baby
mother
wash

Materials

soap
water
paper towels

Good Clean Fun

Turn picking up toys into good clean fun with an upbeat verse from a familiar tune.

Skills encouraged

self-help

Language to use with toddlers

clean up
pick up
help
toys
blocks
dolls
thank you

Materials

none needed

Home connections

Toddlers enjoy cleaning up their toys when they also have the help of an adult and clean up is made into a game by singing, counting, racing against the timer or music box, or with each person cleaning up a different color. Encourage your toddler to clean up after he finishes with a toy or periodically throughout the day to avoid the frustration of cleaning up everything at the end of the day when everyone is tired.

To do

1. Encourage the toddlers to help pick up the toys by singing the following verse (to the tune of the chorus of "My Bonnie Lies Over the Ocean") repeatedly during clean up time.

> *Clean up, clean up,*
> *Clean up the toys*
> *Clean up, Clean up!*

2. Refer to specific items (such as blocks, dolls, books) or specific children's names.

> *Clean up, clean up,*
> *Clean up the blocks*
> *Mikey, clean up!*

3. End with a "Thank You" verse when finished picking up the toys.

> *Thank you, thank you,*
> *Thank you my helpers (child's name)*
> *Thank you, thank you!*

To do again

With older toddlers, sing an introductory verse giving specific direction.

> *Our books are on the floor,*
> *Our puzzles are on the table.*
> *Our toys need to be put away*
> *So let's clean up today.*

> *Clean up, clean up,*
> *Clean up the toys*
> *Clean up, clean up!*

Teaching hints

Clean-up songs enlist the help of toddlers in picking up the toys much more than asking them to do so.

Snuggle Up With a Good Book

Books should be integral to the toddler classroom. Set aside a cozy space with soft pillows for them to enjoy the world of books.

To do

1. Place a small wading pool in a quiet area of the room. Fill the bottom with pillows, stuffed animals and puppets. If a wading pool is not available, define a cozy area with a large bath mat or rug.

2. Fill a basket with books. Chunky or board books work best with younger toddlers. Add a few parenting magazines too if desired. Make books from magazine pictures and squares of poster board bound together with book rings or yarn (see Toddler Books and Lift The Flap Books in *Toddlers Together*).

3. Encourage toddlers to get inside the soft pool to look at books and relax.

4. Get inside with the toddlers to read books to them.

To do again

Use wading pools in a number of ways throughout the classroom and playground:

✓ for toys with multiple pieces, such as plastic interlocking blocks to contain the pieces in one area
✓ for a fun place to have a picnic snack
✓ for a "tearing pool" to practice tearing paper
✓ for a sensory place with lots of textures, soft balls or ribbons
✓ for dramatic play areas, such as a pond or ocean

Teaching hints

Early exposure to books is vital for prereading to help children develop an appreciation of the world of books. Read often to the toddlers as a free choice activity. Start reading to one child and soon a group will gather around. Requiring toddlers to sit for a large group time doesn't work well with toddlers, yet they do enjoy snuggling up around the teacher to listen to a story when they choose to do so.

Home connections

Use a wading pool for all kinds of "dry play" at home inside or out in the yard, from a house for your child's stuffed animals to a special place to play with toys with many pieces. Let your child eat a special snack or meal now and then in the pool.

Skills encouraged

language, relaxation

Language to use with toddlers

books
look at
see
pictures
read
snuggle
relax
soft

Materials

wading pool
pillows
stuffed animals
puppets
basket
books
poster board
magazines

Name That Tune

Songs and chants have unlimited use with toddlers. Vary the words to familiar tunes to have an infinite variety to use at any time.

Skills encouraged

language

Materials

none needed

To do

1. Make up your own songs by changing the words to familiar tunes to fit the specific need. Tunes easy to adapt for other purposes include:

> *Are You Sleeping?*
> *London Bridge*
> *Mary Had a Little Lamb*
> *Farmer in the Dell*
> *Mulberry Bush*

2. Sing often throughout the day. Use the adapted tunes for recognizing individual toddlers and their activities, emphasizing specific topics or themes, help during clean up, hand washing and other transition motor skills and creative movement anytime.

3. Use your imagination.

Teaching hints

Singing calms most toddlers and adults. Just as some people whistle or hum when they are relaxed, happy children and adults sing. Chant if singing is not comfortable for you, verses and rhymes have a tremendous impact on all areas of toddler development.

Home connections

Make up your own songs and chants to use with your toddler at home, especially when the tension level starts to rise.

Chapter Two

Hello, Hello

Toy telephones are not just for play. Adults can model quite elaborate conversations while at the same time reassuring toddlers that their parents will return.

To do

1. Pretend to be talking to the child's parent. For example:

> *Hello,*
> *Oh, hi Brenda's daddy.*
> *Yes, she's doing just fine.*
> *She's playing with the markers.*
> *Yes, she liked her pickles at lunch.*
> *OK, she'll see you after nap.*
> *Do you want to talk to her?*
> *Here she is.*

2. Give child the phone to talk to her daddy.

3. When the child is finished, say "Good-bye."

To do again

Let the toddlers see you writing notes and reminders to their parents to model another way of communicating.

Teaching hints

While many toddlers will just hold the phone up to their ear, they are fascinated with adults pretending to talk on the phone. Hearing you converse with their parents and confirming when they will be back reassures the toddlers, especially those adjusting to the room.

Home connections

Make pretend phone calls to grandparents and other relatives. This helps toddlers develop skills of talking to people on the phone without the pressure of talking right now to someone they can not see.

Skills encouraged

language, pretend play

Language to use with toddlers

Hello
How are you?
doing just fine
playing
friends
mommy
daddy
Bye, bye

Materials

toy telephones

Soothing Sounds

Music influences the emotional quality of the setting. Use various types of music in the toddler classroom to set the tempo of the classroom activities.

Skills encouraged

sensory exploration

Language to use with toddlers

music
hear
listen
songs
sing
loud
soft
instruments

Materials

variety of music

To do

1. Play different types of music throughout the day. Explore more than children's music and try all kinds—classical, ethnic, folk songs or even environmental sounds. See what you and toddlers respond to at different times of the day.

2. Dance with the toddlers if you see them moving to the beat.

3. Play upbeat music to exercise to or for marching.

4. Play quiet, soothing music at mealtimes and rest times.

5. Clap or use shakers to music with a beat. Or, sing with recordings of familiar songs.

6. Even play music outside.

7. Remember to have times without music playing too.

To do again

Play music boxes for the toddlers. Dance to a music box and stop when it stops. Play a game of trying to get all the toys picked up by the time the music stops with older toddlers.

Teaching hints

Music often sets the scene. Keep in mind that not all children's music works for toddler classrooms: upbeat, rock-and-roll tempos found on some children's records and tapes can be overstimulating. Toddlers are busy by nature and do not need fast music to get them moving.

Home connections

Play a variety of music at home. Your toddler may help you expand your horizons.

All Bottled Up

"Bottle up" all sorts of sensory material to make the items safe for toddlers.

To do

1. Gather clear plastic bottles with lids, such as those from sodas, juices, bottled water or sports drinks.

2. Fill the bottles 1/4 to 1/2 full with any of the following materials separately or in combination.

- ✓ colored rice
- ✓ ribbon
- ✓ beads
- ✓ buttons
- ✓ sequins
- ✓ colored sand
- ✓ aquarium gravel
- ✓ small plastic items
- ✓ pieces of plastic straws

3. Secure the lid with a hot glue gun.

4. Store the bottles in a basket or open box. Place the bottles out for the toddlers to explore. Talk with the toddlers about the colors, sounds, items inside the bottles.

5. Encourage the toddlers to shake the bottles to hear the sounds. Use the bottles with the shaker activities in *Toddlers Together*.

6. For older toddlers, provide plastic curlers, plastic straws or ping pong balls to use with a bottle with a large opening, such as large plastic ones from juice. The neck of the bottle should be wide enough for the objects to fit through easily. Encourage the toddlers to dump and fill with the bottles and objects.

To do again

Fill the bottles with colored water and plastic objects or equal parts of colored water and lamp oil. Secure the top with a hot glue gun and duct tape around the cap for extra security.

Skills encouraged

sensory exploration

Language to use with toddlers

bottle
see
inside
shake
sounds
colors

Materials

plastic bottles
variety of materials
hot glue gun
plastic curlers
straws
ribbon
variety of materials

Teaching hints

See what toddlers do with the bottles. They will find unique uses for the bottles, especially in the home living area. Check the bottles often for cracks or the tops coming loose. Discard as needed.

Home connections

Let your toddler practice her pouring skills with plastic bottles and cups at the sink or even in the bathtub.

It's in the Bag

Use paper gift bags and tote bags for toddlers' all-time favorite activities—dump and fill.

Skills encouraged

fine motor, cognitive

Language to use with toddlers

bag
empty
full
put inside
take out, dump out
count
What's inside?

Materials

gift bags with handles
tote bags
purses, sand buckets, baskets

To do

1. Provide old paper gift bags with handles and tote bags for the toddlers. Put clear self-adhesive paper or duct tape where the handle is attached to the gift bag for added durability.

2. Let the toddlers use the bags for dump and fill play.

3. Talk with them about the objects they put inside their bag, how full it is, how many items are in the bag.

4. Ask the toddlers to find certain objects around the room to put inside their bag.

5. Provide purses, baskets, sand buckets for additional dump and fill play.

6. Use two to four bags of different solid colors for older toddlers to sort objects, such as plastic interlocking blocks, plastic blocks, milk jug caps by colors.

To do again

Boxes also are an ideal source for dump and fill play. Large laundry soap boxes with a handle can be covered with colorful self-adhesive paper for a perfect carrying case.

Teaching hints

Have a special bag to store "Wow!" activities, which are special activities to do individually or with a small group of toddlers to capture their interest. It can be playdough, a puzzle, game, puppet or special book, anything that will cause the toddlers to say, "Wow!"

Seeing the World Through Colored Windows

Toddlers are amazed when they see the world change colors through windows covered with colored cellophane.

To do

1. Cut large squares or circles out of different colors of overhead transparencies or colored cellophane wrap.

2. Tape the shapes to a window.

3. Encourage the toddlers to look through the colored windows. Talk with them about how everything changed colors.

4. Attach the cellophane to a mirror if windows are not easily accessible to the toddlers. Talk with them about the color change on their face when they look at themselves through the shape.

5. Attach the colored transparency or cellophane wrap to a frame made from poster board. Let the toddlers look through the color shape. Talk with them about the color changes they notice. Play peekaboo with the toddlers using the color shape.

To do again

Look through sheer scarves. Play peekaboo with sheer scarves.

Skills encouraged

sensory exploration

Language to use with toddlers

colors
look through
see
different
changes

Materials

colored overhead transparencies
colored cellophane
scissors
tape
poster board

Where Are You, My Friend?

Toddlers become keenly aware of their friends as their social skills emerge. Help them learn about their friends with a singing game of looking for friends.

Skills encouraged

language, self-esteem, friendship

Language to use with toddlers

where
names
she
he
hair color
colors
shoes
shirt
shorts
pants
ribbon

Materials

none needed

To do

1. Have the toddlers look for different friends around the room as they sing the following verse to the tune of "Where, oh Where, Has My Little Dog Gone."

> *Where, oh where, has our friend Sharon gone?*
> *Oh where, oh where, can she be?*
> *With her long brown hair and her lobster T-shirt*
> *Oh where, oh where, can she be?*

2. Hide favorite stuffed animals, dolls and puppets behind your back or around the room. Sing the verse about the dolls and animals.

Teaching hints

Give dolls, puppets and stuffed animals a name beyond just dolly or puppy to give them a special identity.

Home connections

Use the verse to reduce panic when favorite security objects or toys are misplaced around the house.

Chapter Two

All by Myself

Two year olds have a strong desire to be independent. Encourage two's autonomy with a special trick to help them learn how to put on their jackets "all by myself."

To do

1. Lay the toddler's coat, jacket or sweater on the floor with opening or zipper facing up. Have the child stand by the top, telling him "At the hood" or "By the tag."

2. Sing the following to the tune of "The Farmer in the Dell" and have the toddler do the actions.

> *I put both hands in, (put both hands in sleeves)*
> *I put it over my head. (raise hands so jacket goes over the head and*
> *   arms go inside sleeves)*
> *Heigh, ho, look at me I did it ALL BY MYSELF!*

3. Show excitement that the child did it by himself. Zip or button coat if needed.

Teaching hints

Some coats and jackets are easier than others, while windbreakers or sweaters may be more difficult. Some toddlers will pick this up quickly, especially in colder climates and when parents have also taught the child to put on a coat the same way. Show the parents the technique and song so they can follow through at home and will know why their child is putting his coat on the floor to put it on.

Home connections

Let your child choose what he wants to wear as often as possible. Make selecting clothing for the next day part of the bedtime routine if your mornings are hectic. Use clothespins to attach matched sets of clothing if mismatched clothing bothers you, because polka dots with stripes won't even phase your toddler. Encourage your toddler to dress and undress himself whenever possible. Offer help by saying "We'll do it together" when needed. Keep in mind that undressing often comes first, often to the dismay of their parents.

Skills encouraged

self-help, self-esteem

Language to use with toddlers

coat
jacket
sweater
put on
hand
sleeves
hood
tag
over
all by myself

Materials

jacket

Boxed In

Toddler classrooms are busy by nature, yet toddlers need time for quiet and to get away from the activity at times. Create a cozy space easily from a large box and soft materials.

Skills encouraged

sensory exploration,
relaxation

Language to use with toddlers

big box
inside
outside
feel
look
rest
relax
all alone

Materials

large boxes
scissors or large knife (for
   teachers only)
fabric
craft fur
felt
ribbons
pillows
duct tape
stuffed animals

To do

1. Find a large appliance box to use in the classroom for a cozy hideaway for one toddler at a time. Place the box on its side in a quiet area of the room.

2. Cut square or round windows out of the top and two sides of the box with a large knife.

3. Cover the opening and windows with strips of ribbon if desired.

4. Cut large shapes out of fabric, felt, craft fur and other texture materials. Tape the textures on the inside of the box with duct tape.

5. Place a few small pillows, stuffed animals and books inside the box.

6. Encourage a toddler to go inside to relax. Talk with him about the textures and the windows.

7. Play peekaboo with the toddler through the window on the top.

8. Use large boxes out on the playground as tunnels or cozy corners.

To do again

Large boxes can be used as a farm, dog house, bear cave, bus—just use your imagination.

Teaching hints

Limit the box to just one toddler at a time as toddlers are easily frustrated and can get aggressive with each other in small spaces.

Home connections

Make a cozy box or box house for your toddler to use at home. Let her decorate the outside with markers.

Toddler in the Box

Toddlers feel you can't see them if their eyes are covered since they can't see you. Playing simple peekaboo games with a box and a blanket will always produce joyful giggles.

To do

1. Place boxes of different sizes for the toddler to explore and climb inside. Talk with them about the sizes, the inside and the outside of the box.

2. Encourage a toddler to get inside the box. Place a blanket over the box. Play peekaboo with the toddler.

3. Show the toddler a jack-in-the-box. Encourage an older toddler to be a jack-in-the-box by hiding in the box and jumping up as you sing "Pop Goes the Weasel."

> *All around the cobbler's bench,*
> *The monkey chased the weasel.*
> *The weasel thought it was all in fun,*
> *Pop! (child jumps up) Goes the weasel!*

4. Play a hiding game with a box and the following verse sung to the tune of "Are You Sleeping?"

> *Where is Kimberly?*
> *Where is Kimberly?*
> *I can't find her.*
> *She must be hiding.*
> *Where can she be?*

5. Say, "Come out, Kimberly." Uncover the child or the child jumps up. "Oh, there you are! Inside the box!"

Suggested books

Read *Inside Outside Upside Down* by Stan and Jan Berenstain and *Baby in the Box* by Frank Asch.

Home connections

Play simple hiding games with your toddler by hiding in closets, under the sheets or even in a clothes hamper.

Skills encouraged ★

language, cognitive, motor skills

Language to use with toddlers

box
inside
outside
hide
cover
peekaboo
pop
up

Materials

boxes
blanket
jack-in-the-box toy

The Ideal Toy

Toddlers love boxes. Sing about this perfectly priced toy for toddlers that entertains them so well.

Skills encouraged

language

Language to use with toddlers

box
colors
patterns
hand
head
tummy
foot
big
little
empty
full

Materials

boxes
self-adhesive paper or wrapping paper and tape

Home connections

Don't be too quick to throw away boxes. Toddlers often enjoy the box of a toy more often than the new toy itself. Bring out a box when your toddler seems to need something to capture his interest.

To do

1. Collect a variety of boxes for the toddlers to explore and use for dump and fill play. Let them get inside larger boxes. Let the toddlers show you what to do with boxes.

2. Cover the boxes with different colors/patterns of self-adhesive or wrapping paper. Give each toddler a special box. Sing about their boxes to the tune of "Mary Wore a Red Dress."

> *Kori has a black and white box, black and white box,*
> *Black and white box.*
> *Kori has a black and white box in her hand.*

3. Substitute other children's names and description of their boxes.

4. Sing about their boxes and parts of their bodies with the following verse sung to the tune of "My Bonnie Lies Over the Ocean."

> *My box is on my head. (hold box on head)*
> *My box is on my tummy. (hold box on tummy)*
> *My box is on my foot. (put box on foot)*
> *Because that is where I put it today.*

5. Compare different types of boxes with the following verse sung to the tune of "Are You Sleeping?"

> *Big box, little box. (point to or hold up small and large box)*
> *Big box, little box.*
> *See them here, see them here.*
> *Big and little, big and little.*

6. Substitute other types of boxes, different colors, empty or full, shapes.

Teaching hints

Boxes are an inexpensive yet very popular toy for toddlers. Use them often in the classroom for a new item to spark excitement in the classroom and on the playground. Boxes have a number of uses, just follow the toddlers' lead.

To do again

See *Toddlers Together* for additional activities and games to do with boxes.

Match Box Fun

Boxes, box tops and juice can lids can be made into a number of match box games.

To do

1. Obtain a variety of boxes with lids. Cover the boxes and lids with different colors or patterns of self-adhesive paper.

2. Place two to five of the boxes out for the toddlers to explore and use for dump and fill play.

3. Encourage older toddlers to take off and put the tops back on by matching the colors or patterns.

4. For younger toddlers, save the lids from juice cans with a pull tab (the edges will be smooth). Encourage the toddlers to drop the lids inside an empty tissue box or a box with a slit cut out of the top.

5. For older toddlers, cover juice can lids and two to four tissue boxes with different colors or patterns of self-adhesive paper. Boxes with tops, such as those from diaper wipes, can also be used by cutting a slit into each box top. Encourage the toddlers to drop the lids into the box of the matching pattern or color.

To do again

Cover three boxes of different sizes with the same pattern of self-adhesive paper. Encourage the toddlers to match the lid to the box of the right size.

Teaching hints

The lids from juice cans with pull tabs can be used in any number of ways in the classroom with toddlers from matching games to pretend cookies. Just use your imagination.

Skills encouraged

fine motor, matching

Language to use with toddlers

box
match
same
inside
top
lid
color
pattern
open
close

Materials

boxes with lids
tissue boxes
juice can lids
self-adhesive paper

Building Blocks

Make lightweight blocks in any number of patterns and colors inexpensively from boxes and empty packages for the toddlers to build up high and of course, knock down.

Skills encouraged

gross motor, creative expression

Language to use with toddlers

blocks
build
stack
on top
line up
next to
knock down
line
round
square
big
little
colors

Materials

assorted boxes and containers
self-adhesive paper
newspaper, optional

To do

1. Collect a variety of the following to use for building blocks
> sturdy small to medium size boxes
> sturdy food packages, such as oatmeal canisters, potato chip cans
> diaper wipe containers
> laundry soap boxes

2. Cover the items with self-adhesive paper. The boxes can be filled with crumpled up newspaper for extra durability if desired.

3. Place the blocks out for the toddlers to use for building. Encourage them to stack the blocks to make towers, line up the blocks to make fences or a road.

4. Talk with the toddlers about the colors, sizes and shapes of the blocks. Count the blocks as they stack them up high.

5. Replace the blocks as needed.

6. Cover the blocks with different colors and patterns of self-adhesive paper according to the season or theme, such as wood tones and tan in fall, shades of blue in winter, pastels in spring and brighter colors in the summer.

To do again

Cover some of the boxes and containers with fabric scraps, felt, fur for texture blocks.

Teaching hints

Keep in mind that knocking the blocks down is more fun for younger toddlers than building, while older toddlers do actually begin to build items. Knocking down is a excellent cause and effect activity for toddlers as they learn that they can make a stack of blocks fall down.

Stepping Blocks

Recycle old phone books to make sturdy blocks for the toddlers to practice their gross motor skills.

To do

1. Cover old phone books with self-adhesive paper. A stack of old magazines taped together can also be covered with self-adhesive paper.

2. Let the toddlers explore the heavy blocks. Talk with them about the heavy weight, the colors and patterns.

3. Encourage the toddlers to step on, step off, step over, jump off the "stepping blocks."

4. Have the toddlers help you line up the "stepping blocks" for them to walk across like a beam.

5. Space the blocks apart like stepping stones. With young toddlers, encourage them to walk between the blocks. With older toddlers, encourage them to step from one block to the next.

To do again

Use old phone book pages for toddlers to practice their tearing skills.

Skills encouraged

gross motor

Language to use with toddlers

block
heavy
colors
pictures
step on
step over
walk on
line up

Materials

old phone books or magazines
tape
self-adhesive paper

Saving for a Rainy Day

Set aside popular toys in a box to always have a special surprise ready for a rainy day.

Skills encouraged

pretend play, sensory exploration, fine motor, language

Language to use with toddlers

surprise
special treat
wow
super
rain
outside
inside

Materials

storage box or basket
toys
ribbon

To do

1. Put special toys and items in a large storage box or basket to bring out on rainy or stormy days. Include items that are not out every day or items the toddlers have especially enjoyed in the past, such as special blocks, fire trucks, a play city, toy piano, playdough.

2. Tie a large ribbon around the box to make it even more like a special treat.

3. Bring out the box during bad weather. Show excitement with all the surprises, saying "Wow" when unpacking the box.

4. Play with the toddlers with the toys and special things. Talk with them about all the neat items.

5. Repack the box when finished to save for another rainy day.

6. Change the items in the box when the items do not seem as special.

To do again

Have a bag with a special book, puppet or other small items to use at the last minute, such as when a meal is late or for last-minute picnics on a nice day.

Teaching hints

Having a box of special toys set aside exclusively for bad weather reduces the need for additional last minute planning. Since its use is restricted, the appearance of the box makes the day special.

Home connections

Put away some of your child's toys. Periodically bring out these new toys to maintain her interest and to use for rainy days or weekends at home. Fill a basket of special toys, such as party favors, stickers or even junk mail (see How Trashy! on page 154.) Have a special tote bag of toys for long car trips too.

For Toddlers Personally

Me, Me, Me

Toddlers are in love with themselves. Using mirrors with a chant about "me" lets them get to know that special person even more.

Skills encouraged

self-esteem, language

Language to use with toddlers

me
two arms
two legs
ten fingers
ten toes
two eyes
two ears
one head
one nose
parts of the body

Materials

none needed

To do

1. Say the following chant with the toddlers.

> *Me, me, me (point to self)*
> *Look at me*
> *And you will see*
> *Fingers, toes (hold up fingers and point to toes)*
> *Head and nose! (touch head and nose)*
> *All on me!*

2. With older toddlers say the rhyme with the addition of numbers and more parts of the body.

> *Me, me, me (point to self)*
> *Look at me*
> *And you will see*
> *10 fingers, 10 toes (hold up fingers and point to toes)*
> *2 arms, 2 legs (hold up arms and point to legs)*
> *2 eyes, 2 ears (point to arms and legs)*
> *1 head and 1 nose! (point to head and nose)*
> *All on me!*

3. Say the rhyme with the toddler while looking in a mirror.

To do again

Have child stand in front of a mirror with you. Say the first part of the verse and talk about other parts of the body.

> *Me, me, me*
> *Look at me*
> *And you will see (point to and label different parts of the child's body;*
> *let her identify parts too)*
> *And that is all of me! (holds hands overhead)*

Teaching hints

Have unbreakable mirrors around the room for toddlers to look at themselves as much as possible. Add one to the dress-up area, cozy area, over the sensory tub or almost anywhere in the room. Plastic hand held make-up mirrors work well when talking about parts of the body or characteristics with the toddlers.

Home connections

This is a perfect rhyme to say in the bathtub and when drying off your child.

Bippity-Boppity-Boo

Turn diaper changes into a special one-on-one time with a chant about toddlers' pride and joy—their belly buttons.

To do

1. When changing a toddler's diaper, chant the following:

> *Belly button, belly button (trace circle around child's navel)*
> *Bippity-boppity-boo (trace in opposite direction)*
> *And I love you! (tap child's belly button or give hug)*

2. During playtime or special one-on-one times, trace circles on the child's back or knee cap. Say the child's name in place of belly button.

Teaching hints

Caregiving routines, such as diaper changing, are premium teaching times with toddlers. Use these times to give quality one-on-one attention by talking, singing, touching and making full eye contact with each toddler.

Skills encouraged

language

Language to use with toddlers

belly button
circle
navel
knee
hug
I love you!

Materials needed

none needed

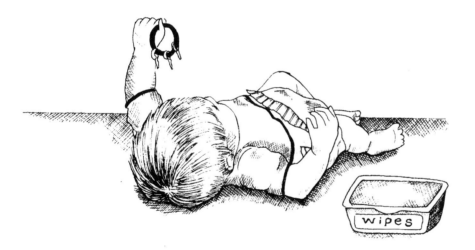

Hey, Hey

Give the toddlers individual recognition with a playful chant about their names, bodies and activities.

Skills encouraged

language, self-esteem

Language to use with toddlers

ears
eyes
tongue
feet
hands
head
knees
clothes
wear
friend
play

Materials needed

none needed

To do

1. Focus on the child's name and parts of her body with the following chant.

> *Hey, hey, Tara, Tara,*
> *Where are your ears today? (point to ears)*

Ask about other parts of the body, such as eyes, tongue, feet.

2. Vary the last line to focus on clothing or favorite items.

> *Hey, hey, Tara, Tara,*
> *What do you have today? (or, what are you wearing today)*

Talk about the child's blanket, snugly or specific items of clothing.

3. Say the chant to acknowledge the toddlers presence and activities in the room.

> *Hey, hey, Shelly and Bobby,*
> *I see you all are playing with the balls today.*

Talk with the toddlers about who they are playing with or what they are doing.

To do again

Say the chant with the child's first and last names to familiarize them with their full names.

Teaching hints

It's best to sing the chant informally as the toddlers play or during caregiving routines rather than singing as a large group since many toddlers will not have the attention span for each child to have a turn.

Home connections

Change the last line to ask for toddler's input: "What shall we eat today?" "What shall we play today?" Or make suggestions for an activity through the chant.

> *Hey, hey, one and all*
> *Let's take a walk today.*

All of Me

Go beyond thumbkin and pinky and identify parts of the body with toddlers.

To do

1. Sing the following to the tune of "Where Is Thumbkin?"

> *Where is your nose? Where is your nose?*
> *There it is. There it is.*
> *Touch it with your finger. Touch it with your finger.*
> *Just like me. Just like me. (touch nose)*

Substitute other parts of the body, such as eyes, hair or belly button.

2. Use the verse to explore actions with the parts of the body.

> *Where are your hands? Where are your hands?*
> *Here they are. Here they are.*
> *Clap them together. Clap them together.*
> *Just like me. Just like me.*

3. Additional suggestions include:

> *...feet...stamp them on the floor...*
> *...head...turn it side to side...*
> *...arms...put them in the air...*
> *...fingers...wiggle them around...*
> *...shoulders...move them up and down...*

4. With older toddlers introduce less familiar parts of the body, such as cheek, elbow, wrist.

To do again

Use the verse with a number of searching games, from friends or specific toys in the class to identifying items in pictures.

Teaching hints

It is important to use correct terminology for parts of the body rather than slang or the "pet" names they use, even with toddlers.

Home connections

An ideal song to use for bath time to learn about parts of the body.

Skills encouraged ★

language

Language to use with toddlers

Where is...?
body
nose
eyes
head
fingers
arms
feet
hands
shoulder
elbow
touch
clap
stamp
Just like me!

Materials needed

none needed

Here's a Story

Most toddlers love recognition! Tell simple stories to recognize the uniqueness of each child with a verse about their hair, eyes and favorite things.

Skills encouraged

self-esteem, language

Language to use with toddlers

story
names
hair
eyes
colors
family
likes
favorite
to do
smile

Materials

photographs of the children
    or a mirror

Teaching hints

Use this chant during playtime to spend one-on-one time with the children as they play. It is also an ideal verse for caregiving routines like diaper changes, toileting, mealtimes.

Home connections

Use the verse as part of your child's bedtime routine and talk about your child's day with the story portion.

To do

1. Have the toddler sit in your lap. Let her look in a mirror or at a photo of herself. Talk about her smile, face, hair color, eye color.

2. Chant the following verse to the child:

>   *Here's a story about Margaret. (child's name)*
>   *Margaret with her blonde hair and green eyes too.*
>   *Let me tell you all about her.*

3. Talk about the child in terms of favorite things to do, favorite foods, family members, clothing.

4. Let older toddlers add other favorite things.

To do again

While holding up a photograph of a toddler, chant the following verse.

>   *Here's a picture of DJ.*
>   *DJ with the brown hair and brown eyes too.*
>   *Show me where DJ is here at school with you.*
>   *(Ask toddlers to find child)*

Continue with photographs of the other toddlers.

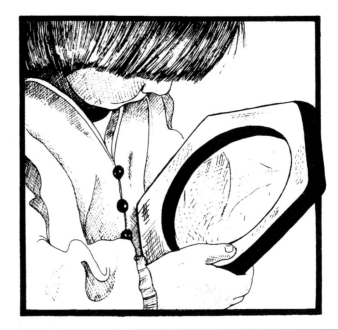

Chapter Three

Playing Footsie

Let the toddlers take off their shoes for special fun playing footsie.

To do

1. Take off shoes and talk with the toddlers about their two feet, ten toes, big toe, little toe.

2. Say the traditional "This Little Piggy" nursery rhyme, or sing "Where Is Big Toe?" to the tune of "Where Is Thumbkin?"

3. Encourage them to wiggle their toes, point or stretch their toes, slide their feet on the ground, walk on tiptoes. Even try "clapping" their feet together.

4. Provide different sensory materials for them to feel with their bare feet, such as a scratchy door mat, furry craft fur, spongy pillow, soft felt. Talk with them about the different textures.

5. Place two small chairs next to a dish tub or baby bath tub with a small (VERY small!) amount of water. Let two toddlers sit together and soak their feet. Provide a towel to dry their feet. Let them rub baby lotion on their feet afterwards if they desire.

To do again

Make foot prints by painting fingerpaint or tempera paint on the bottom of the child's feet. Hold his hand while he walks around on a long sheet of butcher paper. Talk with him about the slippery, cold paint and the prints his feet make. Have the child step into a dish tub of water at the end of the paper to rinse off the paint.

Teaching hints

Even toddlers' feet need time out of shoes. Let them take off their shoes at nap time to give their feet a rest too.

Home connections

Play footsie with your toddler now and then.

Skills encouraged

sensory exploration

Language to use with toddlers

2 feet
10 toes
1,2,3...
feel
tickle
big toe
little toe
scratchy
soft
furry

Materials

sensory materials
two small chairs
dish pan
towel
baby lotion

Ten Little Fingers and Toes

Fingers and toes come in quite handy for counting and getting rid of the wiggles with toddlers.

Skills encouraged

language, fine motor

Language to use with toddlers

fingers
toes
1,2,3...
hand
foot
wiggle
crawl
tap

Materials

none needed

To do

1. Count fingers with the toddlers with the following variations to the traditional "Ten Little" tune.

> *1 little, 2 little, 3 little fingers,*
> *4 little, 5 little, 6 little fingers,*
> *7 little, 8 little, 9 little fingers, (hold up fingers one by one or*
> > *count on child's hand)*
> *10 little fingers on my hand. (hold up 10 fingers)*

2. Add the following verses as desired.

> *They wiggle and they wiggle all together.*
> *They wiggle and they wiggle all together.*
> *They wiggle and they wiggle all together. (wiggle fingers)*
> *10 little fingers on my hand. (hold up 10 fingers)*
>
> *They clap and they clap all together... (clap hands)*
>
> *They crawl and they crawl on my leg/arm... (crawl fingers on leg/arm)*
>
> *They hide and they hide behind my back... (put hands behind back)*

Suggested books

Read *Hand Hand Fingers Thumb* by Al Perkins or *Piggies* by Don and Audrey Wood.

To do again

Take off shoes and count toes with the tune. Wiggle and stamp the toes for additional verses.

Teaching hints

Many toddlers will be able to count by rote indicating they know the "language of counting" without a true understanding of counting objects. Gradually toddlers will develop an awareness that one stands for one object, two for two items and so on. Becoming familiar with the words of counting is a first step to truly counting objects.

Home connections

Count informally throughout the day with your toddler to familiarize her with the "language of counting." Count toys, pieces of food, family members in the car. Count almost anything.

Chapter Three

Don't Skip

Skipping is beyond most toddlers, but they can move in other ways to "Skip to My Lou" so don't skip over this lively tune.

Roll, roll, roll your hands...

Rub, rub, rub your hands...

Shake, shake, shake your hands...

2. Use the tune with other parts of the body:

Stamp, stamp, stamp your feet...

Jump, jump, jump on two feet...

Nod, nod, nod your head...

Crawl, crawl, crawl on your knees...

Wiggle, wiggle, wiggle your body...

3. Use your imagination for other ways to move. Let the toddlers make suggestions.

4. End with a quiet activity of laying down, such as "Rest, rest, rest your body" to refocus the toddlers' energy.

To do again

Use the verse for caregiving routines and transitions:

Pick, pick, pick up the dolls...

Wash, wash, wash your hands...

Skills encouraged
motor skills, language

Language to use with toddlers
hands
clap
shake
roll
feet
stamp
march
crawl
jump
move
body

Materials
none needed

Home connections
Use the tune to ask your toddler to do something or to focus their attention on a task. Music can be calming for both you and your child when "wills" start to clash.

To do
1. Encourage the toddlers to move their hands to the following verses sung to the tune of "Skip to My Lou."

Clap, clap, clap your hands.
Clap, clap, clap your hands.
Clap, clap, clap your hands.
Clap your hands my friends.

It Takes Two to Be Friends

Explore the idea of doing things with friends with a verse about friendly hands.

Skills encouraged

language, fine motor, friendship

Language to use with toddlers

hands
special
clap
roll
rub
hug
friends

Materials

Piggies by Audrey and Don Wood

To do

1. Read *Piggies* by Audrey and Don Wood.

2. Say the following chant about hands with actions to the toddlers:

> *I have two hands.*
> *And they are very special hands.*
> *They can clap together, (clap)*
> *They can roll together, (roll hands)*
> *They can rub together, (rub hands together)*
> *And they can give each other a hug, (hold hands together)*
> *Just like two friends.*

To do again

Fingerpaint and make handprints. Attach a copy of the verse for the parents to the handprints.

Chapter Three

My Body Can Do

No doubt toddlers can keep their bodies in constant motion. Sing a simple verse about all the things their bodies can do.

To do

1. Sing the following verse to "Twinkle Twinkle Little Star."

> *My two hands go clap, clap, clap. (clap)*
> *My two feet go stamp, stamp, stamp. (stamp)*
> *My two hands go thump, thump, thump. (tap head or pound on legs)*
> *My two feet go jump, jump, jump. (jump)*
> *My body can turn around and around. (turn around)*
> *And now my body can sit quietly down. (sit down)*

2. Repeat the verse, ending with "Now my body can lay quietly down" the second time.

To do again

Sing the verse slowly and then quickly.

Teaching hints

A good song to sing to get toddlers to sit down on the floor.

Skills encouraged

language, gross motor

Language to use with toddlers

two hands
two feet
jump
thump
stamp
clap
turn around
sit down

Materials

none needed

A Tall Tale

Toddlers will proclaim how BIG they are—let them show how they have grown with the following tall tale.

Skills encouraged

language, gross motor

Language to use with toddlers

tall
small
I am...
Can't see me!

Materials

none needed

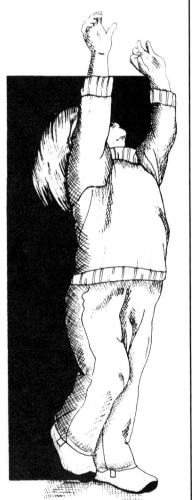

To do

1. Have the toddlers stretch and move with you with the following chant.

> *I am so, so very tall. (reach up high on tiptoes)*
> *I used to be so, so small. (bend down, touch floor)*
> *Now I am tall. (reach up high on tiptoes)*
> *Now I am small. (bend down)*
> *And now you can't see me at all! (curl up into ball with head down)*

2. Repeat the verse again as the toddlers show interest. With older toddlers, say it faster each time.

Wiggle Waggles

Have toddlers wiggle and waggle to release some of their natural energy.

To do

1. Sing and wiggle to the following verse sung to the tune of "Jingle Bells."

> *Wiggle waggles, (wiggle body)*
> *Wiggle waggles,*
> *Wiggle your body.*
> *Oh what fun it is to wiggle*
> *Your body every day, Hey!*

2. Repeat the tune with other wiggly parts of the body, such as fingers, toes, head.

To do again

Use the "Jingle Bells" tune with other actions, such as clapping hands, stamping feet, swaying arms, marching legs. For example:

> *Clapping hands, (clap hands)*
> *Clapping hands,*
> *Clap your hands.*
> *Oh what fun it is to clap*
> *Your hands every day, Hey!*

Teaching hints

This is a perfect tune to focus toddlers' random energy on rainy days, when lunch is late or at any time the toddlers' need to move.

Home connections

A fun song to do exercises in the car seat when your toddler is tired of sitting.

Skills encouraged

gross motor

Language to use with toddlers

wiggle
fingers
toes
body
every day

Materials

none needed

Dr. Toddler

Pretending to be doctors for dolls and stuffed animals with tummy aches and boo boos is an ideal way to talk about healthy bodies with toddlers.

Skills encouraged

pretend play, social skills

Language to use with toddlers

doctor
healthy
take care
fever
sick
hurt
feel better
bandage
rest
immunization
good food

Materials

white butcher paper
dolls or stuffed animals
ace bandages
white fabric
gauze strips
band-aids
children's doctor kit
stethoscope
books about visiting the
    doctor

Home connections

Let your toddler pretend to take care of you or a willing sibling, especially before check ups at the doctor.

To do

1. Cover a play table or doll bed with white butcher paper. Place dolls or stuffed animals on the examination table.

2. Add some of the following items to the doctor's office.
    ✓ ace bandages
    ✓ strips of white fabric for bandages
    ✓ gauze strips
    ✓ band-aid boxes
    ✓ children's doctor kit
    ✓ stethoscope
    ✓ white shirts (shorten if needed)
    ✓ other toddler-safe supplies

3. Show the toddlers how to use the stethoscope and other items in the doctor's kit. Have them put on the white shirt for a doctor's coat.

4. Tell the toddlers that the dolls are sick or hurt. Encourage them to take care of the dolls with the supplies. Help them tie bandages or put band-aids on the dolls hurt leg or bumped head.

5. Emphasize how the doll needs to eat good food like fruits and vegetables to grow and stay healthy. Pretend to give the doll an immunization so it won't get sick.

6. Pretend you have a boo boo or don't feel well and let the toddlers be your doctor.

Suggested books

Read *I am a Doctor* by Cynthia Benjamin and other books about visiting the doctor with the toddlers. Talk with them about their visits to the doctor.

To do again

Use the same supplies to take care of stuffed animals for a veterinarian's office.

Teaching hints

Use simple medical supplies and illnesses for toddlers, emphasizing more the head bumps, scrapes, stomachaches that they may have experienced themselves. Toddlers enjoy taking care of sick and hurt dolls more than being a patient for another toddler to be the doctor.

Chapter Three

Bump of Knowledge

Hardly a day goes by without at least one toddler getting a little "bump of knowledge." Let them learn about simple first aid as they pretend to do first aid on their dolls that get boo boos too.

To do

1. Fill a few resealable bags with ice cubes.

2. Place one or two dolls in a dish tub, baby bath tub or sensory tub with damp wash cloths and the bags of ice.

3. Tell the toddler the baby has a scratch or bump on her leg or arm or forehead. Encourage him to wash the boo boo with the wash cloth and put the ice on it to make it all better.

4. If desired, let the toddler put a bandage or two on the baby's "bump of knowledge."

5. Talk with them about how the ice and bandage help make the doll feel better.

6. Fill large resealable bags with ice for the toddlers to explore at other times, especially on hot days outside.

To do again

Place cotton balls, gauze squares and strips of gauze in the sensory tub for the toddlers to feel. Add large tongs for them to use to pick up the items or add a doll to use with the first aid supplies.

Teaching hints

Ice works wonders with all the "bumps of knowledge" that toddlers get so easily, especially when they first start to walk. Letting a toddler put ice on you or suck on an ice cube while applying ice to their bumps helps redirect their attention if they resist the cold ice being applied to their skin.

Home connections

Bags of frozen peas or corn work well as ice bags at home too.

Skills encouraged

sensory exploration, pretend play

Language to use with toddlers

bump of knowledge
scratch
scrape
bleeding
boo boo
wash
ice
bandage
all better

Materials

resealable bag
ice cubes
dolls
dish tub or baby bath tub
wash cloth
bandages

Creative First Aid

First aid supplies can be used in a number of creative ways for collages and painting activities.

Skills encouraged

creative expression, fine motor

Language to use with toddlers

cotton swab
cotton ball
gauze
bandage
paint
collage
stick

Materials

paint
glue
flat tray or container
paper
cotton swab
cotton ball
gauze squares

To do

1. Mix two to three different colors of paint. Add a small amount of glue to the paint. Pour into flat tray or container.

2. Let the toddler choose what color of paper and paint she wants to use.

3. Dip a cotton swab into paint. Encourage her to paint with the swab by making dots or moving it side to side.

4. Have her leave the swab on the paper. It will stick because of the glue.

5. Let her paint with another swab if she desires.

6. The toddler can also use the glue-paint with cotton balls or gauze squares held with a clothespin.

To do again

Make a collage of bandages. No glue is required and peeling the backing off truly challenges toddlers' fine motor skills. Make a collage of first aid supplies using cotton balls, gauze pieces, bandages, bandage wrappers and cotton swabs with the sticky side of self-adhesive paper as the backing.

Chapter Three

Follow the Path

Toddlers learn about concepts of space as they follow the path with their feet.

To do

1. Trace the soles of a toddler-size pair of shoes on a piece of poster board. Cut a large square around the feet. Laminate or cover the poster board with clear self-adhesive paper.

2. Place the feet on the floor. Encourage a toddler to step onto the feet and then jump off the paper feet.

3. Cut shoe-shapes out of self-adhesive paper. Place the feet in a path along the floor.

4. Encourage the toddlers to walk along the foot path.

To do again

Place a wide strip of masking tape on the floor in a line for the toddlers to walk across, step over and jump over the line. Put the tape down into squares for the toddlers to step inside, walk around or even sit inside the box.

Teaching hints

Place two feet in front of the sink to show the toddlers where to stand for washing hands.

Skills encouraged

gross motor, language

Language to use with toddlers

feet
stand
follow
walk on
step over
inside
around
across
square

Materials

toddler-size shoes
poster board
scissors
tape
self-adhesive paper

Toddler Yoga

Toddlers are constantly on the go! Help them relax with a very simplified version of yoga geared just for toddlers.

Skills developed

gross motor

Language to use with toddlers

stretch
wiggle
shake
arms
hands
leg
up
down

Materials

none needed

To do

1. Encourage toddlers to relax their bodies by doing the following movements with you. Count to five for each activity.

arms
> *hold arms overhead up (1,2,3,4,5)*
> *hold arms to the side (1,2,3,4,5)*
> *hold arms in front (1,2,3,4,5)*
> *wrap arms around your body (1,2,3,4,5)*

legs
> *hold one leg up (1,2,3,4,5)*
> *wiggle foot (1,2,3,4,5)*
> *put leg down (1,2,3,4,5)*
> *move foot back and forth (1,2,3,4,5)*

head
> *look up (1,2,3,4,5)*
> *look down (1,2,3,4,5)*
> *look to the side (1,2,3,4,5)*
> *look to the other side (1,2,3,4,5)*
> *move head up and down (1,2,3,4,5)*
> *move head side to side (1,2,3,4,5)*

2. Play relaxing instrumental music.

To do again

Have the toddlers follow you while you stretch your muscles by bending over, standing on tiptoes, leaning side to side.

Teaching hints

State the movement verbally, "Look up" and then do the action for the toddler to follow. Give the child time to copy your actions by counting to five. Use a very calm voice as this is intended to be a quiet activity. This will help many active toddlers to relax, even for just a few minutes.

Home connections

Lay in bed with your toddler in the morning or after nap. Stretch different parts of your body as you both wake up. Spend time relaxing and stretching together on a blanket on the floor after a busy day.

Chapter Three

Home, Sweet Home

Stories and pictures from home help bridge the gap between home and school for the toddlers and their families.

To do

1. Read books about houses and families, such as:

✓ *The Napping House* by Audrey Wood
✓ *Outside, Inside* by Carolyn Crimi
✓ *I Love My Daddy Because...* and *I Love My Mommy Because...* by Gaylord Porter
✓ *Mommy and Me, Daddy and Me, Grandpa and Me, Grandma and Me*, and other books by Neil Ricklen

2. Cut simple house shapes out of paper or wallpaper samples. The bottom square should be at least 7" x 7" to hold a picture.

3. Have the parents send a picture of their child or family, preferably taken in front of their house.

4. Glue the pictures on the house shapes.

5. Put the houses together on the wall or a bulletin board for all the toddlers to look at.

6. Talk with the toddlers about who they live with and what can be seen in the pictures.

7. Have the parents bring in other pictures of their child at home with a pet, in their bedroom, in the kitchen and with extended family members to put on the house shapes over a period of time.

To do again

Cut out pictures of houses from real estate buyers guides. Let older toddlers make a collage with the pictures.

Teaching hints

Start early with the notification of the need for the pictures. Some parents will be able to send the pictures the next day while others may need to take a picture or even need reminders!

Home connections

Look at photo albums with your child often. See if he can identify what room or where the picture was taken.

Skills encouraged

language, self-esteem

Language to use with toddlers

house
live
home
family
inside
pet
room
kitchen
bedroom

Materials

books about houses and families
paper
wallpaper samples
scissors
glue

Attraction

With an endless number of shapes and colors, magnets attract toddlers attention for lots of endless fun practicing fine motor skills.

Skills encouraged

fine motor, language

Language to use with toddlers

magnet
stick
pull up
pictures
shapes
refrigerator

Materials

magnets
cookie sheet

To do

1. Gather a variety of plastic magnets that pass the choke test for the toddlers.

2. Put them out for the toddlers to explore on an old cookie sheet. Encourage them to take the magnets off the cookie sheet and then put them back on.

3. Talk with the toddlers about the different pictures, colors and shapes of the magnets.

To do again

Make magnets by attaching magnetic strips to wooden craft shapes. Make picture magnets from magazine pictures or photos of the toddlers—glue poster board with a magnet strip on the back. Shapes can also be cut out of magnetic sheets (found at art or craft supply stores). Attach magnetic strips to felt story patterns. Use with a cookie sheet to tell stories with older toddlers.

Block Party

Promote toddlers' budding building skills with a "block party" of building houses for each other and the dolls.

To do

1 Put large blocks in a large square around you. Invite the toddlers to come sit with you inside your house.

2. Encourage the toddlers to build houses for each other or the dolls in the class.

3. Have them build homes and cages for the stuffed animal pets as well.

4. Provide child hammers for the toddlers to practice hammering on a pounding bench or on the blocks.

5. Suggest they also build "high rises" by stacking the blocks like towers or a bed by laying the blocks flat on the floor.

To do again

Let the toddlers print with colored plastic or smaller wooden blocks. Match the color of the paint to the blocks if possible. Provide square and triangle shapes cut out of wallpaper for the toddlers to make a shape collage. Some older toddlers may put the two shapes together like a house but do not require that so it remains their expression rather than the teachers' creation.

Teaching hints

Large cardboard blocks works best for this activity with the toddlers. See Building Blocks on page 48 on how to make inexpensive cardboard blocks. Older toddlers also enjoy building with the smaller wooden and plastic blocks as well. Younger toddlers tend to stack the blocks up high just to knock them down, while older toddlers do start lining up blocks and making things.

Skills encouraged

fine motor, creative expression

Language to use with toddlers

blocks
build
houses
hammer
wall
fence
inside
outside
visit
doll
pet
shapes

Materials

blocks

Oh Where, Oh Where?

Toddlers enjoy singing about the antics of the missing pets with a traditional tune.

Skills encouraged

language

Language to use with toddlers

dog
where
tail
short
ears
long
find

Materials

puppet or stuffed dog and cat

Teaching hints

For the children who do not have a pet, let them bring in a picture of their favorite stuffed animal pet.

To do

1. Look at pictures and books about dogs and cats. Have the parents send in a picture of their family pet. Talk with the toddlers about the pictures and their own pets.

2. Chant or sing the following traditional verse:

> *Oh where, oh where has my little dog gone? (shake head "no")*
> *Oh where can he be?*
> *With his tail so short, (hand behind back, wiggle fingers)*
> *And his ears so long, (put hands like dog ears on the side of head)*
> *Oh where, oh where can he be? (hands to side)*

3. Sing about a cat with a few changes to the verse.

> *Oh where, oh where has my big cat gone? (shake head "no")*
> *Oh where can she be?*
> *With her tail so long, (show length with hands)*
> *And her ears so short (hold one finger on each side of your*
>   *head for cat's ears)*
> *Oh where, oh where can she be? (hands to side)*

4. Use a stuffed cat and dog or puppet with the verses. Hide the animal behind your back. Have the cat or dog come out at the end of the verse for the toddlers to hug and pet.

5. Have a pet parade of the toddlers' favorite stuffed animal pets.

To do again

Cut out pictures of cats and dogs from magazines for the toddlers to glue onto paper for a collage. Mount the pictures onto small poster board squares to put together into a pet book with yarn or book rings. See Toddler Books in *Toddlers Together* for detailed instructions.

Chapter Three

Pet Rock

Toddlers can be quite nurturing. Let them show their tender, loving side with a pet rock and a few simple rocks.

To do

1. Gather enough rocks and boxes to have at least one for each toddler.

2. Cut the fabric into 4" x 6" squares.

3. Let the toddler pick out the rock he would like to have for his pet, a box for its cage, and a fabric square for a blanket.

4. Provide markers, scraps of fabric and shapes from gift wrap for the toddler to use to decorate the cages.

5. Cut felt into shapes of food such as green circles and yellow triangles.

6. Encourage the toddler to take care of his pet rock by covering it with the blanket, carrying it in the box and feeding it the food cut out of felt. Talk with the toddler about his rock and what he calls it.

7. Sing songs to the pet rock, such as any of the songs for babies on pages 74-76.

8. Provide a dish tub with a small amount of water, cloths and toothbrushes for the toddlers to bathe their pet rocks.

To do again

Let the toddlers decorate their pet rocks with markers, collage materials like felt, ribbons, yarn. Avoid the temptation to make the rocks look like an animal. Remember it is the toddler's pet rock and it should remain his creation.

Teaching hints

For younger toddlers or those needing more concrete pets, provide plastic animals or small stuffed animals that they can take care of in their boxes. Have them bring one from home if needed.

Skills encouraged

creative expression, pretend play

Language to use with toddlers

rock
pet
take care
feed
box
sleep
bathe
decorate

Materials

rocks
fabric
scissors
glue
markers
paint
felt
shoe or small boxes
dish tub, water, cloths

Hush Little Baby

Music soothes as well as entertains. The familiarity of traditional lullabies encourages the wholehearted participation of toddlers, teachers and parents, especially those with limited musical skills or interest.

Skills encouraged

language

Language to use with toddlers

hush
baby
sing
happy
bedtime

Materials

doll or stuffed animal

To do

1. Pretend to rock a baby while saying the following rhyme.

> *Hush little baby (ies),*
> *Don't you cry,*
> *For I'm (we're) going*
> *To sing a lullaby!*

2. Sing lullabies while pretending to rock a baby or use a doll or stuffed animal in your arms. Sing the traditional "Rock-a-bye Baby," "Bye Baby Bunting" or any from your own childhood or culture.

3. Make up additional verses to the above verse, such as:

> *Hush little baby*
> *I want to tell you*
> *How very much*
> *I love you.*

or

> *Hush little baby*
> *I can't see you (cover eyes)*
> *And this is how*
> *We play peekaboo! (uncover eyes)*

To do again

Additional lullabies follow in this chapter as well as any in Lullaby and Good Night on page 135 or Good Night, Friends on page 136.

Teaching hints

Use the verses and lullabies individually with the toddlers while rocking or holding them in your lap for ideal one-on-one attention and to calm an upset child, especially with times of separation anxiety that can appear or reappear anytime during the year with toddlers.

Home connections

As in the toddler classroom, music reduces tension and brings peaceful harmony into the home with toddlers as well as promoting language development. Sing or chant often with your toddler. Lullabies and nursery rhymes work especially well since they are familiar to most adults and help even the musically timid feel comfortable with singing.

You Are My Sunshine

Toddlers enjoy singing a variations of a familiar lullaby to their babies and friends.

To do

1. Provide receiving blankets for the toddlers to wrap their babies and stuffed animals to keep them warm.

2. Encourage the toddlers to rock or cuddle their baby doll or stuffed animal as they sing with you or sway to the beat of the following traditional lullaby:

> *You are my sunshine, my only sunshine.*
> *You make me happy when skies are gray.*
> *You'll never know dear how much I love you.*
> *So please don't take my sunshine away!*

3. Substitute the names and special qualities of individual children sitting in your lap or nearby, such as:

> *You are our Aaron, our only Aaron.*
> *You make us happy when skies are gray.*
> *You'll never know dear how much we love you.*
> *So please don't take your special smiles away!*

Or, use "friends" or "buddies" to refer to a larger group of children.

Teaching hints

Holding, rocking and gentle back rubs while singing familiar lullabies and songs helps soothe almost any distraught toddler, especially during their adjustment to a new class.

Home connections

Personalize this and other lullabies at home with the child's name for an easy way to boost a child's self-esteem. Use the song to also help with a toddlers' adjustment to a new sibling with the following verses:

> *You are my big brother, my only big brother....*
or
> *You are my baby brother, my only baby brother....*

Change the words to refer to any family member from baby to mama or papa. Look at pictures of the specific family member while singing the verses.

Skills encouraged

language, social

Language to use with toddlers

song
rock
you
baby
special
happy
my sunshine
friend
name

Materials

dolls
blankets
stuffed animals

Baby's Music

Toddlers enjoy singing about babies, especially when the song involves simple hand actions of clapping and the all-time favorite game of peekaboo.

Skills encouraged

language, fine motor

Language to use with toddlers

baby
music
game
clapping
peekaboo
rock a baby bye
cradle

Materials

none needed

To do

1. Chant or sing in a sing-song fashion the following verse with the related actions.

> *Here's the baby's music with hands clapping too. (clap)*
> *Here's the way the baby plays at ... (pause) peekaboo*
> *(cover eyes, then uncover)*
> *Here's a bear for baby, big and soft and round. (rub tummy)*
> *Here's baby's drum, pound, pound, pound. (pound floor*
> *or fists together)*
> *Here's the baby's hat that keeps her head dry. (hands on head)*
> *Here's the baby's daddy, rock a baby bye! (pretend to rock baby)*

2. When older toddlers are very familiar with the verse, whisper the words while doing the actions. It is fun to hear the toddlers say the words themselves.

Teaching hints

Shorten the verse if needed for younger toddlers by eliminating one or two of the lines. Be sure to leave in the clapping, peekaboo and rocking lines as those tend to be especially popular and easy to copy for the younger ages.

Home connections

Sing the verse about your toddler or younger sibling by substituting the child's name in place of "baby."

Chapter Three

Knock at the Door

Toddlers still enjoy the playful interaction and touch of tickle type games as long as they are gentle and respectful of toddlers' wishes to end the game.

To do

1. Read *More, More Said the Baby* by Vera Williams.

2. Do the following traditional tickle rhyme with a toddler.

> *Knock at the door (gently tap on the child's forehead)*
> *Peep in (lift child's eyelid or touch side of eye)*
> *Lift up the latch (gently push up on the end of the child's nose)*
> *And walk in. (pretend to "walk" on child's chin with two fingers)*

3. Repeat the verse with the toddler as she desires.

4. Encourage the toddlers to do the rhyme to their doll or stuffed animals.

To do again

Do other touch-tickle rhymes with the toddlers, such as Bumble Tickle or Like a Teddy Bear in *Toddlers Together* and Here Comes the Bumble Bee! on page 227.

Teaching hints

Remember to respect the toddlers' wishes as to whether they want to be tickled and always keep your touch gentle.

Home connections

Playful games such as these work especially well at home when a toddler is refusing to get dressed, having to wait or just to change the mood.

Skills encouraged

language, social interaction

Language to use with toddlers

knock
door
peep
lift
walk in
tickle
gentle
play
giggle
creep
mouse
bumble bee

Materials

More, More Said the Baby by Vera Williams
doll or stuffed animals

Exploring the Past

Although they proclaim themselves as no longer babies, toddlers still enjoy the action response component of many infant toys as they practice their fine motor skills with a traditional busy box.

Skills encouraged

fine motor, cognitive

Language to use with toddlers

busy box
baby
sounds
turn
move
bell
see
pictures

Materials

action-reaction toys
instrumental music
baby care items

Home connections

Use baby toys as a way to help big brother or sister prepare for the arrival of the new sibling or to talk with a toddler about how much she has grown. Let the toddler or child freely explore her old toy's before and after the arrival of the new sibling. Stress to her how she once played with these toys when she was a baby and soon she can teach the baby how to play with the toys. If possible, show the toddler pictures of her playing with the toys when she was an infant. Talk about how much she has grown and learned because all toddlers love to feel big.

To do

1. Bring out two or more busy boxes, pop-up toys or other action-reaction toys. Provide at least two to avoid problems with sharing.

2. Let the toddlers explore the busy box toys on their own.

3. Talk with the toddlers about the actions they are doing, such as turning and sliding and the sounds made by their actions.

4. Put on upbeat instrumental music and play the busy boxes to the music.

5. Add the busy boxes to a Toddler Nursery with other baby toys and baby care items, such as empty powder and lotion bottles, diaper wraps, newborn disposable diapers, bottles, empty box of baby cereal, receiving blankets and books about babies for the toddlers to use to take care of the dolls and stuffed animals (see We're Not Babies in *Toddlers Together*).

Teaching hints

Even though busy boxes and pop-up items are considered infant toys, even older toddlers can benefit from exploring the cause and effect, object permanence (the concept that objects still exist when they are out of sight) and fine motor elements of these toys.

Shake, Rattle and Roll

Baby rattles are a perfect shaker for toddlers to explore cause and effect and use with music.

To do

1. Place a variety of infant rattles in a basket for the toddlers to explore on their own.

2. Talk with the toddlers about the sounds made when they shake the rattles.

3. Sing songs, nursery rhymes or put on music to shake the rattles with the beat.

To do again

Make shakers to compare sounds and to show the toddlers how rattles are made. Use the rattles in any of the activities for shakers in *Toddlers Together*.

Skills encouraged

fine motor, cognitive

Language to use with toddlers

rattle
baby toy
shaker
shake
sounds
music

Materials

baby rattles
basket

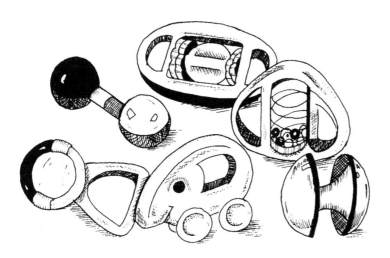

Oh So Smooth

Baby lotion provides soothing sensory experiences for toddlers and their babies.

Skills encouraged

sensory, language

Language to use with toddlers

lotion
smooth
smell
rub
hand
arm
shoulder
back
foot
leg
massage

Materials

baby lotion
doll
empty baby lotion bottles

To do

1. Place a small amount of baby lotion in the toddler's palm. Encourage him to rub the lotion on his hands, arms and legs.

2. Talk with him about the parts of his body he is rubbing the lotion on and the smell of the lotion.

3. Rub some lotion on his back, shoulder or hand for a "toddler massage." Talk with him about your actions.

4. Let the toddler rub a small amount of lotion on a washable doll. Talk with him about the parts of the doll's body. The toddlers can also wash their doll in a small amount of soapy water in a dish tub or small baby bath tub (see Bathing Beauties in *Toddlers Together*).

5. Provide empty baby lotion bottles with the dolls for the toddlers to pretend to rub lotion on their babies. Be sure to glue the lid on the bottles as they can present a choking hazard.

To do again

Fingerpaint with baby lotion (see Lotion Motion on page 86).

Teaching hints

The tactile experience of the lotion and massage is soothing for many toddlers. Try it with an overactive or upset toddler to help calm the child.

Home connections

A body, hand or even foot massage is fun for many parents and toddlers after a long day at school and work. Name different parts of the body as you rub lotion on your child.

Chapter Three

You Must Have Been a Beautiful Baby

While toddlers enjoy looking at pictures of babies, they will look at their own pictures in disbelief for they often have difficulty imagining they were ever a baby.

To do

1. Encourage parents to send in a baby picture and a recent photo of their child.

2. Put the pictures up on the wall or bulletin board next to each other for all the toddlers to see.

3. Talk with the toddlers about the pictures, emphasizing how small each child was when they were a baby and how much each has grown. Help the toddlers find their own picture and identify their friends.

4. Put out parenting magazines in the book or cozy area for the toddlers to look at pictures of babies and children. Talk with the toddlers about the pictures.

5. Make a Baby Book from magazine pictures of infants, especially large, simple pictures of one baby. Glue the pictures onto poster board squares. Laminate or cover the squares with clear self-adhesive paper for durability if desired. Put the pages together like a book with yarn or book rings (see Toddler Books in *Toddlers Together*).

6. Add the Baby Book to the book or cozy area for the toddlers to enjoy. Talk with them about the pictures, emphasizing what babies do and parts of their face.

To do again

Let older toddlers glue magazine pictures of babies on construction paper for a baby collage. Put their collages on the bulletin board or wall near the home living area or in the Toddler Nursery (see Exploring the Past, page 78).

Teaching hints

Toddlers seem to prefer pictures of real children and animals. Parenting magazines are an ideal source for photos of infants and children. Keep this in mind when selecting books and pictures for toddlers.

Home connections

Toddlers enjoy looking at pictures of themselves with their parents. This is an ideal time to emphasize how special they are, how much they have grown and name family members. Looking at newborn and early infancy pictures is also an ideal way to help prepare a toddler for a new sibling. Parents can make a "My Own Baby Book" for their toddler by placing special photos of the child and family members in a small, inexpensive album. The toddlers can keep this book of photos as their own. Make one each year for the child as he grows.

Skills encouraged

language

Language to use with toddlers

baby
tiny
crawl
cry
sleep
eyes
nose
mouth

Materials

photographs of the children
clear self-adhesive paper
magazines
poster board
glue
book rings
yarn
paper

Peekaboo, I Love You

Playing peekaboo still excites toddlers and promotes their understanding of object permanence, the notion the objects out of sight continue to exist.

Skills encouraged

cognitive, fine motor

Language to use with toddlers

pictures
wall
bulletin board
fabric
peekaboo
face
smile
happy
sad

Materials

magazines
tape
fabric
photos

To do

1. Collect large pictures of infants from parenting magazines or have parents send in pictures of their toddler as an infant.

2. Attach the pictures to the wall or bulletin board at the toddlers' level.

3. Cover each picture with a large piece of fabric.

4. Encourage the toddlers to play peekaboo with the baby in the picture by lifting up the cloth and saying "Peekaboo, I love you!"

5. Talk with the toddlers about the facial features and expression of the baby.

To do again

Use other pictures related to the different themes, such as animals or teddy bears, for the peekaboo wall.

Home connections

Play peekaboo and hiding games at home with toddlers for simple enjoyment. Toddlers also enjoy looking for hidden objects around the house that can be easily found.

Baby Blanket

Toddlers enjoy covering up the dolls and stuffed animals to keep them warm and will take pride in making a special keepsake baby blanket for them.

Skills encouraged

creative expression, pretend play

Language to use with toddlers

handprint
blanket
fabric
colors
special
cover up
keep warm
rectangle
extra special

Materials

children's favorite blankets
old white sheet or piece of muslin
fray check or pinking shears
fabric paint

To do

1. Have the toddlers bring in their special baby blanket. Talk with each one about his blanket, the softness, the colors, the fabric and how special it is to him.

2. Cut up an old white sheet or muslin into rectangles the size of an infant receiving blanket. Cutting with pinking shears or using fray check on the edges can be done if desired.

3. Spread fabric paint on one or both hands of the toddler and encourage him to make hand prints on the cloth. If more than one color of paint is available, let the toddler choose what color he wants to use and if he wants to make handprints in different colors.

4. Talk with the toddler about his handprints and how it makes his blanket extra special.

5. When the paint is dry, let the toddler use his blanket to cover up his baby or favorite stuffed animal to keep it warm.

6. Use the blankets with bedtime activities in the winter chapter or the activities related to blankets in *Toddlers Together*.

To do again

Use craft sponges with fabric paints for other designs, especially those shaped like hands and feet. The sponges can also be used to print on construction paper to relate to a theme or activity.

Baby Boogie

Dancing and moving like babies allows toddlers to crawl and practice other important motor skills.

Skills encouraged

gross motor

Language to use with toddlers

like a baby
crawl
bounce
wiggle
clap
music

Materials

pictures of infants
upbeat music

To do

1. Show the toddlers pictures of infants at different ages and levels of motor development. Talk with them about how new babies lay on their back and wiggle while others can sit, crawl or even stand.

2. Play upbeat instrumental music for the toddlers to "dance like babies" to the beat with you in some of the following ways:

> *lay down and wiggle body to the beat*
> *sit and clap or bounce upper body to the beat*
> *crawl while the music plays*
> *stand in one place and bounce body to the beat*

To do again

Move like babies with the following verses sung to the tune of "Here We Go 'Round the Mulberry Bush."

> *This is the way the baby stretches, the baby stretches, the baby*
> *   stretches.*
> *This is the way the baby stretches when he lays on his blanket.*
> *   (lay on floor and stretch arms and legs)*

Additional suggestions

> *...the baby crawls...when she is on the floor.*
> *...the baby rocks...when he sits up. (sway side to side)*
> *...the baby claps...when she hears music.*
> *...the baby walks...when he's almost one. (walk slowly)*
> end with
> *...the baby sleeps...in her crib.*

Teaching hints

Crawling is still an important motor skill activity for toddlers. Encourage them to crawl often with various movement activities.

Bottle Cap Designs

The caps and rings to old bottles can be used to print circles and other designs.

To do

1. Collect old plastic baby bottles. Parents of toddlers are often a good source for bottles that are no longer needed.

2. Examine the different bottles with the toddlers. Talk about the sizes, colors and pictures on the bottles. Have them practice taking off and putting back on the caps or covers and the rings for the nipples.

3. Gather different color bottle covers and nipple rings. The caps to the bottles used with disposable bags often have designs for printing.
Note: Keep all disposable bottle bags and nipples away from toddlers.

4. Mix paint to match the different colors of the bottle covers and rings. Put the covers and rings in the matching color of paint. Place the covers to bottles with disposable bags with the design down if any are being used.

5. Let the toddler pick what color of background paper she wants to use for printing.

6. Encourage the toddler to print with the bottle covers and rings by chanting "Paint paper, paint paper."

7. Talk with her about the colors, the circles, the sizes and the designs made with the bottle covers and rings.

To do again

Print circles of different sizes from the covers to food packages, such as peanut butter jars, spice containers, ketchup bottles. Match the color of the paint to the plastic cover.

Teaching hints

Although many toddlers no longer drink from a bottle by this age, some still do. Never make these children feel like a baby, but do encourage them to drink from a cup when they are thirsty and at mealtime. Avoid letting them walk around the classroom with a bottle in their mouth. Limit the use of the bottle to nap time or certain areas of the room if needed. Work closely with the parents in weaning their toddlers from the bottles. Often it is the parent who is not quite ready to give up the bottle, and they need encouragement too.

Skills encouraged

fine motor, creative expression

Language to use with toddlers

baby
bottle
cover
cap
ring
print
circles
big
little
designs
colors

Materials

old plastic baby bottles
paint
paper
flat tray

Home connections

Weaning from the bottle can be difficult for some families. Limit using the bottle to certain times of day, to just water and to specific areas of the house. Just be sure to stay with the process and don't give in to your toddler's tears.

Lotion Motion

Fingerpainting with baby lotion provides a soothing and sweet smelling sensory experience for toddlers.

Skills encouraged

sensory, fine motor

Language to use with toddlers

baby lotion
smooth
smear
rub
back and forth
smell
sweet
color
cold

Materials

baby lotion
flat tray or table top
towel

To do

1. Place about a spoonful of lotion on a table top or tray.

2. Encourage the toddler to paint with the lotion by moving his hands back and forth, up and down, and in circles in the lotion on the smooth surface.

3. Talk with the toddler about his movements, the smell, the color and the feel of the lotion.

4. Play soothing lullaby or instrumental music while the child explores the lotion.

5. When finished, encourage the toddler to rub the lotion on his hands, onto your hands, his legs, his tummy. The excess can be rubbed off with a towel.

To do again

Chill a bottle of lotion in the refrigerator. Let the toddler paint with the cold lotion or add a small amount to the room temperature lotion as the child fingerpaints. Talk with the toddler about the different temperatures.

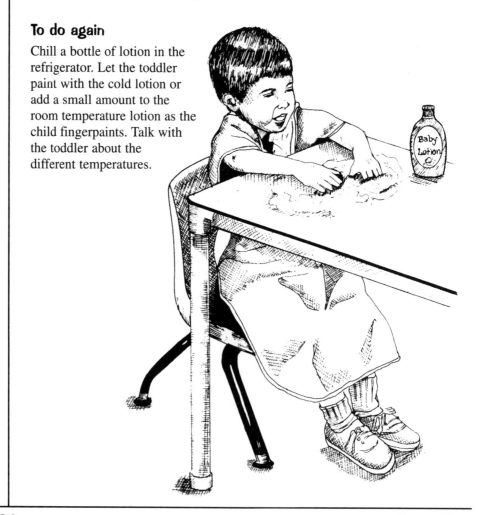

Here's My Baby

Toddlers enjoy rocking their pretend tiny baby to sleep in the following fingerplay.

To do

1. Say the following fingerplay with toddlers.

> *Here is my tiny baby. (hold up index finger)*
> *Here's how I'll put him to bed. (lay index finger*
>   *in palm of other hand)*
> *I'll cover him up, (fold fingers over index finger except for the tip)*
> *Under his blanket except for his tiny head. (wiggle tip of index finger)*
> *If he should start to cry, I'll hold him right here, (place index*
>   *finger on shoulder like holding a baby)*
> *And rock him like my Daddy who loves me so very dear.*
>   *(sway body to rock imaginary baby)*

2. Repeat with Mommy, Grandma or Grandpa as needed or desired to cover all the family patterns represented in the class. Mommy and Daddy can be used together in the last line.

3. Use the rhyme with a doll or stuffed animal and a blanket.

Suggested book

Read *A, B, C, D Tummy, Toes, Hands and Knees* by B. G. Hennessy.

Home connections

Use the verse at bedtime with your toddler. Personalize the fingerplay with your child's name, such as "Here is my love Lucas...."

Skills encouraged

language, fine motor

Language to use with toddlers

baby
finger
bed
cover
kiss
cry
hold
Daddy
Mommy

Materials

none needed

For Toddlers in Fall

Tree-mendous Trees

Help toddler develop an appreciation of nature early on by exploring the tremendous beauty of trees.

Skills encouraged

sensory exploration

Language to use with toddlers

trees
leaves
trunk
hug
feel
rough
branch
twigs
look up
birds
squirrels

Materials

blanket
basket
broccoli
bread sticks
napkins
unshelled peanuts, nuts and sunflower seeds
basket

To do

1. Examine the trees on the playground or take a walk around the school to look at more trees. Talk with the toddlers about the trees, leaves, trunks, branches, twigs. Talk with them about the animals that live in the tree, such as squirrels and birds.

2. Encourage them to feel the trunk by rubbing it and even hugging it. Talk with them about the rough or smooth texture, small or big trunk, tall tree and other observations.

3. Spread a blanket underneath the tree to have a picnic. Taste broccoli shaped like trees or bread sticks shaped like tree branches.

4. Encourage the toddlers to lie down and look up at the leaves on the branches.

5. Read a book and sing songs under the tree. Listen and look for birds.

6. Leave some unshelled peanuts, nuts and sunflower seeds under the tree for the squirrels and birds.

7. Let the toddlers collect acorns, leaves, twigs, pine cones, moss balls that have fallen from the trees. Save the larger items in a basket in the classroom for the toddlers to explore or use some of the items for a nature collage (see Natural Textures and Nature Collage in *Toddlers Together*).

To do again

Lay down and look at the clouds with older toddlers.

Home connections

Take a short hike or walk through a wooded area with your toddler. Have a picnic lunch under the trees around your house. Let your toddler take out some of his plastic or stuffed animals to play with under the trees.

A Beautiful Creation

Toddlers' scribbles are their most important marks (MIMs), just as a tree is an important natural resource. Display toddlers' MIMs on a tree like precious leaves in autumn for a beautiful creation.

To do

1. Cut a large tree trunk out of brown butcher paper or use white butcher paper painted brown.

2. Attach the tree to the wall or bulletin board.

3. Cut different leaf shapes (or oval shapes) out of light colors of paper, such as tan, yellow, white.

4. Let the toddler pick out what leaf she wants to color. Provide markers and crayons in fall colors (brown, red, orange, yellow) for the toddler to color the leaf shape.

5. Talk with her about the leaf, the colors she is using and the marks she is making.

6. When she is finished, let the toddler show you where she wants to put her leaf on or near the tree trunk.

7. Let her color another leaf shape if he desires.

To do again

Provide red and yellow fingerpaint for the toddler to use on a cookie sheet or large flat tray. Encourage her to smear the paint with her hands. Talk with her about the colors mixing to make orange, the feel of the paint and so on. Encourage her to make handprints on a large leave shape, or place a large leaf shape in fingerpaint to make a print of the toddler's fingerpainting (see Magic Prints in *Toddlers Together*). Display the fingerpainting on the tree trunk as well.

Teaching hints

Toddlers enjoy seeing pictures of themselves and their families. Display photos of the children and their families on leaf shapes on a large tree trunk for a Family Tree. Also, trace and cut out the toddler's hands for a unique leaf to add to the family tree.

Home connections

Make a truly unique family tree to look at with your toddler by attaching photos of different family members to leaf shapes. Attach to a paper tree trunk. Put the family tree in your child's room for him to look at often.

Skills encouraged

creative expression, fine motor, self-esteem

Language to use with toddlers

tree
leaves
colors
paint
draw
picture
lines
fingerpaint
handprint

Materials

butcher paper
paint
tape
paper
markers
crayons

For Toddlers in the Fall

To See What He Could See

The traditional song of "The Bear Went Over the Mountain" has endless possibilities of what toddlers can imagine a bear seeing on his journeys.

Skills encouraged

language, gross motor

Language to use with toddlers

bear
mountain
over
see
What did he see?
tree
lake

Materials

large pillows
pictures of animals, trees
pillows

To do again

Sing about other animals that relate to another theme or to other places, such as the bear went in the forest, squirrel went up the tree, bird in the sky, cat went over the fence.

To do

1. Sing "The Bear Went Over the Mountain" with the following actions.

> *The bear went over the mountain, (crawl two fingers in arc like*
>   *bear walking over mountain)*
> *The bear went over the mountain,*
> *The bear went over the mountain,*
> *To see what he could see. (hands over eyes)*

2. Show pictures while singing the next verses.

> *He saw another bear, (hold up picture of bear)*
> *He saw another bear,*
> *He saw another bear,*
> *When he went over the mountain.*

Sing additional verses using some of the following examples, lots of trees, big blue lake, bird in the sky. Use pictures when possible.

3. Let older toddlers make suggestions of what the bear saw. Sing the verses with their suggestions.

4. Place large pillows on the floor to be a mountain. Encourage toddlers to crawl over the mountain of pillows while singing the first verse of "The Bear Went over the Mountain." Use the children's names in place of the bear as they crawl over the pillows.

Suggested book

Read *Brown Bear, Brown Bear What Do You See?* by Bill Martin.

Home connections

Vary the song to entertain your toddler while in the car, such as:

> *The red car went down the street...*
> *To see what we could see. (sing about what can be*
> *seen from the car window)*

> *We saw lots of cars and trucks...*
> *We saw a pig on the sign...*
> *We saw an eighteen wheeler...*

Chapter Four

Tommy the Tree

Explore trees and falling leaves with sensory activities and a movement song.

To do

1. Chant or sing the following song to the tune of "Twinkle, Twinkle, Little Star" and do the actions.

> *Tommy the tree stands tall, tall, tall. (stand up tall)*
> *His trunk is big and strong, strong, strong. (hands on waist)*
> *His branches up high are long, long, long. (hold up arms)*
> *And when the wind begins to blow, (sway side to side)*
> *His leaves begin to fall, fall, fall. (wiggle fingers down*
> *   towards the ground)*

2. Give each toddler two large leaves to hold and let fall to the ground as they say the chant.

3. Cut a tree trunk and a few leaves out of felt to use with the chant at the flannel board.

4. Make a Tommy the Tree collage. Cut out a simple tree trunk shape from brown paper for the toddler. Have him place the paper trunk on the sticky side of self-adhesive paper. Encourage the toddler to put small leaves, pieces of torn leaves or pieces of torn paper around the tree trunk on the sticky side of the self-adhesive paper.

5. Collect leaves that have fallen from the trees. Fill buckets, baskets, dump truck, wagons and other containers with the leaves. Talk with the toddlers about the colors, textures and sizes of the leaves.

To do again

Add leaves to the sensory table or a dish tub for the toddlers to explore. Add tongs for the toddlers to use to try to pick up the leaves. Encourage the toddlers to tear and crumple the leaves. Place very dry leaves in resealable bags. Let the toddlers smash the leaves with a child's rolling pin.

Skills encouraged

language, gross motor

Language to use with toddlers

tree
tall
branches
leaves
fall

Materials

leaves
felt
scissors
flannel board
self-adhesive paper
paper
buckets, baskets

Home connections

Let your toddler help you rake and gather leaves from your yard. Of course, your toddler will also enjoy playing and jumping in the piles of leaves.

Falling Leaves

Toddlers enjoy twirling and dancing as they pretend to be falling leaves in the fall.

Skills encouraged

motor skills, creative movement

Language to use with toddlers

leaves
tree
down
ground
blow
wind
dance
scarves

Materials

scarves

To do

1. Pretend to be leaves in autumn with the following movement song sung to the tune of "London Bridge."

> *The leaves are in the trees, in the trees, in the trees.*
> *The leaves are in the trees, way up high. (hold hands up and*
>   *sway side to side)*
>
> *The leaves blow in the wind, in the wind, in the wind.*
> *The leaves blow in the wind, all around. (sway side to side*
>   *or spin around)*
>
> *The leaves are falling down, falling down, falling down.*
> *The leaves are falling down, on the ground. (flutter fingers*
>   *down to the ground)*
>
> *The leaves are on the ground, on the ground, on the ground.*
> *The leaves are on the ground in the fall. (lay down)*

2. Use scarves as leaves.

3. Make a pile of leaves with the scarves, then toss the leaves up in the air.

To do again

Play upbeat instrumental music, such as a waltz. Dance like leaves blowing in the wind using scarves.

Chapter Four

Squirrel Play

Chant about the antics of squirrels playing around trees for a fun activity verse.

To do

1. Look at pictures of squirrels. Watch live squirrels around trees if possible.

2. Say the following action verse about squirrels.

The squirrel climbs up the tree. (wiggle fingers upward; hold arms overhead)
He's as happy as can be.

> *The squirrel creeps down the tree. (wiggle fingers slowly*
> *down to ground; put hands on floor)*
> *He's as careful as can be.*
>
> *The squirrel runs around the tree. (spin around or roll hands)*
> *He's as silly as can be.*
>
> *The squirrel curls up under the tree. (bend over, cover*
> *head with hands)*
> *He's as sleepy as can be.*

Suggested book

Read *Squirrels* by Brian Wildsmith.

To do again

See additional activities for squirrels in *Toddlers Together*.

Skills encouraged

language, fine motor

Language to use with toddlers

squirrel
bushy tail
climbs
tree
up
happy
down
careful
runs around
silly
curls up
under
sleepy

Materials

pictures of squirrels

Forest Friends

Toddlers learn about animals of the forest and their activities as they pretend to be creatures looking for food, homes and sleeping places.

Skills encouraged

gross motor, creative movement

Language to use with toddlers

forest
bear
creeps
berries
squirrels
run
circles
trees
rabbits
hop
home
deer
sleep
quietly

Materials

pictures of forest animals

To do

1. Look at pictures of forest animals. Talk with the toddlers about the animals, how they move, where they live, what they eat.

2. Pretend to be animals of the forest by singing the following to the tune of "Farmer in the Dell."

> *The squirrels run in circles, the squirrels run in circles,*
> *Looking for a tree to climb,*
> *The squirrels run in circles. (crawl quickly around room in circles)*
>
> *The bear creeps through the trees, the bear creeps through the trees,*
> *Looking for some berries to eat,*
> *The bear creeps through the trees. (crawl slowly with legs straight)*
>
> *The birds fly around, the birds fly around,*
> *Looking for their nest in the trees,*
> *The birds fly around. (fly like birds around room)*
>
> *The rabbit hops around, the rabbit hops around,*
> *Looking for home under the ground,*
> *The rabbit hops around. (hop)*
>
> *The deer sleep on the ground, the deer sleep on the ground,*
> *Curled up underneath the trees,*
> *The deer sleep on the ground. (lay down)*

Suggested book

Read *Home for a Bunny* by Margaret Wise Brown.

To do again

Move like a specific forest animal looking for food, eating, stretching, sleeping. See Beary Fun Animal Antics and All Creatures Great and Small in *Toddlers Together*.

Home connections

Take a walk through the forest, even if it is just an undeveloped patch of trees on the edge of your town. Look for different insects, birds and tree-dwelling creatures.

Deep in the Woods

Bring the peacefulness of the forest into the busy toddler classroom with a few stuffed animals and nature items.

To do

1. Place a dark sheet or blanket on the floor in a corner of the room. Cover a small table for a cave, if desired.

2. Put up pictures of forest animals, such as bears, rabbits, squirrels, deer, birds in the area.

3. Place a few large rocks, tree branches, leaves, pine cones and other large nature items on the sheet to resemble the woods. Add stuffed bears, rabbits and other forest animals to the woods.

4. Encourage toddlers to go "deep in the woods" with you. Talk with them about the animals and the nature items that are in the forest.

5. Add leaves, rocks and small twigs to the sensory tub or a dish tub with some potting soil or sand for the toddlers to explore.

6. Encourage toddlers to be an animal while in the woods:
   ✓ crawl like a bear with back legs straight
   ✓ crawl quickly like deer
   ✓ fly like birds
   ✓ hop like rabbits
   ✓ stand on knees, bend up and down like squirrels

7. Have an inside picnic "deep in the woods" with the animals and read books in the peaceful forest.

To do again

Use leaves, rocks and small twigs with playdough for a nature collage (see more activities for Rocks, Stones and Treasures in *Toddlers Together*).

Home connections

Make a dark forest with a large blanket over the kitchen table or a couple of chairs. Add stuffed animals to play with in the forest. Read books to your toddler in the forest.

Skills encouraged

pretend play

Language to use with toddlers

forest
woods
trees
leaves
bears
squirrels
birds
deer
rabbits
dark
pine cones

Materials

dark sheet or blanket
pictures of forest animals
stuffed animals
nature items
sensory table or dish tub
potting soil or sand

Out on a Limb

Use small tree branches for a unique painting experience with older toddlers.

Skills encouraged

creative expression

Language to use with toddlers

tree
branch
leaves
pine tree
paint
sway
side to side
tap

Materials

small tree branches
paint
flat trays
paper

To do

1. Gather two or three small tree branch with leaves.

2. Pour green, brown, red, orange paint (leaf colors) into flat trays. Add one tree branch to each color of paint.

3. Let the toddler choose what color of paper she wants to use. Large sizes of paper work best.

4. Encourage the toddler to paint with the tree branch by swaying it side to side over the paper. Chant, "Side to side, just like the branches sway side to side." Or, encourage her to tap the branch on the paper.

5. Let her paint with more colors if she desires.

6. Talk with her about the colors of paint, her actions, the designs left by the branches.

To do again

Paint with branches from pine trees.

Home connections

Let your toddler play with a few branches, using them as trees for her plastic or stuffed animals.

All Sorts of Leaves

With the natural variation in the sizes and shapes of leaves, leaves can be made into a simple sorting game for toddlers.

To do

1. Gather four to five leaves of two distinctly different types of trees, either by size or shape.

2. Glue one leaf at the bottom of a small box, such as a shoe box, or on the side of a paper bag. Do the same with a different type of leaf in another box or on bag.

3. Place the extra leaves in a small basket.

4. Encourage the toddler to sort the leaves into the two bags or boxes by matching the leaves with the ones on the box or bag.

5. Talk with the toddler about the different sizes and shapes of the leaves, the colors, the dry leaves, where they come from.

To do again

Cut leaf shapes out of two to four different colors of construction paper. Encourage the toddlers to sort the paper leaves by color.

Skills encouraged

cognitive, sorting

Language to use with toddlers

trees
leaves
maple
oak
aspen
sycamore
brown
red
dry
big
little
fall
ground

Materials

leaves
small boxes or paper bags
glue
basket

Fruit Basket

A basket of fruit can be quite a sensory experience of textures, shapes, colors and tastes.

Skills encouraged

sensory exploration, language

Language to use with toddlers

apples
oranges
pears
tangerines
colors
smell
taste
basket
sweet
juicy
trees
bumpy
smooth
shiny
good food

Materials

baskets
fruit
paper bag
cups
blender
cinnamon
spoons and bowls
markers
craft sponges
paint
paper

To do

1. Place a variety of harvest fruit, such as apples, oranges, tangerines, pears in a basket.

2. Talk with the toddlers about the juicy oranges, the shiny apples, emphasizing the colors, sizes, textures. Ask the toddlers to help find a specific fruit in the basket.

3. Leave a few of the sturdy fruits, such as the apples and oranges, out for the toddlers to explore on their own.

4. Hide a piece of fruit in a paper lunch sack. Encourage the older toddlers to feel it and guess what kind of fruit it is.

5. Have a tasting party with the fruits. Emphasize how the fruits are good food that helps them grow strong.

6. Make fresh squeezed orange juice for snack. Let the toddlers lick the inside of the orange half after it has been squeezed. Make applesauce with peeled apples in a blender, adding a sprinkle of cinnamon.

7. Provide markers in the colors of the fruits (orange, red, green, yellow) for the toddlers to color on a large tan oval shape (basket).

8. Mix paints in the fruit colors for the toddlers to paint on tan paper or to print with craft sponges shaped like fruit.

To do again

Add other harvest foods to the basket, such as vegetables and nuts. Talk with the toddlers about the names, colors, textures of the vegetables and nuts.

Home connections

Toddlers are developing their lifelong eating habits so expose your child to a variety of fruits and vegetables, especially if you do not like the foods yourself.

Vegetable Garden

Because they love to play in the dirt, toddlers are natural gardeners. Let them pretend to be tending a garden with plastic vegetables and potting soil.

To do

1. Fill the sensory table or small dish tub with a small amount of potting soil. Wading pools also work well, especially outside.

2. Add plastic vegetables and shovels to the soil. Real potatoes are a nice addition if desired as they withstand the toddlers play and have a "dirt smell" to them.

3. Let the toddlers explore the soil and vegetables.

4. Talk with them about the names and colors of the vegetables, how they grow in the ground, how to take care of them.

To do again

Let the toddlers wash plastic fruits or vegetables in a dish pan with a small amount of water and scrub brushes or washcloths. Have the toddlers scrub real vegetables that can be boiled or steamed for them to taste, such as carrots, small red potatoes, squash.

Home connections

Plant a simple garden with your toddler. Let her help dig the soil and drop in the seeds. Herbs and quick growing plants work best. Strawberry plants are easy for toddlers to care for and then enjoy the fruits of their labors.

Skills encouraged

sensory exploration

Language to use with toddlers

soil
dirt
potatoes
carrots
squash
cucumber
plant
grow
eat
crunchy
wash
scrub
dry

Materials

plastic vegetables and real
  potatoes
sensory table or dish pan
wading pool
potting soil
shovels
vegetable brush

Farmer's Market

Toddlers learn about all sorts of fruits and vegetables as they pretend to go shopping at a Farmer's Market.

Skills encouraged

pretend play, language

Language to use with toddlers

fruit
apples
oranges
pears
vegetables
carrots
potatoes
celery
cucumbers
squash
buy
share
piece
bag

Materials

baskets, paper sacks
plastic fruit and vegetables
felt
craft sponges
dish pan
soil

To do

1. Place a variety of small baskets out with plastic fruits and vegetables. Fruit and vegetable shapes, such as carrots, apples, oranges can also be cut out of felt to put in the baskets.

2. Talk with the toddlers about the names, colors, textures of the fruits and vegetables.

3. Encourage the toddlers to shop for the fruits and vegetables. Provide paper lunch sacks, gift bags or tote bags for them to put their produce in to take home.

4. Encourage them to give their friends a piece of fruit or taste of a vegetable.

5. Encourage older toddlers to sort the same fruits and vegetables into the same basket. This could be a separate game using baskets to sort fruits and vegetables cut out of felt.

6. Taste real fruits and vegetables (see Fruit Basket on page 100).

To do again

Say the "To Market, to Market" nursery rhyme using specific fruits and vegetables (see Going to the Market on page 153).

Home connections

Visit a roadside stand to buy a fruits and vegetables for a special picnic snack. Look at all the different fruits and vegetables at the stand with your toddler.

Chapter Four

Sing a Song

Can four and twenty blackbirds really be baked in a pie? Change the traditional nursery rhyme to talk about pies with toddlers.

To do

1. Say the following nursery rhyme with the toddlers. Clap or pat legs to the beat.

> *Sing a song of sixpence,*
> *A pocket full of rye.*
> *Four and twenty blackbirds*
> *Baked in a pie.*

2. Show the toddlers a picture of a pie or a real pie. Let them have a small taste of pie or taste a pie filling, such as pumpkin, apple, cherry.

3. Modify the rhyme to refer to a real pie filling, for example:

> *Sing a song of sixpence,*
> *A pocket full of rye.*
> *Lots and lots of pumpkins*
> *Baked in a pie. (or cherries, apples, pecans)*

4. Cut out felt fruit pieces to use with the rhyme. Place the felt pumpkins or other fruit in a pie tin and cover with a large yellow circle for the crust. Show the toddlers the pie filling and pie as you say the verse.

5. Let older toddlers make pies with the felt fruit shapes, yellow circle crust and pie tins.

To do again

Cut a circle out of paper to fit inside a pie tin. Dip a large marble (supervise carefully or use a golf ball or ping pong ball) in paint and place in the pie tin. Encourage the toddler to roll the large marble by moving the pie tin from side to side. Dip the large marbles in other colors of paint as desired.

Home connections

Make a simple pie with premade crust and filling with your toddler.

Skills encouraged

language

Language to use with toddlers

sing a song
blackbirds
pie
pumpkin
cherries
apples
taste
yummy

Materials

picture of a pie
pie or pie filling
felt
scissors
pie tin

1½+

Little Boy Blue

Stimulate toddlers' interest in "Little Boy Blue" with sounds and actions.

Skills encouraged

language

Language to use with toddlers

boy
horn
sheep
meadow
cow
corn

Materials

pictures of a little boy, a horn, sheep, cow and corn

To do

1. Say the "Little Boy Blue" nursery rhyme with the following actions.

> *Little boy blue,*
> *Come blow your horn. (hold fist up to mouth and make a*
> *   toot toot toot sound)*
> *The sheep is in the meadow,*
> *And the cow is in the corn. (bend over and pretend to be*
> *   cow or sheep eating)*

2. Show pictures of a little boy, horn, sheep, cow and corn with the rhyme.

To do again

Substitute toddlers' full names in place of "Little Boy Blue."

Home connections

Stop and watch cows or other animals grazing while traveling or visit a farm. Many children grow up without ever really seeing farm animals.

Chapter Four

Pieces of Fruit

Toddlers experiment with the possibilities of halves and wholes with simple apple and fruit puzzles.

To do

1. Cut a large red apple shape, a small brown stem and green leaf out of felt. Glue the stem and leaf to the apple.

2. Cut the apple shape in half.

3. Glue one side of the felt apple to a small piece of poster board.

4. Encourage the toddler to put the two halves together to make a whole apple.

5. With older toddlers, cut red, green and yellow apples out of felt. Cut the apples into halves. Attach one half of each color to poster board. Encourage the toddlers to put the apples back together by matching the colors.

6. Cut other fruits such as oranges, pears, strawberries out of felt to make matching halves puzzles.

To do again

Cut large simple pictures of people, animals or objects in half for toddlers to match halves. Mount the pictures on poster board. Cover with clear self-adhesive paper or laminate for durability before cutting the picture in half. Pictures of single objects work best to make these simple puzzles for toddlers.

Skills encouraged

cognitive

Language to use with toddlers

apples
green
red
yellow
oranges
halves
put together
whole
one
two

Materials

felt
scissors
glue
paper
poster board

Dump Salad

Toddlers enjoy working together to make a salad just by dumping fruit in a large bowl for an easy cooking activity.

Skills encouraged

sensory exploration

Language to use with toddlers

pears
peaches
oranges
bananas
apples
yogurt
stir
dump
yummy
taste

Materials

canned and fresh fruits
strainer
plastic knives
yogurt
bowl
mixing spoon
cups and spoons

Teaching hints

Make sure the children thoroughly wash their hands before they help with any cooking activity. The toddlers can work individually or in small groups dumping the ingredients into the salad rather than all at one time.

To do

1. Collect the following ingredients.
    - ✓ canned mandarin oranges
    - ✓ canned pears
    - ✓ canned peaches
    - ✓ canned pineapple chunks, optional
    - ✓ canned apricots, optional
    - ✓ bananas
    - ✓ apples
    - ✓ large container of vanilla yogurt

2. For a group salad, each family could be assigned (or sign up) to bring one of the ingredients. More than one family can bring the same fruit. Each child can help prepare the Dump Salad and add his fruit to the salad.

3. Wash hands.

4. Have the toddler dump the canned fruit into a strainer and then pour the strained fruit into a large bowl. Stir after each addition.

5. Let older toddlers help cut the bananas into circles with a plastic knife. The teacher will need to peel and cut the apples into wedges. Have older toddlers cut the apples into smaller chunks.

6. Dump the bananas and apples into the salad.

7. Dump in yogurt to moisten all the fruit. Stir.

8. Serve the fruit in individual cups and enjoy the Dump Salad that everyone helped make.

9. Talk with the toddlers about all the nutritious fruits they added to the salad.

To do again

Make a fresh fruit salad with other seasonal fruits in the spring and summer. Have each child bring a specific fruit.

Home connections

Have your toddler help you wash fresh fruits and vegetables when cooking or for snacks.

Chapter Four

Apple Sandwiches

Try apples and peanut butter for a simple snack that is quite yummy.

To do

1. Wash hands.

2. The teacher cuts apples into thin wedges.

3. Give each toddler two apple slices.

4. Encourage her to spread peanut butter on one of the slices with a plastic knife. Have her put the other apple slice on top to make an apple sandwich.

5. Before putting the top apple slice on, let her sprinkle one of the following on the peanut butter, if she desires.
> ✓ sunflower seeds
> ✓ granola cereal

6. Taste the apple sandwich and enjoy.

7. Talk with the toddlers about the sweet apple taste, the sticky peanut butter, the crunchy granola.

To do again

Let the toddler put a slice of cheese between the apple wedges for another tasty apple sandwich, or make ants on a log with celery, peanut butter and raisins (see Ants on a Log on page 232).

Skills encouraged

sensory exploration, fine motor

Language to use with toddlers

peanut butter
sticky
spread
knife
celery
raisins
apples
sunflower seeds
granola cereal
eat
yummy
nutritious

Materials

apples
shape knife (for teacher only)
celery
peanut butter
plastic knife
raisins
sunflower seeds
granola cereal

Home connections

Spread peanut butter on crackers or rice cakes. Make shapes or patterns with raisins on the peanut butter.

Snap Crackle Pop

Snapping green beans and shelling peas challenges toddlers' fine motor skills as they help prepare a taste treat for snack or lunch.

Skills encouraged

sensory exploration, fine motor

Language to use with toddlers

green beans
peas
snap
bend
crack
bowl
cook
boil
taste
eat
nutritious
wash

Materials

fresh green beans
bowl
strainer
pan
steamer

To do

1. Wash hands.

2. Give each toddler a handful of fresh green beans. Encourage him to break the green beans into smaller pieces by bending it in half to make it crack or snap.

3. Let the toddler break a handful of green beans.

4. Wash all of the green beans in a strainer.

5. Steam or boil the green beans until soft.

6. Serve for snack or with lunch.

To do again

Have the toddlers try shelling fresh peas to cook and serve for snack or with lunch.

Home connections

Have your toddler help you wash and scrub fresh vegetables for a salad, casserole or soup. He can help tear lettuce and add cut vegetables into the pan or bowl.

Chapter Four

Turtle Shells

Explore the homes of turtles with small blankets and the colors of green and yellow.

To do

1. Look at pictures of turtles. Talk with the toddlers about their shells, how it is like their home, how they hide inside it, the colors.

2. Bend over and put a small blanket on your back like a turtle shell. Hide your head with the blanket and play peekaboo.

3. Let the toddlers pretend to be turtles hiding bent over on their knees with the blanket over their back. Call them out of the shell with the "Little Turtle" chant from *Toddlers Together* or with the following variation.

> *Little turtle, little turtle*
> *Come on out.*
> *Little turtle, little turtle*
> *I see you.*

4. Put small blankets on the toddlers' backs and your back. Crawl around slowly like turtles.

To do again

Cut paper into large circles or ovals like a turtle shell. Let the toddlers fingerpaint and make handprints on the paper with green and yellow fingerpaint. Or, let them do a collage of green and yellow shapes on the large shape. Talk with them about the colors, the designs, shapes and how they resemble a turtle's shell.

Skills encouraged

sensory exploration, creative expression

Language to use with toddlers

turtle shell
home
hide inside
paint
handprints
green
yellow
design

Materials

pictures of turtles
small blankets or pieces of fabric

It's Keen Being Green

It's an ideal time to focus on the color green when planning activities centered around frogs and reptiles.

Skills encouraged

sensory exploration

Language to use with toddlers

green
light
dark
frogs
alligators
grass
apples
kiwi
pickles
broccoli
goop

Materials

green items
basket or dish tub
plastic grass
berry baskets
plastic cups and containers
green playdough
green cookie cutters
corn starch
green food coloring
paint and brushes
paper

To do

1. Place a variety of green things from around the house, such as green socks, green bows or ribbon and green toys out in a basket or in a dish tub for the toddlers to explore. Talk with them about the color green and the items.

2. Add green Easter basket plastic grass to a dish tub or the sensory tub for the toddlers to explore with green berry baskets. Encourage the toddlers to fill the baskets with grass. Add plastic cups and containers, preferably green, with lids if desired.

3. Make green playdough for the toddlers to explore, preferably with green cookie cutters. See the playdough recipe on page 161.

4. Make Green Goop. Pour a full box of cornstarch in a dish tub. Mix with water until it resembles batter. Add drops of green food coloring. Let the toddlers explore the Green Goop with their hands.

5. Taste green foods, such as honeydew melon, apples, kiwi, pickles.

6. Let the toddlers paint with shades of green by adding white, black or yellow paint to green paint to make different shades of the green. Or, let the toddlers fingerpaint with green and then mix in the other colors with their hands to see the changes in the green color.

7. Make a green collage of green ribbons, green yarn, green fabric scraps, green shapes.

8. Have a green day where everyone wears green and has pistachio pudding for snack. Dance with green ribbons or scarves and be sure to pretend to be green frogs jumping around the playground.

To do again

Change the focus color to relate to the theme or season.

Home connections

Have green eggs and ham for breakfast after reading the classic *Green Eggs and Ham* by Dr. Seuss to your toddler.

Little Turtle

Toddlers will love this traditional rhyme about a snapping turtle.

Skills encouraged

language, fine motor

Language to use with
toddlers
turtle
swim
climb
snap
catch
clap
me

Materials

pictures of turtles

To do

1. Look at pictures of turtles. Talk about their shells, where they live, what they eat.

2. Chant the following traditional verse with the toddlers.

> *I have a little turtle. (cup hands)*
> *He lives in a box.*
> *He swims in the puddle. (make swimming action with hands)*
> *He climbs on the rocks. (crawl fingers over other fist)*
>
> *He snaps at the mosquito. (clap hands together)*
> *He snaps at the flea.*
> *He snaps at the fly.*
> *And he snaps at me! (point to self)*
>
> *He caught the mosquito. (clap hands together)*
> *He caught the flea.*
> *He caught the fly.*
> *But he didn't catch me! (shake head no)*

Tough Skins

Toddlers explore a variety of actions as they pretend to be reptiles and frogs.

Skills encouraged

gross motor

Language to use with toddlers

snake
slink
turtle
creep
frog
leap
hop
lizard
crawl

Materials

pictures of snakes, turtles, lizards and frogs

To do

1. Look at pictures of snakes, turtles, lizards and frogs with the toddlers. Talk with the children about how the different creatures move.

2. Move like the creatures with the following chant.

> *Crawl like a lizard,*
> *Crawl like a lizard,*
> *Very, very quickly. (crawl quickly)*
>
> *Creep like a turtle,*
> *Creep like a turtle,*
> *Very, very slowly. (crawl slowly)*
>
> *Slink like a snake,*
> *Slink like a snake,*
> *On the ground. (lay down and scoot body)*
>
> *Leap like a frog,*
> *Leap like a frog,*
> *Off of the ground. (hop)*

3. Do other actions associated with the above creatures, such as:
> *Hide like a turtle...in your shell (bend over and cover head)*
> *Curl like a snake...in a circle (curl up body)*
> *Eat like a frog...catching bugs with your tongue (pretend to catch bugs with tongue)*
> *Freeze like a lizard...and not move at all (arch head and don't move)*

To do again

Vary the words of the chant to apply to other groups of animals.

Teaching hints

Use the chant for transitions when the toddlers have to walk together to the playground or other place. Encourage them to move like slow animals with the chant, such as slow turtles, huge elephants, giant whales.

Doing What He Oughta'

Explore what water animals and reptiles oughta' do in the water with variations to the classic song of "Little White Duck."

To do

1. Sing the following verses to the tune of "Little White Duck" or say the verses as a chant.

> *Little green frog, doing what he oughta'*
> *Little green frog, jumping in the water. (making jumping*
> *motion with hand)*
>
> *Little tiny turtle, doing what he oughta'*
> *Little tiny turtle, hiding in the water. (hide head like turtle)*
>
> *Little alligator...snapping in the water. (clap hands together)*
>
> *Little friendly fish...swimming in the water. (make swimming*
> *action with hand)*
>
> *Little crocodile...sleeping in the water. (pretend to sleep)*

2. If desired, cut shapes of the animals out of felt or use pictures as a visual stimulus.

Suggested book

Read *Splash* by Ann Jones for a book about all kinds of animals in the water.

To do again

Change the verses to any groups of animals and their actions in or out of the water, such as pets, zoo animals, farm animals. For example,

> *Big playful dog, doing what she oughta'*
>
> *Big playful dog, chasing sticks and balls.*

Skills encouraged ★

language, creative movement

Language to use with toddlers

green
frog
jumping
water
turtle
hiding
alligator
sleeping
fish
swimming

Materials

felt
scissors
pictures of a frog, turtle,
alligator, fish, crocodile

Home connections

Use the verse with your child's name to ask your older toddler to do something or to help him stay focused on a task, such as:

Big girl Bonnie, doing what she oughta'

Big girl Bonnie, putting away her boats.

Snake Farm

Although snakes do frighten most adults, many young children are fascinated by them so it is important that early on we teach appreciation for snakes rather than our own apprehensions.

Skills encouraged

sensory exploration

Language to use with toddlers

snake
long
smooth
slide
head
grass
rocks
dirt

Materials

toy snakes
sensory table or dish tub
rocks and twigs
plastic grass
sand
potting soil

To do

1. Gather toy snakes at least six inches long. Some of the families with older siblings at home may have plastic snakes the class can borrow.

2. Add the toy snakes to a sensory table or dish tub with rocks and twigs and one of the following sensory environments.
    ✓ plastic Easter basket grass
    ✓ potting soil for dirt
    ✓ sand

3. Encourage the toddlers to explore the snakes and sensory materials. Talk with them about the snakes, their features, how they hide under rocks. Emphasize to the toddlers that these are only pretend snakes (see teaching hints).

4. Add a small amount of water to the sensory table or dish tub for a different type of environment. Add rocks.

To do again

Encourage the toddlers to move like snakes:
    ✓ lay down on the ground and stretch as long as they can and curl up
    ✓ slither on the floor
    ✓ lay on tummy and move head side to side
    ✓ crawl under a larger pillow or table for a rock

Teaching hints

The Snake Farm offers an ideal time to stress to the toddlers that many snakes can be dangerous and should always be left alone unless an adult says it can be touched. Emphasize that if they ever see a real snake anywhere they should always tell a mommy, daddy, teacher or adult.

Snake Patterns

Rubber snakes make interesting trails and patterns when mixed with paint and a toddler's imagination.

To do

1. Find two or more plastic snakes about six inches in length.

2. Mix paint in colors close to the color of the snakes. Pour the paint into a tray or pie tin. Add one snake to each color.

3. Let the toddler choose if she wants to paint with the snakes on green paper for grass, blue paper for water or black paper for dirt.

4. Encourage the toddler to paint with the snake by placing it on the paper to make prints or sliding it around to make trails with the paint on the snakes.

5. Talk with the toddlers about the colors, snakes, patterns.

To do again

Provide markers in snake colors (brown, black, red) for toddlers to color on green paper for grass or tan paper for dirt. Talk with them about the lines they are making and how some look like snakes. Let the toddlers color snake lines on long strips of butcher paper on the ground outside. Keep as a group mural of most important snake marks.

Teaching hints

Painting with the snakes can be messy so let the toddlers hold on to the snakes with a clothespin if desired.

Skills encouraged

fine motor, creative expression

Language to use with toddlers

snake
prints
trails
long
curly
prints
trails
paint
paper
pattern
color

Materials

toy snakes
paint
trays or pie tins
paper

Toddler-assic Park

Something magical happens with many two year olds—they discover dinosaurs. While their fascination is not on the level of preschoolers, older toddlers still enjoy exploring the power of these huge creatures.

Skills encouraged

pretend play

Language to use with toddlers

dinosaurs
Triceratops
Tyrannosaurus Rex
Brontosaurus
huge
long ago
dead
growl
leaves
meat
bones

Materials

wading pool
toy dinosaurs
rocks
twigs
felt
scissors
poster board
wet sand, aquarium gravel or
    potting soil

Teaching hints

Keep the discussion about dinosaurs simple as toddlers see them as just another animal and are not interested in why they are extinct. Don't worry about knowing the names of all the dinosaurs. Some toddlers will probably already know many of the names, especially Tyrannosaurus Rex, Brontosaurus and Triceratops and will enjoy teaching the adults.

To do

1. Place a small wading pool in the classroom to make a toddler-assic park with some of the following.
    ✓ large plastic dinosaurs
    ✓ stuffed dinosaurs
    ✓ large rocks
    ✓ large twigs
    ✓ leaves cut out of felt
    ✓ bones cut out of poster board
    ✓ a small amount of sand
    ✓ pictures of dinosaurs on the wall nearby

2. Let the toddlers play with the dinosaurs inside or out of the pool. Talk with them about the dinosaurs, how they lived long ago, what they ate.

3. Take the plastic dinosaurs outside for the toddlers to play with in the sandbox.

4. Add some of the smaller plastic dinosaurs that pass the choke test to the sensory tub or dish tub with wet sand, aquarium gravel or potting soil. Include rocks and twigs if desired.

To do again

Print with the plastic dinosaurs dipped in paint (see Animal Prints on page 130).

Lily Pads

Frogs and lily pads make for fun matching, one-to-one correspondence and motor skills games for older toddlers.

To do

1. Gather two to five plastic or stuffed frogs. The frogs can also be cut out of construction paper and covered with clear self-adhesive paper for durability.

2. Cut the same number of irregular shapes out of green felt for lily pads.

3. Encourage the toddler to place one frog on each pad for a one-to-one correspondence activity. Have the toddler count the frogs. Talk with him how each frog needs to take a rest on its own lily pad.

4. Explore prepositions with the toddler by encouraging him to have one of the frogs jump on, jump off, jump over or jump around a lily pad.

5. Vary the lily pad game with two or three different sizes of frogs and lily pads cut out of felt or paper for matching by size. Or, use different colors of frogs and colors for a color matching activity.

6. Sing songs about frogs using the frogs and lily pads as props, such as "Freckled Frogs" and "Gagunck, Quack and All That" in *Toddlers Together* or Doing What He Oughta' on page 113.

To do again

Cut two or three large lily pads out of green fabric or felt. Encourage the older toddler to be a frog jumping on, off, over or from pad to pad. Sit on a pad next to the toddler and pretend to be a frog by saying "ribet," blinking your eyes and trying to catch flies with your tongue.

Skills encouraged

cognitive, matching, gross motor

Language to use with toddlers

frogs
lily pads
rest
one on each
count
jump on
jump over
over
around
water
big
little
colors

Materials

plastic or stuffed frogs
construction paper
scissors
self-adhesive paper
felt

Dinosaur Stomp

Introduce toddlers to a few facts about dinosaurs with a song about "Ten Little Dinosaurs."

Skills encouraged

language, gross motor

Language to use with toddlers

dinosaurs
stomp
ate
meat
leaves
grew
huge
loud
roar
crawl

Materials

pictures and books about dinosaurs
plastic dinosaurs

To do

1. Look at pictures and books about dinosaurs. Talk with the toddlers about the special features of different dinosaurs, such as their long necks, big teeth, horns.

2. Gather ten plastic dinosaurs and sing "Ten Little Dinosaurs" using the dinosaurs as a visual prop.

3. Add the following verses to the tune.

> *They stomped and they stomped*
> *On the ground.*
> *They stomped and they stomped*
> *On the ground.*
> *They stomped and they stomped*
> *On the ground.*
> *Ten little dinosaurs. (stamp feet or make toy dinosaurs walk)*
>
> *They ate and they ate*
> *Meat or leaves...*
> *Ten little dinosaurs. (pretend to eat)*
>
> *They grew and they grew*
> *Very huge...*
> *Ten little dinosaurs. (hold arms out to show size)*

Suggested books

Read *Bones, Bones, Dinosaur Bones* or *Dinosaurs, Dinosaurs*, both by Byron Barton.

To do again

Pretend to be dinosaurs with the toddlers by:
✓ crawling around slowly
✓ walking on knees with large steps
✓ growling
✓ swaying head side to side

The World of Make-Believe

The activities of Halloween each fall is an ideal time to explore make-believe with toddlers through dress-up and creative movement activities.

To do

1. While hats should be available year-round in toddler classrooms, this is an ideal time to introduce silly or unusual hats, or hats related to occupations, such as firefighter hats or hard hats. Parents are often a good resource for unusual hats. Also, make crowns out of poster board for older toddlers.

2. Encourage the toddlers to try on the hats and look at themselves in the mirror. Pretend to take pictures of the toddlers with old or toy cameras.

3. Talk with the toddlers about the hats they are wearing. Emphasize the colors, size and special qualities of the hat.

4. For older toddlers provide additional silly or unusual dress-up items that they can fit over their regular clothing, such as:
   - ✓ ballet tutus   ✓ bow ties
   - ✓ bright clothing   ✓ slippers
   - ✓ old one-piece swimsuits
   - ✓ novelty or character-related boxer shorts
   - ✓ sunglasses or glasses with the lenses removed

Use your imagination. Even consider old Halloween costumes. Parents of older children are often a good resource for old costumes.

5. Encourage toddlers to dress-up and make-believe to be clowns. Talk with children about what they are wearing, the bright colors and how unusual they look.

Suggested books

Look at *Dress-up Time* or *Little Grown-up*s by Tony Arma for pictures of toddlers dressed in costumes.

To do again

Have a Clown Day or Silly Dress-up Day for the children to wear silly hats and mismatched clothing to school.

Teaching hints

Keep the clothing simple and loose but not too large so the toddlers can dress themselves as much as possible. Keep in mind that they are much better at taking off clothing than putting it on.

Skills encouraged

pretend play, creative movement

Language to use with toddlers

clowns
dress-up
pretend
hats
move like
Who's that?
Just me!

Materials

hats
poster board
scissors
stapler
unbreakable mirrors
old or toy cameras
clothing

Home connections

Clowns and people dressed up in costumes or masks often frighten toddlers since the character with strange clothing and face make-up is unfamiliar to the toddler, even it is a parent behind the costume. Giving toddlers opportunities to dress up and pretend to be clowns helps them understand how people can put on special clothing to change their appearance but still be the same person.

Clowning Around

Clowns capture the attention of many toddlers, yet frighten others. Explore clowns on a simple level to help toddlers understand their pretend nature and lessen their fear.

Skills encouraged

language

Language to use with toddlers

clown
happy
sad
face
hair
silly
eyes
nose
hair
pretend
colors
hat

Materials

toy clowns
pictures of clowns
old circus programs
felt
scissors
felt board

To do

1. Place stuffed and toy clowns out for the toddlers to play with on their own. Talk with the toddlers about the special features of the clowns, such as big nose, bright hair, funny hat, big shoes.

2. Look at pictures of clowns in old circus programs. Talk with the toddlers about all the different looks of clowns, emphasizing to the toddlers that they are just people dressed up silly.

3. Cut the following pieces out of felt:
   - ✓ large white circle for face
   - ✓ small red circle for nose
   - ✓ large yellow smile
   - ✓ hat shape out of brown
   - ✓ purple bow tie
   - ✓ small blue or black circles for eyes
   - ✓ irregular shape out of green or orange for hair

4. Encourage older toddlers to help put the clown features cut out of felt on a felt board. Talk with them about the different features and colors. Have them point to their own noses, eyes like on the clown's face.

5. Say the following rhyme about a clown with the toddlers.

   CeCe the crazy clown,
   Had a tiny hat but couldn't keep it on. (shake head no)
   She put it on her head, (touch head)
   But it just kept falling down. (touch ground)

Use the felt pieces with the rhyme if desired.

Home connections

Toddlers are frightened with the different looks of clowns because they are unfamiliar. Older children have more experiences to remember and know that it is safe to talk with the "creature" or stand for a picture with it. Most toddlers do not have this understanding. Accept your toddlers reluctance or refusal. Provide them experiences to draw from through books, pictures, pretend play and casual exposure depending on your child's comfort level.

Chapter Four

Be a Clown

Toddlers can be a clown with variations to a familiar song.

To do

1. Let the toddlers act like a clown by singing the following to the tune of "If You're Happy and You Know It."

If you're a clown and you know it,
Dance around. (dance)
If you're a clown and you know it,
Dance around.
If you're a clown and you know it,
Then your silliness will really show it.
If you're a clown and you know it,
Dance around.

Substitute other clownish actions, such as:
- ✓ jump up and down
- ✓ twirl around
- ✓ wiggle all around
- ✓ bend over
- ✓ fall down

Use your imagination or let older toddlers suggest movements.

2. End with the following to refocus the toddlers' energy.

If you're a clown and you know it,
Lay right down. (lay on ground)
If you're a clown and you know it,
Lay right down.
If you're a clown and you know it,
Then your body needs to rest.
If you're a clown and you know it,
Lay right down.

3. With younger toddlers, simplify the actions as needed to clap your hands, touch your nose, touch your head, shake your head.

To do again

Dress up like clowns or put on hats with the song.

Skills encouraged

language, gross motor

Language to use with toddlers

clown
jump
dance
wiggle
spin

Materials

none needed

Festive Dancing Rings

Attach bright ribbons to rings for a festive touch to dancing activities.

Skills encouraged

gross motor

Language to use with toddlers

rings
ribbons
colors
dance
wave
side to side
up and down
parade

Materials

canning rings
embroidery hoops
large craft rings
ribbons
leftover fabric
scissors

To do

1. Cut leftover ribbons from crafts and gift wrapping into strips of 12 inches or more. Strips of leftover fabric or old sheets can also be used.

2. Tie the ribbons or fabric strips around old canning rings, embroidery rings or large rings used for crafts. "Rings" can also be cut out from the sections of six-pack holders.

3. Give each toddler a ring to use while dancing or pretending to be clowns in the circus. Encourage the toddlers to wave the colorful rings up and down, side to side.

4. Place the rings out in a basket near the dress-up and music area for the toddler to explore on their own. Talk with the toddlers about the colors on the rings.

5. Use the colorful rings in a parade of festive colors, just like at the circus.

To do again

Make the rings with ribbons or fabric strips of all one color when emphasizing a specific color with the toddlers.

Teaching hints

Avoid streamers as the dye runs easily when they get wet.

Circus Animals

Toddlers can pretend to be animal trainers caring for their circus animals while they wash and feed them in the sensory tub.

To do

1. Place a small amount of hay or shredded paper in a dish tub or sensory table.

2. Add plastic animals related to the circus, such as elephants, monkeys, dogs, lions, tigers, horses.

3. Add small boxes, shoe boxes or berry baskets for the toddlers to use as cages.

4. Let the toddlers explore the animals and hay or paper on their own. Talk with them about the circus animals, the sounds they make, their colors, what they eat.

5. Encourage the toddlers to line the animals up like in a parade.

6. Look at old circus programs to find pictures of some of the animals in the circus.

To do again

On another day, let the toddlers wash the circus animals in the sensory tub with a small amount of water and cloths or sponges. Old toothbrushes can be added if desired.

Teaching hints

Large plastic animals work best to prevent the risk of choking.

Home connections

Toddlers can play with plastic animals at the sink with a small amount of water or in a baby bath tub outside on a warm day. Or, let the toddler take a few special plastic animals in the bathtub for a special treat.

Skills encouraged

sensory, fine motor

Language to use with toddlers

elephants
monkeys
horses
dogs
tigers
lions
sounds
hay
feed
wash
cages

Materials

hay or shredded paper
sensory table or dish tub
plastic animal
small boxes, shoe boxes or
   berry baskets

Hoopla

Hula hoops provide a simple way to introduce prepositions and early cooperation skills with toddlers.

Skills encouraged

gross motor, social skills

Language to use with toddlers

hula hoop
circle
big
inside
outside
through
around dance
together

Materials

hula hoops
recorded music

To do

1. Place a hula hoop on the ground.

2. Encourage the toddler to stand inside the hoop, outside the hoop, walk around the hoop, jump inside the hoop.

3. Hold the hula hoop up on its side. Encourage the toddler to walk through the hoop.

4. Have a small group of older toddlers hold on to the side of a hula hoop together. Put on some music for them to dance while holding on to the hoop. Or, sing "Ring Around The Rosie" while holding on to the hoop.

5. Leave a few hoops out for the toddlers to explore on their own.

To do again

Put hoops out on the playground for the toddlers to use on their own. Encourage pairs of older toddlers to walk together inside the hoop. They will develop their own way of negotiating which way to go. Provide a ball or beanbags with the hoop for the toddlers to toss inside or through the hoop.

Teaching hints

Hoops smaller than traditional hula hoops are ideal for the toddlers to explore on their own.

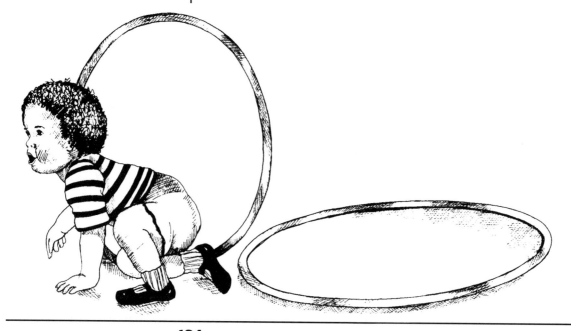

Chapter Four

Silly Clowns

Toddlers can release some of the boundless energy and practice their developing motor skills as they pretend to be silly clowns.

To do

1. Do the silly clown actions with the following chant:

> *The clowns dance, dance, dance.*
> *The clowns dance, dance, dance.*
> *Silly clowns see and silly clowns do*
> *They like to do just like you!*
>
> *The clowns spin, spin, spin.*
> *The clowns spin, spin, spin.*
> *Silly clowns see and silly clowns do*
> *They like to do just like you!*

Substitute other actions, such as wiggle, crawl, jump, march.

2. Let individual toddlers make suggestions of the movements and say the child's name in place of "you."

3. End the motor skills chant with a calmer movement to refocus the toddlers energy, such as rest or sleep.

To do again

Change the clowns to our friends, for example:

Our friends clap, clap, clap.
Our friends clap, clap, clap.
Our friends see and our friends do
We like to do just like you! (child's name)

Teaching hints

Use the chant for gross motor skills or as a less active activity by doing only hand, head and upper body movements when needed.

Skills encouraged

gross motor

Language to use with toddlers

clowns
silly
dance
jump
twirl
crawl
wiggle

Materials

none needed

Circus Magic

Do a painting activity involving surprise to introduce the element of magic associated with the circus.

Skills encouraged

fine motor, creative expression

Language to use with toddlers

surprise
magic
Wow!
paint
fold
rub
open
see

Materials

paper
scissors
thick paint
squeeze bottles

To do

1. Fold construction paper in half. The paper can be cut into circles to relate to the circus rings and balls.

2. Fill small squeeze bottles with paint the thickness of yogurt. Provide at least three colors, with white as an option since it mixes well with all colors.

3. Let the toddler pick out what color paper and paint he wants to use to make circus magic.

4. Encourage the toddler to make drops of paint on the paper with the squeeze bottles.

5. Have him help fold the paper in half when he's finished making drops. Rub the paper to mix the paint.

6. Open the folded paper to reveal the magical surprise.

7. Talk with the toddler about the colors and magical designs created on the paper.

8. Let the toddler make more circus magic as he desires.

To do again

Use the magic painting technique with other shapes, such as hearts, squares folded into a triangle or oval.

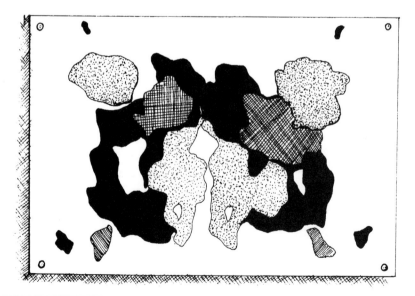

Chapter Four

Joining the Circus

Toddlers explore the circus and exercise their developing motor skills as they move like clowns and animals related to the circus.

To do

1. Look at old circus programs and pictures of things related to the circus, such as clowns, animals, trains, dancers.

2. Encourage the toddlers to pretend to be in the circus with the following movement song, sung to the tune of "Here We Go 'Round the Mulberry Bush."

> *This is the way the clowns dance,*
> *The clowns dance, the clowns dance.*
> *This is the way the clowns dance,*
> *To make us all laugh. (dance)*
>
> *This is the way the performers march...*
> *In the circus parade. (march around room)*
>
> *This is the way the monkeys jump...*
> *In the circus act. (jump)*
>
> *This is the way the elephants walk...*
> *In the circus act. (take big steps with head down and arm*
> *extended from nose like a trunk)*

3. Make up other verses as the toddlers show interest, such as ponies prance, dogs twirl, children clap. Just use your imagination for other ways to perform.

To do again

Put on marching music and pretend to have a circus parade.

Teaching hints

Use the following verse with animals walking, marching, trotting as a transition when going from place to place with the toddlers to help reduce running.

Home connections

Use the verse at home to pretend to be different animals as a playful way to encourage your toddler to go or do what's needed in a playful way, such as:
> *This is the way the clowns take a bath...*
> *This is the way the tigers shine their teeth...*

Skills encouraged

gross motor, creative movement

Language to use with toddlers

circus
clowns
dance
jump
act silly
monkeys
dogs
horses

Materials

pictures of the circus
old circus programs

Clown Faces

Toddlers can enjoy a nutritious snack and explore facial features as they make clown faces to eat.

Skills encouraged

sensory, fine motor

Language to use with toddlers

clown face
nose
eyes
smile
banana
peanut butter
cream cheese
spread
apple
grape
raisin
coconut
rice cake

Materials

bananas
apples
sharp knife (for teacher only)
large rice cakes
peanut butter or cream cheese
plastic knife
grapes
raisins
coconut
food color

To do

1. Cut bananas into circles and apples into slices.

2. Have a few toddlers wash their hands.

3. Working with just a few toddlers at a time, give each toddler a rice cake. Have each one help you spread peanut butter or cream cheese on their rice cake with a plastic knife.

4. Give each toddler two slices of banana for eyes, a grape cut in half for a nose and an apple slice for a smile. Let them put the fruit on their rice cake to make their own clown face creations. Talk with them about the different fruits and facial features they represent as they are making their faces.

5. If desired, let the toddlers sprinkle coconut colored with food colors on top for clown hair.

6. Enjoy the yummy clown faces.

To do again

Use rice cakes with peanut butter and raisins for the toddlers to make any type of design with the raisins. Or, just put cut up bananas on top of the rice cakes with peanut butter for a tasty treat.

Teaching hints

Let the toddlers make their own faces with the ingredients as much as possible to reduce frustration. Don't expect perfect faces as it is the process of creating the face that is important. It's okay for the banana eyes to be stacked upon each other touching the apple smile. Clowns are meant to be silly looking anyway.

Home connections

Make happy faces or rice cake fruit pizzas at home for a nutritious snack. Children are more likely to eat what they have helped make.

It's a Circus out There

Use hula hoops with circus-related toys for the toddlers to have their own three ring circus

To do

1. Place two or three hula hoops on the ground. Group similar circus-related toys in each hoop, for example: plastic or stuffed animals, such as lions, bears, horses, monkeys, dogs, trains and stuffed clowns.

2. Put up pictures of clowns and circus activities nearby. Old circus programs provide a wonderful source of pictures or as a book of pictures to look at with the toddlers.

3. Allow the toddlers to play with the different toys. Talk with them about the items and what they do in the circus.

4. Encourage older toddlers to sort related toys into separate hoops, such as all the clowns in one and the animals in another.

5. Encourage the toddlers to line up the toys for a circus parade.

Suggested book

Read *Circus Girl* by Michael Garland.

To do again

Use hoops for sorting large objects, such as blocks, balls, boxes covered with paper.

Skills encouraged ★

pretend play

Language to use with toddlers

circus
animals
elephants
monkeys
horses
clowns
train
inside
pretend

Materials

hula hoops
circus-related toys
pictures of clowns
old circus programs

Teaching hints

This is an ideal activity to do during the time the circus is in the area as some of the families may be going to the circus and the toddlers will be able to build upon their first-hand experience.

Home connections

See the circus with your toddler. Try to sit close to the front and leave at the intermission if your toddler becomes too restless.

Animal Prints

Toddlers can make a circus picture of the animals performing in the three rings.

Skills encouraged

fine motor, creative expression

Language to use with toddlers

footprints
four
paws
circus animals
horses
lions
elephants
big
small
colors
perform
jumping
running
walking

Materials

plastic circus animals
paint
flat dishes or trays
paper
scissors

To do

1. Gather three to four plastic circus animals. Mix paint to match the predominate color of the animals, such as gray for elephant, yellow for lion.

2. Pour a thin amount of paint in a flat dish or tray. Place the animal that matches the color on top of the paint.

3. Cut construction paper into large circles for rings at the circus.

4. Let the toddler pick out the color of paper she wants to use to print on and the animal she wants to use first.

5. Encourage the toddler to print with the animals by having them perform by walking, jumping and running around the circus ring(circle).

6. Talk with the toddler about the specific animal, the colors, the sound it makes, its size, the tricks it can do.

7. Let the toddler switch to other animals as she desires. Keep in mind some toddlers may want to just do one of the animal in each circle so provide another circus ring for other animals if the toddler desires.

To do again

Print with plastic farm animals to make tracks in the "mud" with brown or black paint while talking about the farm with toddlers.

Teaching hints

See the circle activities in *Toddlers Together* for additional ideas to emphasize the circular shape in relation to circus ring.

Lion Tamer

Wishing they could be as fearless, toddlers enjoy acting out the bravery of the lion tamer at the circus.

To do

1. Look at old circus programs with the toddlers. Talk about the lion tamers and how they teach lions and tigers how to do tricks.

2. Chant the following with the toddlers.

> *Lion, lion, lion tamer.*
> *He says there is nothing braver.*
> *Than a lion with him every day.*
> *Hip, hip, hooray.*

3. Let a toddler hold a hoop like a lion tamer and sing the verse with the child's name, such as:

> *Alan, Alan, lion tamer...*

4. If possible provide plastic or stuffed lions and tigers for the toddlers to play with on their own.

To do again

Pretend to be lions and tigers. Have the toddlers follow you while crawling slowly around like large lions, stretching up on their knees, growling, going in circles, sleeping. Hold a hoop up for the toddlers to crawl through like a lion or tiger. Sing and read about lions (see Leo the Lion on page 239).

Skills encouraged

language

Language to use with toddlers

lion tamer
lions
tigers
tricks
hoops
brave
circus
teach

Materials

old circus programs
hula hoops
plastic or stuffed lions and
   tigers

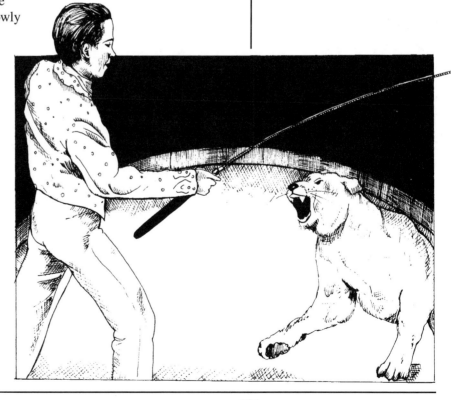

For Toddlers in Winter

Too Many in the Bed

Ten in the bed is just too many for toddlers. Start with less than ten using the traditional song of "Ten in the Bed" with toddlers.

Skills encouraged

language

Language to use with toddlers

three
two
one
bed
goodnight
sleeping

Materials

felt
scissors
flannel board

Teaching hints

Many counting songs for preschoolers can be adjusted for toddlers by starting with lower numbers. These songs often work well with toddlers since they are repetitive.

To do

1. Sing the following shortened version of "Ten in the Bed" with the toddlers. It can also be chanted or sung in a sing-song fashion if the tune is unfamiliar:

> *There were three in the bed, (hold up three fingers)*
> *And the little one said,*
> *"Roll over, roll over."*
> *So they all rolled over*
> *And one fell out.*
>
> *There were two in the bed, (hold up two fingers)*
> *And the little one said,*
> *"Roll over, roll over.*
> *So they all rolled over*
> *And one fell out.*
>
> *There was one in the bed, (hold up pinky)*
> *And the little one said,*
> *Good night." (place hand to head and pretend to sleep)*

2. For older toddlers, start the verse with five in the bed.

3. Cut out felt figures for the number in the bed (three or five) and a square for the bed to use with the song at the flannel board.

Suggested book

Read *The Napping House* by Audrey Wood to also show what happens when there are just too many in the bed.

To do again

Have the toddlers practice rolling on the ground for a related motor skills activity. With older toddlers, sing the song and encourage them to lay still or roll over according to the words.

Chapter Five

Lullaby and Good Night

Lullabies are an ideal way to soothe toddlers and to introduce a nighttime theme with baby dolls or stuffed animals.

To do

1. Sing or chant any of the following traditional nursery rhymes and lullabies with toddlers.

> *"Good Night"*
> *Good night, sleep tight*
> *Wake up bright,*
> *With the morning light*
> *To do what's right*
> *With all your might.*

> *"Wee Willie"*
> *Wee Willie Winkie runs through town,*
> *Upstairs, downstairs in his nightgown.*
> *Tapping at the window, peeking through the lock*
> *Are all the children in bed*
> *For it's now eight o'clock! (tap the beat of the rhyme on your or a child's leg)*

> *"God Bless Me"*
> *I see the moon and the moon sees me.*
> *God bless the moon and God bless me! (substitute children's names)*

2. Sing other lullabies and nighttime songs, such as "Twinkle, Twinkle, Little Star," "Are You Sleeping?" and "Hush Little Baby" with toddlers. The nursery rhymes of "Diddle Diddle Dumpling" and "Little Boy Blue" work well too. Substitute individual children's names when possible if singing to one child.

3. For fun, turn off the lights in the room and pretend to be sleeping when singing the lullabies or nursery rhymes to make it more like bedtime.

4. Encourage the toddlers to wrap up their dolls or stuffed animals in blankets and rock them to sleep while singing the lullabies.

5. Older toddlers may enjoy covering each other with blankets and telling each other "Night, night." Encourage them to sing some of the song to their "sleeping" friends.

Suggested books

Read books about bedtime with the toddlers, such as
> *Good Night Moon* by Margaret Wise Brown
> *Ten, Nine, Eight* by Molly Bang.
> *Sleep Song* by Karen Ray
> *Teddy Bear, Teddy Bear* illustrated by Michael Hague

Skills encouraged

language

Language to use with toddlers

Good night
sleep
relax
tired
blanket
bed

Materials

dolls, stuffed animals
blankets
felt
pictures of people and
  animals sleeping

Teaching hints

Lullabies and similar songs about sleeping work wonders when comforting a hurt, sad or sick toddler, especially while rocking or giving them a back rub. Or, sing a lullaby or two to the entire group before nap time to help everyone relax.

Home connections

Sing lullabies at home at times other than bedtime, such as with "morning snuggles," when playing with dolls or any time your toddler needs extra attention.

Good Night, Friends

The familiar tune of "Good Night, Ladies" can be adapted to a number of uses in a toddler classroom.

Skills encouraged

language, gross motor

Language to use with toddlers

Good night
names
sit down
lay down
stand up
baby
rock
names

Materials

none needed

Home connections

Use this tune to help with requests and gentle reminders all day in the home from "Get in bed sugar plum" to "Wake up sleepy head."

To do

1. As the toddlers are pretending to rock their baby doll or stuffed animal to sleep, sing the following to the tune of "Good Night, Ladies."

> *Good night, baby, Good night, baby,*
> *Good night, baby, It's time to say good night.*
> *(substitute teddy bear, puppy dog or the name of the stuffed animal that the child is holding)*

2. Sing the verse using the children's names as they pretend to "sleep" or even snuggle down for their real nap time.

3. Change the verse to a "good morning" song to sing individually to the children as they are playing. For example,

> *Good morning, Drew. Good morning, Drew.*
> *Good morning, Drew. Let's play with the cat puppet!*
> *(change the names and objects to reflect the children's activities)*

4. Use the verse for a motor skills activity, such as:

> *Stretch up high with me stretch up high with me,*
> *Stretch up high with me, it's time to move our bodies.*
> *(include other actions such as crawl with me, dance with me, spin with me, clap with me, nod with me)*

Use your imagination; let older toddlers make suggestions.

5. To help the toddlers settle down after the movement activity, end with:

> *Good night, friends. (lay down and pretend to sleep)*
> *Good night, friends. Good night, friends.*
> *It's time to rest our bodies.*

To do again

Use the verse for a variety of transitions, such as:

> *Walk slowly, friends. (tiptoe) Walk slowly, friends.*
> *Walk slowly, friends. It's time to go to the playground.*

The tune can be used to give toddlers subtle reminders, such as:
> *Sit down Aden...It's time to eat your lunch.*
> or *Bring the diaper Karen...It's time to have a change.*

Chapter Five

Snug as a Bug

Toddlers love to play peekaboo and hiding games. Use blankets to promote these games in the classroom.

To do

1. Cover a table with a blanket or sheet.

2. Encourage the toddlers to crawl under the table. Play peekaboo with them while they are under there.

3. Let the toddlers play under the blanket if they desire. Teddy bears and other animals are ideal to take inside the pretend cave. Talk with older toddlers about how animals go inside caves and holes in trees to keep warm in the winter.

4. Cover a toddler with a blanket. Pretend that you cannot find the child. Have the other children help you look for the child.

5. Sing the following to the tune of "Where Is Thumbkin?"

> *Where is Freddy? Where is Freddy?*
> *I cannot see him. He is hiding.*
> *Is he under the blanket? Shall we peek. (lift blanket)*
> *There he is. We found him.*

6. Encourage the toddlers to cover and "hunt" for each other or their dolls and stuffed animals.

Suggested book

Read *Sleepy Bear* by Lydia Dabcovich about a bear sleeping in his cave.

Skills encouraged

gross motor, object permanence

Language to use with toddlers

blanket
hide
underneath
crawl through
tunnel
cave
where is

Materials

large blanket or sheet
table

To do again

Use large boxes or blankets and sheets over a table or chairs to make caves for the children to be animals keeping warm, especially with the forest and bear activities (see Deep in the Woods on page 97).

Home connections

Peekaboo and hiding games are easy to do at home to entertain your toddler with little preparation and clean up but lots of guaranteed giggles.

Toddler Sock Hop

Toddlers love to take off their shoes. Give them a treat, and let them play without shoes in the classroom on a cold winter day for a change of pace.

Skills encouraged

sensory exploration, gross motor, self-help

Language to use with toddlers

sock
patterns
colors
soft
warm
slippery
dance
baby booties
feet

Materials

slippers, shoes
baby booties
baskets

To do

1. Plan for a special "Sock Hop" by asking parents to send their child in their favorite socks. Older toddlers can have a "Crazy Sock Hop" by wearing mismatched socks.

2. Let the toddlers take off their shoes and wear only their special socks in the classroom. Talk with the children about the colors, patterns, pictures on their socks. Emphasize how socks keep our feet warm in the winter.

3. Provide adult tube socks, slippers and low-heeled dress-up shoes for the children to put on over their socks if they desire. (It is amazing that once they have permission to take their shoes off that many toddlers want to wear shoes anyway.)

4. Sing about the toddlers' socks with any song about clothing or with the following variation to "Mary Wore Her Red Dress."

> *Louisa wore her kangaroo socks, her kangaroo socks,*
> *her kangaroo socks.*
> *Louisa wore her kangaroo socks*
> *All day long.*

5. Provide baby booties that the toddlers can put on the dolls and stuffed animals.

6. Have older toddlers sort baby booties or socks and larger socks into two different small baskets according to size.

7. Have a toddler-style sock hop by encouraging the children to dance to lively music with their socks on(carpeted floor to prevent slipping).

To do again

See additional sensory, matching, painting and motor skills activities with socks in *Toddlers Together*.

Warm Clothing

Talking about keeping warm presents an ideal opportunity to help older toddlers with their self-help and dressing skills with winter clothing.

To do

1. Collect a variety of small adult or large children's T-shirts, vests, sweaters, thin jackets, winter hats, gloves. Encourage the toddlers to practice dressing by putting the clothing over their own. Help the children as needed with dressing and undressing.

2. Add the items to the homeliving area for the children to practice on their own. Emphasize how it's important to dress warm in cold weather.

3. Use the dress-up coats and sweaters or their own outerwear to show the older toddlers how to put their jackets on by themselves (see All By Myself on page 43).

To do again

Collect infant T-shirts and simple clothing for the toddlers to dress baby dolls and teddy bears so they can keep warm too.

Teaching hints

Larger T-shirts, vests and outwear that fit very loosely are easier for toddlers to practice with than items close to their own size. The same is true for doll clothing. Keep in mind that toddlers will often be more skilled at undressing than dressing.

Home connections

Many "dressing battles" with toddlers disappear as they learn more self-help skills. Encourage your toddler to dress and especially undress as much as he is able when time is not a factor, for toddlers need more time to dress.

Skills encouraged ★

fine motor, self help

Language to use with toddlers

coat
put on
take off
socks
hat
dress
baby
T-shirt
dressing warm

Materials

T-shirts
vests
socks
sweaters
jackets
baby clothes
doll

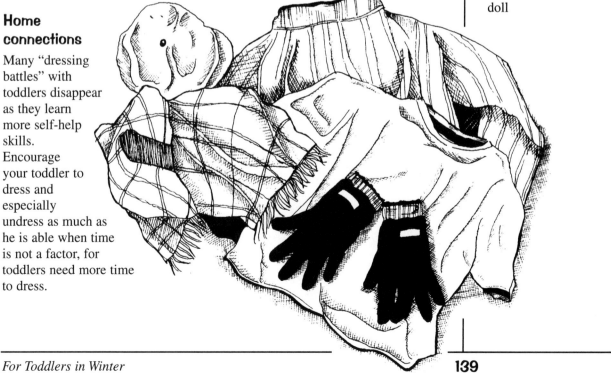

Scarf Walk

Scarves can be used more than for just dress-up play by adding them to motor skill activities.

Skills encouraged

gross motor

Language to use with toddlers

scarf
long
knitted
soft
silky
walk
step over
square
on
off
next to
up high
down low
swing

Materials

winter scarves
dress-up scarves

To do

1. Place a variety of scarves, both the winter knitted and dress-up types, out in the homeliving for the toddlers to use for dress-up play. Talk about the colors and textures with the children.

2. Put on music and encourage the toddlers to dance with the scarves. Swing them up high, down low, up and down.

3. Place one or two long knitted scarves on the floor to make a line. Encourage the toddlers to walk all the way across the scarf or to step over the scarf line. See if any can jump over the scarf. The toddlers can also crawl along the scarf.

4. Place three or four square dress-up scarves on the floor in a line about four inches apart. Encourage the toddlers to walk across the scarves by stepping onto each one. See if they can jump to each scarf.

5. Encourage older toddlers to practice folding the scarves when finished with the activity.

To do again

With older toddlers, to check for color recognition, place three or more square scarves of distinctly different colors on the floor. Ask a toddler to sit or stand on a scarf of a specific color. Toddlers will be able to recognize or point to a specific color before they can verbalize the name of the color.

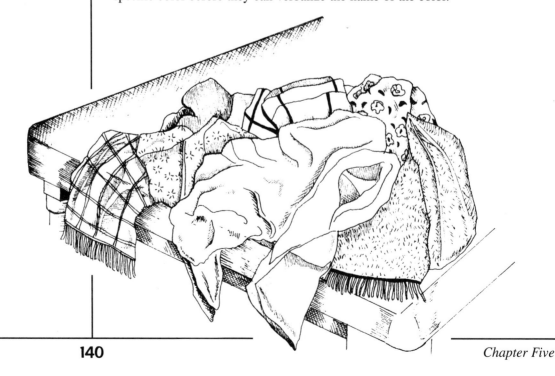

ZZZZZZZZ

Toddlers can explore the ways different creatures sleep with this enjoyable and calming creative movement activity.

To do

1. Look at pictures of different animals and people sleeping. Talk about the position (laying down, curled up, standing up, upside down) and where the creature is sleeping (bed, floor, cave, tree) with the toddlers.

2. Encourage the toddlers to pretend to be different people and animals sleeping with the following variations of "Mulberry Bush."

> *This is the way the baby sleeps,*
> *The baby sleeps, the baby sleeps, (curl up with knees to the chest)*
> *This is the way the baby sleeps*
> *In his little crib!*

> *This is the way the daddy sleeps... (on back, arms outstretched)*
> *In his big bed!*

> *This is the way dogs sleep... (lay on side)*
> *On the floor!*

> *This is the way the horses sleep... (on knees and hands with*
> * head down)*
> *In the barn!*

> *This is the way the ducks sleep... (stand on one leg with head down)*
> *In the tall grass!*

Use your imagination and sing about all types of sleeping animals. Let toddlers make suggestions.

3. End the activity with:

> *This is the way I sleep... (any position)*
> *In my bed! (pretend to sleep for a few seconds)*

4. Pretend to be an animal, such as a cat or bear, that is sleeping then slowly stretch to wake up; stretch one arm, then the other, on leg, then the other, arch the back, yawn. Move like the animal slowly then lay back down to finish resting.

To do again

Encourage parents to bring in pictures of the children sleeping, especially as an infant. It often amazes the toddlers that it is actually them in the picture.

Skills encouraged

language, gross motor

Language to use with toddlers

sleep
snore
lay down
curl up
stand
one leg

Materials

pictures of people and animals sleeping

Suggested books

Read *Where Does the Brown Bear Go?* by Nicki Weiss or *Pretend You're a Cat* by Jean Marzollo and Jerry Pinkney. Move around and sleep like the animals represented in the books.

All Night and All Day

Explore the concepts of day and night with toddlers by sorting pictures of activities related to the times of day.

Skills encouraged

sorting, language

Language to use with toddlers

daytime
nighttime
dark
moon
stars
sleeping
sun
play outside

Materials

magazine pictures
clear self-adhesive paper
basket or shoe box
poster board or large sheet
  of paper
markers

To do

1. Collect pictures of children, families and animals involved in activities related to nighttime (sleeping, wearing pajamas, nocturnal animals in the dark, using flashlights) and daytime (playing outside, hiking, animals in daylight). Some pictures will be clearly either night or day while others can be more open-ended (bathing).

2. Laminate or cover the pictures with clear self-adhesive paper for durability if desired.

3. Put the pictures out in a basket or shoe box for the toddlers to look at on their own. Talk with the toddlers about the activities in the pictures.

4. Divide a poster board or large sheet of paper into two sections. On one side draw a large sun, blue sky and clouds and on the other side draw a dark sky with stars and a moon.

5. Encourage the toddlers to place the pictures of daytime activities on the "sunny side" and the night pictures on the "dark side."

Suggested book

Read *Big Red Barn* by Margaret Wise Brown for an excellent story showing the differences between daytime and nighttime.

Chapter Five

The Kitchen Band

Toddlers love exploring sounds and making music with everyday kitchen items.

To do

1. Gather a variety of metal pots, pans, lids, bowls, large spoons, spatulas found in the kitchen.

2. Encourage the toddlers to experiment with the sounds they can make with the kitchen items. Talk about the loud and soft sounds, fast and slow beat.

3. Sing the following to the tune of "Row, Row, Row Your Boat" while keeping the beat by banging a spoon on the pan:

> *Bang, bang, bang on the pan.*
> *Bang with the spoon.*
> *We can make music*
> *In the kitchen*
> *With just a pan and spoon!*

4. Sing other songs and make music with the kitchen band. Play a marching record and have a parade with the kitchen instruments.

To do again

Add the metal pans and utensils to the homeliving area for the toddlers to use for pretend cooking.

Skills encouraged

sensory exploration, fine motor

Language to use with toddlers

pots
pans
spoon
bang
beat
sound
march
band
parade

Materials

metal pots and pans
metal bowls
large spoons
spatulas

Home connections

Toddlers can entertain themselves with a few simple kitchen items for "music making" or pretend cooking while you are busy preparing meals. Plastic food storage containers are quieter and provide just as much fun.

Puppet Mitts

Novelty hot mitts make ideal puppets to use with toddlers and are often less expensive than traditional puppets.

Skills encouraged

language, fine motor

Language to use with toddlers

puppets
talk
animals
pig
dog
kiss
hug
nose
head

Materials

hot mitts representing animals
basket

To do

1. Obtain a few hot pad mitts that represent animals for use in the classroom. To build a collection ask parents to donate one to the class for their child's birthday or another special occasion.

2. Put the hot pad puppets in a basket in the cozy or library area for the toddlers to explore on their own, or place a few in the homeliving area.

3. Use the puppets to sing songs and talk with the toddlers. Relate songs or nursery rhymes to the type of animal if possible. "Old MacDonald Had a Farm" is an easy song to use with animal puppets.

4. Say the following chant using one of the animal hot pad mitts (change the words to match the puppet being used):

> *Pink pig, pink pig*
> *Pink pig, pink pig.*
> *Pink pig, pink pig*
> *Pink pig, pig! (move the puppet side to side to the beat)*

Or end with the child's name and a body part.

> *Puppy dog, puppy dog*
> *puppy dog, puppy dog.*
> *Puppy dog, puppy dog*
> *Andre's nose!*

Move the puppet to the beat and have the puppet give the child a kiss on that part of the body at the end.

Teaching hints

Use puppets to redirect toddlers when they are "asserting their autonomy" against doing something required, such as putting away a toy, sitting at the lunch table, putting on their coat. It is amazing how they will often do what is asked of them by someone else, even a puppet.

Home connections

Use puppets for lots of playful language interactions at home. See teaching hints for how to use puppets at home to help with your toddler's emerging autonomy.

Chapter Five

Polly Put the Kettle On

Emphasize individual names and cooking warm foods with a variation on a familiar nursery rhyme.

To do

1. Chant the following nursery rhyme.

> *Polly put the kettle on,*
> *Polly put the kettle on,*
> *Polly put the kettle on,*
> *We'll all have tea!*

2. Change the verse to include the children's names and their favorite warm food (change kettle to pan if desired).

> *Mary put the pan on,*
> *Mary put the pan on,*
> *Mary put the pan on,*
> *We'll all have oatmeal! (tap beat to rhyme on the leg of the child)*

3. With older toddlers, pretend to eat the oatmeal (cup one hand like a bowl and move other hand like a spoon to mouth). Pretend the oatmeal is too hot and blow in the pretend bowl. Say yummy and rub stomach when finished.

4. Repeat the verse with other children's suggested foods (soup, spaghetti, hot chocolate) and their name.

To do again

Attach a large red circle to a cardboard box for a stove. While saying the verse with the child's name, have her hold a pan on the stove. Let her stir with a large spoon if desired.

Teaching hints

Talk to the toddlers about how real stoves can get hot and they need to stay away so they do not get burned. Add the stove, pan and spoon to the homeliving area for the toddlers to use on their own.

Home connections

Say the rhyme when heating up food, especially with a hungry toddler who is impatient.

Skills encouraged

language

Language to use with toddlers

names
kettle
pan
hot soup
oatmeal

Materials

pan
large circle
box

Peas Porridge

Vary the traditional rhyme of "Peas Porridge" to explore the concepts of hot and cold as well as different foods with toddlers.

Skills encouraged

language

Language to use with toddlers

chant
clap
hot
cold
peas porridge
spaghetti
noodle soup

Materials

pictures of foods

Home connections

Use this and other familiar nursery rhymes at home spontaneously, especially during the more chaotic times before meals or while travelling in the car.

To do

1. Clap or tap the beat of the following nursery rhyme on your or a toddler's leg.

> *Peas porridge hot,*
> *Peas porridge cold,*
> *Peas porridge in the pot,*
> *Nine days old.*

2. Change the rhyme to any number of different foods. Let the toddlers make suggestions.

> *Noodle soup hot,*
> *Noodle soup cold,*
> *Noodle soup in the pot,*
> *Nine days old!*

3. Add in the following verse with older toddlers.

> *We like it hot! Yes!*
> *We don't like it cold! No!*
> *Noodle soup in the pot*
> *Not very old!*

4. Show pictures of various foods such as spaghetti, macaroni and cheese while saying the rhyme, .

Chapter Five

Hickory Dickory

Liven up the mouse on the clock with simple actions and even some peekaboo fun.

To do

1. Say the traditional "Hickory Dickory" nursery rhyme chant about a kitchen clock, adding the following actions.

> *Hickory, dickory, dock, (rock side to side)*
> *The mouse ran up the clock. (run fingers up arm)*
> *The clock struck one, (show one finger and then clap once)*
> *The mouse ran down, (run fingers down leg)*
> *Hickory, dickory, dock. (sway side to side)*

2. Have the clock strike two for older toddlers.

> *Hickory, dickory...*
> *The clock struck two, (show two fingers and clap twice)*
> *The mouse said (hide eyes and pause) peekaboo, (play peekaboo)*
> *Hickory, dickory, dock.*

3. If desired, say the rhyme as "kitchen clock" to emphasize the kitchen concept.

To do again

Do the rhyme individually with a toddler, having the mouse (your fingers) "run" up and down her body. Great for diaper changes.

Home connections

Say the rhyme while holding your toddler and rocking side to side. Lift him up in the air with the mouse running up the clock. Slide him down your leg for the mouse going down the clock.

Skills encouraged

language, fine motor

Language to use with toddlers

mouse
clock
tick
tock
ran

Materials

none needed

Just Right

Toddlers can explore sizes and matching with pans, lids and measuring cups until they fit together just right.

Skills encouraged

cognitive, matching, nesting

Language to use with toddlers

too big
too small
just right
fit together
inside
sizes

Materials

different sizes of pans with
   lids

To do

1. Collect different sizes of pans with lids. Young toddlers need only two while older toddlers enjoy the challenge of three or more.

2. Place the pans out on the table or in a large dish tub for the toddlers to explore.

3. Encourage the toddlers to match the lids to the right size. Talk about the sizes as: "Too big," "Too small" or "Just right" while they are fitting the lids on top of the pans.

To do again

Read *Pots and Pans* by Anne Rockwell. Provide measuring cups that nest together for the toddlers to put back together. Talk about the sizes of the cups and how the smaller ones fit inside the larger ones.

Home connections

Play these matching games at home while waiting for meals to finish cooking. Have your older toddler help find the pans and matching lids you need for cooking.

Chapter Five

Chef's Surprise

Mix a few simple ingredients of paper, paint and a plastic egg in a pan for an easy "chef's surprise."

To do

1. Cut circles out of two or three different colors of construction paper to fit inside the bottom of an old pan.

2. Mix paint in two or three different colors. White is always a good choice since it mixes well with other colors.

3. Place one plastic egg (preferably to match the color of paint) or golf ball in each color of paint.

4. Let the toddler choose the color of paper he wants to use. Place the paper in the bottom of the pan.

5. Have the toddler pick out the color of egg or ball he wants to use first. Put the egg or ball inside the pan. Place a lid on top of the pan if desired.

6. Encourage the toddler to shake the pan to get the egg or ball to roll around.

7. Look inside and talk about the marks made by the paint on the egg or ball.

8. Let the toddler use another color of paint if he desires.

9. Remove the paper from the bottom of the pan when finished. Talk with him about the colors and lines of his magical "Chef's Surprise."

Skills encouraged

fine motor, creative expression

Language to use with toddlers

pan
lid
close
egg
paint
surprise
shake

Materials

construction paper
scissors
old pan with lid
paint
plastic eggs or golf balls

More Than Just for Dishes

Print unique designs with scrubbers and sponge wands used for washing dishes.

Skills encouraged

fine motor, creative
expression

Language to use with toddlers

washing dishes
sponge
scrubber
print
paint
paper
design
pattern
colors

Materials

plastic scrubbers, sponge
balls or wands
paint
flat dishes or pie tins
paper

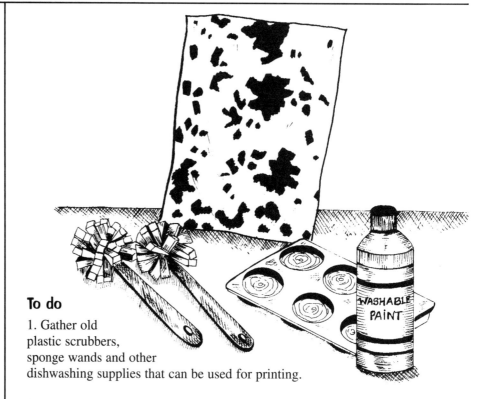

To do

1. Gather old
plastic scrubbers,
sponge wands and other
dishwashing supplies that can be used for printing.

2. Mix two or three different colors of paint to match the scrubbers and sponges
if possible. Pour each color into a flat dish or pie tin. Place the scrubbers and
sponge wands in the paint.

3. Have the toddler pick out the color of paper she wants to use and the paint
she wants to use first.

4. Encourage her to print with the scrubbers and sponge balls with the chant
"Paint paper, paint paper."

5. Talk about the unique designs made by the scrubbers and sponge balls on the
paper.

To do again

Print with crumpled up paper towels for another different printing effect.

Teaching hint

This works best with extra thick paint and thick paper towels. To keep hands
clean use clothespins to hold the paper towels.

Chapter Five

Soup's On!

With a few simple additions to the homeliving area, toddlers can pretend to make hot soup to keep warm in the winter.

To do

1. Add a few of the following to the homeliving area.
    - ✓ large pans, with or without lids
    - ✓ large mixing spoons and plastic ladles
    - ✓ three or four small plastic bowls
    - ✓ plastic vegetables
    - ✓ empty soup cans (place silver duct tape over any rough edges)
    - ✓ boxes of instant soup
    - ✓ hot pan holders

2. Cut out of felt or paper.
    - ✓ yellow noodles
    - ✓ large brown beans
    - ✓ vegetables

Add the felt pieces to the soup pans. Remember to cut pieces at least three inches or larger.

3. Encourage the toddlers to make soup and serve it to each other. Remind them to stir the soup and use the hot pad holders so they "don't get burned." Talk about not touching the hot burner too.

4. Pretend to eat soup with children. Talk about the different kinds of soup (bean, noodle, chicken). Remember to blow on the soup if it's too hot.

To do again

Read *My Kitchen* by Harlow Rockwell. Make a group vegetable soup for snack or lunch time. Have each child bring a vegetable from home to add to the soup. Let the child help you wash the vegetable before you cut it to add to the broth. Be sure to make the soup well enough in advance so it can cool some before the toddlers are ready to eat.

Home connections

Add a few ice cubes to soup at home to help it cool quickly.

Skills encouraged

pretend play, socialization

Language to use with toddlers

soup
hot
stir
Blow on it
yummy
bowl
spoon
bean soup
chicken soup

Materials

large pans
large mixing spoons
plastic bowls
empty soup cans
plastic vegetables
hot pad holders
felt or construction paper
scissors

Toddler Market Place

Boxes, plastic containers and other usual throwaways fascinate toddlers. Save these items for toddlers to explore and dump and fill with sacks in a grocery store just for toddlers.

Skills encouraged

social interaction, language, fine motor

Language to use with toddlers

foods
boxes
cans
containers
bags
take home
put away
good food

Materials

food packages
bread sacks
tape
styrofoam or newspaper
paper sacks
tote bags
plastic fruits and vegetables
shopping carts
pictures of food or grocery
  advertisements

To do

1. Collect a variety of food packages, especially items toddlers will recognize such as cereals, crackers, juice, yogurt, ice cream, milk. Make sure all the packages are clean and safe for toddlers.

2. For older toddlers, fill empty bread sacks with styrofoam squares or crumpled up newspaper to resemble a full loaf of bread. Tie the end in a knot. The same can be done with empty packages of frozen vegetables or bags of carrots. Tape the end closed.

3. Add the packages to the homeliving area along with paper sacks and tote bags for the children to go grocery shopping.

4. Other items that can be added as desired are:
    ✓ plastic fruits and vegetables
    ✓ child-size grocery carts or even small wagons
    ✓ purses

5. Place pictures on the wall of grocery advertisements and food items.

6. Talk to the toddlers about the food items as they shop. This is an excellent time to explore nutrition by emphasizing that good food helps our bodies grow big and strong.

7. Replace the food packages as needed.

To do again

Play a simple sorting game with older toddlers by having them put similar food packages in separate bags, for example milk cartons in one sack and juice cans in another.

Teaching hints

Since grocery packages are easy to collect, it is easy to put too many items out and overwhelm the toddlers. Save some of the packages for replacements since they tear easily. Other usual items in the homeliving area, such as dishes, can be put away while the grocery store is set up. It is important that the area is not too cluttered.

Home connections

Use empty food packages at home for pretend cooking and shopping. Toddlers will use the items in a number of ways; an empty cereal box can become a hat for a young toddler or a cave for an older toddler's dinosaur.

Going to the Market

Explore grocery shopping and different types of nutritious foods with toddlers using variations on traditional nursery rhymes.

To do

1. Chant the following variation of the nursery rhyme "To Market, to Market" with the children.

> *To market, to market to buy a big ham.*
> *Home again, home again Jiggety Jam!*
>
> *To market, to market to buy yellow bananas.*
> *Home again, home again Jiggety Jananas!*

Substitute other foods that the toddlers suggest and end with a rhyming sound at the end.

2. Sing the following to the tune of "The Farmer in the Dell."

> *We're going to the market (store).*
> *We're going to the market (store).*
> *Heigh ho the derry-o*
> *We're going to the market (store).*
>
> *We'll buy some beans and oranges.*
> *We'll buy some beans and oranges.*
> *Heigh ho the derry-o*
> *We'll buy some beans and oranges.*

Substitute other foods that the children suggest.

3. While singing the songs, hold up pictures, plastic fruits or vegetables that relate to the song, or use the songs with the flannel board.

To do again

Use these and other songs or chants related to foods while the toddlers are shopping at the Toddler Market Place (see page 152).

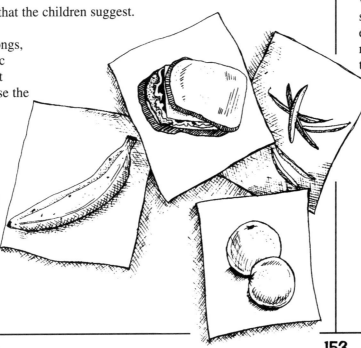

Skills encouraged

language

Language to use with toddlers

market
store
groceries
foods
going
buy
ham
bananas
oranges
fruits
vegetables

Materials

pictures of foods

Home connections

Use these nursery rhyme variations while grocery shopping with your toddler, especially to refocus a restless child at the end of the shopping trip.

How Trashy!

Toddlers need opportunities to tear paper before developing cutting skills with scissors. Let them practice tearing empty paper food packages and food advertisements.

Skills encouraged

fine motor

Language to use with toddlers

food boxes
tear
pieces
crumple
throw away
trash

Materials

paper food packages
food advertisements from the
    newspaper
paper sack or small trash can

Home connections

Keep a shoe box or basket of junk mail for your toddler to open, tear up or crumple as an easy to do fine motor activity at any time, especially when you may be busy paying bills or sorting through papers. Young toddlers will often enjoy "helping" by just putting things in the trash for you.

To do

1. Collect cardboard food boxes and food advertisements from the newspaper.

2. Encourage toddlers to tear the boxes into pieces. The box tops usually tear off quite easily.

3. Younger toddlers may find tearing the boxes frustrating. Encourage them to crumple food advertisement and coupons from the newspaper.

4. Have the children throw their torn pieces and crumpled papers in a nearby paper sack or small trash can.

5. In a class of older toddlers, leave the items to tear and crumple out in a sensory tub or large box on the floor for the children to use as a free-choice activity.

To do again

Have the toddlers crumple up old pieces of paper into a ball, especially leftover giftwrap from holidays or birthdays. Encourage them to toss the balls into a wide, round trash can or a laundry basket. Have older toddlers stand further back as they become successful at closer distances.

Teaching hints

Use this activity for redirecting a toddler who has torn a book. Tell the child, "I will not let you tear books, but you can tear these old boxes and papers all you want." Toddlers have an intense desire to refine their developing fine motor skills but have difficulty at times understanding what objects they can use to practice those skills.

It's All in the Can

Food cans with a lid may be empty of food but offer endless possibilities for toddler play.

To do

1. Collect a variety of empty cans with a plastic lid, such as those from potato chips, snack foods, coffee and powdered drink mixes.

2. Smooth the inside edge of the can with a knife or spoon and cover with silver duct tape two or three times if needed.

3. Cover the cans with self-adhesive paper on the outside if desired.

4. Use the cans in a number of ways, including:
✓ Fill the cans with objects that pass the choke test, such as blocks, spray can tops, sponges, various toys for the toddlers to play dump and fill and to use as shakers.
✓ Cut a hole about the size of a quarter in the top of the plastic lid. Cut out fabric squares (about 4" x 4"). Encourage the toddlers to poke the fabric through the lid to put it inside the can.
✓ Collect the metal lids from pull-tab juice cans (the edges will already be smooth). Cut a slit in the plastic top to fit the metal lids. Have the toddlers push the lids inside the can through the slot, pretending they are cookies or coins.
✓ Provide inexpensive plastic curlers and a can with a hole in the lid for the toddlers to push the curlers through. Use one size curler for younger toddlers while older toddlers can sort two or three different sizes.

5. Sorting activities:
✓ Collect three to five different sizes of cans with lids of distinctly different diameters. Encourage the toddlers to match the lid to the can that it fits.
✓ Cover two or three cans with different colors of construction paper or solid self-adhesive paper. Collect any of the following in the same color: fabric squares, ribbons, colored blocks, bows, construction paper circles. Have the toddlers sort the objects into the cans by color.

6. Provide cans and lids for the toddlers to play with. They can come up with many new ideas.

To do again

Use the larger cans that have the lids taped on in the block area for stacking.

Home connections

Let your toddler explore cans with plastic lids for dump and fill play, pretend cooking and for special collections, such as nature items found on walks around the neighborhood.

Skills encouraged

fine motor, sorting, dump and fill

Language to use with toddlers

can
top
put back on
shake
inside
sort
colors

Materials

empty food can with a lid
knife or spoon
duct tape
self-adhesive paper
objects
fabric
scissors

Food Container Prints

Use empty food containers for a simple printing activity.

Skills encouraged

fine motor, creative
expression

Language to use with toddlers

food containers
print
paint
paper
circles
big
little
colors

Materials

plastic food containers and
   cans
flat dishes or pie tins
paint
paper
paper sacks

To do

1. Collect a variety of plastic food containers and cans for printing. Some specialty coffees come in rectangular cans.

2. Mix two or three different colors of paint. Pour a small amount into a flat dish or pie tin. Place two to three food containers or cans of different sizes and diameters into each color of paint.

3. Let the toddler choose the color of paper he wants to print on and the colors of paint he wants to use. He can also print on paper sacks cut open or left intact.

4. Encourage him to print with the containers by chanting "Paint paper, paint paper" as he prints.

5. Talk with him about the colors, sizes of circles and the shape of the prints he is making on the paper.

Chapter Five

Going Crackers!

Use the variety of crackers available to introduce and explore shapes with toddlers.

To do

1. Taste crackers of different shapes, such as squares, circles and rectangles. Talk to the toddlers about the different shapes and colors of the crackers.

2. Save the boxes from two or three different types of crackers. Cover the boxes with clear self-adhesive paper for durability.

3. Cut shapes out of construction paper to match the shapes and color to match the crackers from the packages. For example, brown rectangles for a graham cracker box or white squares for a box of saltines. Make five to ten of each kind of cracker. Laminate or cover the crackers with clear self-adhesive paper.

4. Cut a slit in the side of the box for the crackers to fit through.

5. Encourage the toddlers to put the crackers in their corresponding boxes. Some toddlers will do best with just two types of crackers while some prefer the challenge of sorting three types. Talk to the children about the shapes and colors as they sort the crackers.

6. Young toddlers will enjoy just fitting the cracker through the slot as a dump and fill activity.

To do again

Make a similar sorting game out of dog and cat food boxes. Have the children sort bones for the dogs and fish for the cats into each box.

Home connections

Explore shapes at home with crackers, slices of cheese and the way bread is cut. Foods offer a natural way to explore shapes and especially colors with curious toddlers.

Skills encouraged

sorting, fine motor

Language to use with toddlers

crackers
round
square
rectangle
cracker box
inside
taste
colors

Materials

different shaped crackers
cracker packages
self-adhesive paper
construction paper
scissors
markers

Check Out That Label

Food labels provide an easy way to explore environmental print and emergent literacy with toddlers.

Skills encouraged

emergent literacy, fine motor

Language to use with toddlers

food types
package
What is this?
Do you eat...?

Materials

food labels and coupons from
   familiar foods
poster board
clear self-adhesive paper
yarn

To do

1. Collect food labels and coupons of foods that are familiar to toddlers, such as Cheerios and other cereals, graham and other crackers, soups and juices. Ask the parents for the brand names of foods that their children often eat and which they can recognize. Coupons from fast food restaurants can also be used if desired.

2. Attach the labels to poster board squares. Cover with clear self-adhesive paper. Leave the pictures separate for a picture file or put the squares together into a book with yarn or book rings.

3. Look at the labels with the toddler. Ask her if she can tell you what food is. Talk about the different foods, how it tastes and how we eat it.

4. Put the pictures or book of labels out in the cozy or book area for the toddlers to explore on their own.

To do again

Save labels and coupons for the toddlers to glue on a shoe box, paper sack or piece of cardboard for a label collage. The toddlers can make individual collages or a group label collage on a large box.

Teaching hints

This activity should not be intended to have the older toddlers read. The emphasis should be to explore the environmental print that many toddlers are already aware of in a fun and natural away. The awareness of environmental print will vary greatly among the individual children.

Home connections

Older toddlers become aware of environmental print from food labels, restaurant signs, store signs. This is an early step of prereading. Point out and explore these labels and signs with your older toddler as she shows interest to promote her emerging literacy in a casual way rather than through direct instruction.

Bread Tasting Party

Toddlers love to explore different types of bread and foods from various cultures with simple tasting parties at snack.

To do

1. Provide a variety of breads for the toddlers to taste, such as white, wheat, oatmeal, rye, raisin, pumpernickel. Cut the breads into bite-size slices for the toddlers to taste for snack time.

2. Let older toddlers spread honey or butter on their bread with a plastic knife if desired.

3. Taste breads from other cultures on another day or over a period of days. Include tortillas, sweet bread, pita bread, garlic bread sticks, pretzels, gingerbread, croissants to name just a few. Cut the breads into bite-size pieces for the toddlers.

4. Talk to the children about the tastes, colors, shapes and textures of the different breads.

5. Be sure to sing a few songs about breads during the tasting party (see Dough Re Mi, page 160) and read a version of the "Little Red Hen" before the snack.

To do again

Have a muffin or fruit bread tasting party with different types of homemade muffins, such as apple cinnamon, banana, pumpkin, oatmeal, bran. Cut the muffins into bite-size pieces for the muffin tasting party.

Skills encouraged

sensory

Language to use with toddlers

white bread
wheat bread
rye bread
raisin bread
tortilla
croissant
pretzel
bread stick
muffins
honey
butter

Materials

different types and varieties
  of breads
plastic knife
butter
honey

Teaching hints

Ask if any of the parents would be willing to make homemade breads or bring breads from their cultural traditions for the bread tasting party. Do the same for the muffin tasting party.

Home connections

Bake bread or muffins with your toddler. Older toddlers can help with many of the easy box mixes for muffins and fruit breads.

Dough Re Mi

A number of traditional nursery rhymes about foods add to the exploration of breads with toddlers.

Skills encouraged

language, fine motor

Language to use with toddlers

sing
hot cross buns
muffin man
pat a cake
hands
tap

Materials

none needed

Teaching hints

Rhymes and songs about foods work especially well during meal time transitions.

Home connections

Rediscover the nursery rhymes and songs from your own childhood to chant and sing with your toddler while cooking meals, bathing, traveling in the car. Use them anytime to promote language development as well as a to calm a busy toddler.

To do

1. Chant the following traditional rhyme.

> *"Pat A Cake"*
> *Pat a cake, pat a cake, baker's man.*
> *Bake me a cake as fast as you can. (pat hands together to the rhythm of the chant)*
> *Roll it up and pat it, (roll hands)*
> *And mark it with a B. (pat hands)*
> *Put it in the oven (slide hands forward)*
> *For all my friends and me.*

The names of individual children can be used in the last line. Use the first letter of their name in place of the B.

2. Chant about baking all kinds of breads with:

> *"Hot Cross Buns"*
> *Hot cross buns, hot cross buns*
> *One a penny, two a penny*
> *Hot cross buns.*

Substitute different types of breads or muffins in place of hot cross buns, such as:
> *Gingerbread, gingerbread*
> *One a penny, two a penny*
> *Gingerbread.*

3. Sing about the muffin baker with the following traditional tune.

> *"Muffin Man"*
> *Oh, have you seen the muffin man, the muffin man, the muffin man?*
> *Oh, have you seen the muffin man?*
> *He lives down the lane. (pretend to search with hand over eyes)*
>
> *Oh yes, I've seen the muffin man, the muffin man, the muffin man.*
> *Oh yes, I've seen the muffin man*
> *Who lives down the lane! (shake head yes)*

To do again

Read books with these three nursery rhymes and others to the toddlers.

Dough Play

Toddlers can pretend to make bread and muffins with a few simple props and playdough.

To do

1. Follow the following basic homemade playdough recipe to make a white dough for toddlers to use for their pretend baking.

> *1 cup flour*
> *1 tablespoon oil*
> *1 cup water*
> *1/2 cup salt*
> *2 teaspoons cream of tartar*

Combine all ingredients in a saucepan or electric skillet. Cook over medium heat. Stir continually. Mixture will form into a ball. Put oil on hands and knead the dough until smooth. Store in a closed container. (Brown dough can be made by adding dry brown tempera paint; other colors can be made with the addition of dry tempera paint or food colors.)

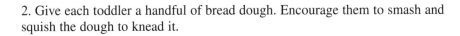

2. Give each toddler a handful of bread dough. Encourage them to smash and squish the dough to knead it.

3. Provide muffin tins and metal bread pans for them to put their dough in to pretend to make muffins and bread.

4. Sing songs about making bread (see Dough Re Mi, page 160) while playing with the dough.

To do again

The dough, mixing bowls, muffin tins, bread pans can be added to the homeliving area for the older toddlers to play with. Extra supervision will be required to make sure the dough stays in that area but it is a fun addition to the homeliving area.

Skills encouraged

fine motor, sensory exploration, dramatic play

Language to use with toddlers

dough
squish and smash
knead
roll
muffin tin
bread pan
cook

Materials

playdough ingredients
saucepan and stove or
  electric skillet
muffin tin
metal bread pan

Home connections

Make playdough for your toddler at home. Let him help you with the kneading step. Different colors of playdough can be made by adding food coloring. Playdough will often keep toddlers entertained at the kitchen table while the parent is nearby cooking dinner.

Muffin Tin Crayon Chips

Recycle old crayons into a new shape that is easier for many toddlers to use for their "most important marks."

Skills encouraged

fine motor, prewriting, creative expression

Language to use with toddlers

round crayons
draw
write
mark
paper
colors
lines

Materials

old crayons
old muffin tins
vegetable spray
oven
paper

To do

1. Collect old crayons. Peel off the paper.

2. Spray the muffin tin sections with a vegetable spray.

3. Break the crayons into smaller pieces to fit inside the muffin tin section. Put three to four small pieces of the same color into each section or make new colors by mixing crayon pieces.

4. Place in a cold oven so the crayons melt gradually. Turn the oven to 300° F.

5. Check the melting crayons regularly. As they start to melt, stir the mixture periodically to mix the color and wax.

6. When all the crayons have melted, stir each section thoroughly and turn off the oven. Leave the melted crayons in the oven to cool.

7. Remove the new crayon chips when cool.

8. Provide different shapes and sizes of paper for the toddlers to use with the crayon chips. Talk to the children about the colors and marks on their paper.

Teaching hints

The crayon chips work especially well with younger toddlers. Leave the chips out regularly for free-choice for older toddlers since they are larger and less likely to break.

Home connections

Toddlers early marks on blank paper with crayons are their "most important marks" or MIMs before their early writing attempts. Let your toddler draw with crayons or markers often, especially when you are writing as well. They love to copy their parents. Save some of these MIMs as you would other creations.

Muffin Tin Games

Sections of muffin tins and paper muffin cups provide easy one-to-one correspondence and matching games for toddlers.

To do

1. Place a muffin tin with the same number (six or twelve) of muffin cups near the tin on the table.

2. Encourage the toddler to put one muffin cup in each space to fill each section.

3. When finished, count the spaces with the toddler.

4. Take the cups out and let the child do the process again if she desires.

5. This same type of one-to-one correspondence activity can be done by putting ping pong or plastic golf-size balls in each section. Provide the same number of balls as sections. Count the sections and ball with the toddler.

To do again

Cut out the bottom section of different colors or designs of muffin cups. Tape the circles to the bottom of the sections of a small muffin pan (six sections or use just half of a large muffin pan) so that each section has a different color or design. The colors or designs can be repeated in a pattern as well. Provide the same colors and numbers of muffin cups. Encourage older toddlers to match each muffin cup to the bottom of each section of the pan.

Teaching hints

Smaller muffin pans with six sections work best for this activity with many toddlers.

Skills encouraged

fine motor, one-to-one correspondence, matching

Language to use with toddlers

muffin tin
muffin cup
one in each space
count
all full
match
colors

Materials

muffin tins
muffin papers
ping pong or plastic golf-size
   balls

Dough Dance

Toddlers use their large motor skills as they pretend to mix the dough for bread with their bodies.

Skills encouraged

gross motor, creative
expression, language

Language to use with toddlers

pour flour
sift
bowl
dough
mix
knead
rise
share

Materials

none needed

To do

1. Sing the following to the tune of "Mulberry Bush." Do the following actions and encourage the toddlers to follow you.

This is the way to pour the flour, pour the flour, pour the flour.
*This is the way to pour the flour into the bowl. (bend at waist to
   the side while standing)*

This is the way the flour is sifted, flour is sifted, flour is sifted.
This is the way the flour is sifted into the bowl. (jump)

This is the way to mix the dough...(spin)

This is the way to knead the dough...(pound floor)

*This is the way the bread is baked, the bread is baked, the bread
   is baked.*
*This is the way the bread is baked in the hot oven. (curl up in
   ball and lay on the floor)*

This is how we eat the bread, eat the bread, eat the bread.
*This is the way we eat the bread when it is finished. (pretend to
   eat bread)*

2. Ask a parent to make fresh bread for the toddlers to have for snack or make bread in a bread maker with the toddlers.

Pizza Pan Man

Change a familiar nursery rhyme to highlight pizza, a food toddlers love.

To do

1. Sing the following to the tune of "Muffin Man."

Oh do you know the pizza man, the pizza man, the pizza man?
Oh do you know the pizza man who likes to eat pizza everyday?

Oh yes I know the pizza man, the pizza man, the pizza man.
Oh yes I know the pizza man, his name is Tony.

2. Substitute individual children's names. For girls, change the verse to pizza woman or girl if desired.

3. Glue a picture of a whole pizza from an advertisement to cardboard. Let the child hold the pizza while you sing the verse to him. Pass the pizza to another child to sing about the next child.

To do again

Encourage the children to flatten large balls of playdough into pizza crust. Sing the following verse with the children as they flatten their playdough: Oh do you know the pizza makers, the pizza makers, the pizza makers?

Oh do you know the pizza makers...who smash the dough like this.

Oh yes I know the pizza makers...

For older toddlers, provide plastic knives for them to pretend to cut their pizzas into slices. Sing the following:

Oh do you know the pizza cutters, the pizza cutters, the pizza cutters,
Oh do you know the pizza cutters who slice the dough like this?

Oh yes I know the pizza cutters...

Teaching hints

Use this same variation of "Muffin Man" at mealtimes to highlight what the children are eating, with variations such as:

Oh do you know the cheese eaters...

Home connections

Sing this verse when eating pizza with your toddler. Or, sing about your toddler's favorite meals, such as spaghetti eaters or pancake eaters. This verse can also be helpful with finicky eaters to encourage them to try new foods.

Skills encouraged

language, fine motor

Language to use with toddlers

pizza man
Do you know?
children's names
pizza
smash
flat

Materials

cardboard
pizza advertisement
glue

Pizza Toppings

Toddlers can use their "most important marks" with markers or paint on large circles to create pizzas.

Skills encouraged

fine motor, creative expression

Language to use with toddlers

circle
round
big
little
red
yellow
paint
draw

Materials

tan or white paper cut into
   large and or small circles
markers
crayons
paint and brushes

Teaching hints

Vary the sizes of paper offered as the large size at the easel encourages whole arm movements while the smaller pieces at the table promote wrist actions.

Home connections

Let your toddler make his "most important marks" on circles and other shapes of paper at home rather than coloring books.

To do

1. Cut large and small circles out of tan or white butcher paper.

2. Let the toddlers draw with markers or crayons on the circles with red for tomato sauce and yellow for cheese on the large pizzas (circles) at the easel or on the floor.

3. Talk to the children about their marks on the paper, emphasizing the round circle shape and the colors they are using.

4. Also have the smaller circles available for the toddlers to color or use at another time.

5. The children can also use red and yellow paint on large circles at the easel.

To do again

The toddlers can add toppings to the pizza they have colored or painted on another day. Print brown and black circles with paint using spools, bingo blotters, sponges or other circular objects to make pepperoni or olives. Or, cut out brown circles for pepperoni, black circles for olives, pink squares for ham from construction paper for the toddlers to glue on to the pizza(circle). Older toddlers can tear pieces of construction paper scraps or tissue paper for the toppings as well.

Chapter Five

Personal Pizzas

With just a few simple ingredients, toddlers can make their own personal pizzas.

To do

1. Working individually or in pairs, have toddlers wash their hands with you.

2. Let the child help you spread a tablespoon of pizza or spaghetti sauce on top of one half of an English muffin. Some toddlers will be able to do this on their own.

3. Place a handful of grated cheese on a small plate. Encourage the toddler to sprinkle the cheese on top of their pizza.

4. Some older toddlers may want to add a slice of pepperoni, pieces of ham or olives.

5. Place the child's personal pizza on a cookie sheet. Label with her name using masking tape placed on the cookie sheet.

6. After each child has made his personal pizza, warm the pizzas in the oven at 350° F until the cheese melts.

7. Enjoy!

Teaching hints

Some toddlers will really enjoy this simple cooking activity so let them use the leftover ingredients to make extras for the teachers and other friends. Expect that toddlers will want to taste a pinch of the grated cheese while they are making their pizzas.

Home connections

Have your toddler help you make fresh pizza for dinner with frozen pizza dough or English muffins. Try quesadillas. Let your toddler sprinkle grated cheese on a corn or flour tortilla. Put on a cookie sheet. Heat at 350° F until melted. Enjoy when cool.

Skills encouraged

fine motor, sensory

Language to use with toddlers

pizza
bake
English muffin
sauce
spread
sprinkle cheese
red
yellow
warm
yummy

Materials

English muffins
pizza or spaghetti sauce (jar variety works best)
grated cheddar or mozzarella cheese
pepperoni, small pieces of ham and olives
cookie sheet
oven

Pizza Play

A simple sequencing game for older toddlers can be made with a few pieces of felt made into pizza ingredients.

Skills encouraged

fine motor, language, sequencing

Language to use with toddlers

pizza
crust
circle
tomato sauce
red
cheese
sprinkle
pepperoni
make
ingredients
first
next

Materials

felt pieces
scissors
round cake pan

To do

1. Cut out the following items from felt to represent pizza ingredients:
    ✓ crust—large tan circle to fit inside cake pan
    ✓ tomato sauce—irregular red, round shape smaller than the crust
    ✓ cheese—three to five squares or irregular yellow pieces
    ✓ pepperoni—red circles about the size of a half dollar

2. Encourage the toddler to build a pizza by putting the crust in the pan first, the tomato sauce on next, etc. Talk to the child about the ingredients, the colors and the sequence of making a pizza.

3. Leave the felt ingredients for two to three pizzas out in the quiet or library area for the older toddlers to explore on their own.

4. Store the pieces in an old pizza box with a picture of a pizza on top.

To do again

Add the felt ingredients to the Toddlers' Pizza Place, page 169, in the homeliving area.

Teaching hints

Keep the pieces large and simple for toddlers rather than small pieces of felt for olives or mushrooms.

Teaching hints

Send home one of the felt pizzas with a "birthday child" or one who especially enjoys pizza or this activity. Let the parent use the felt ingredients with their child over a few days to see how easily teaching games can be made for their child.

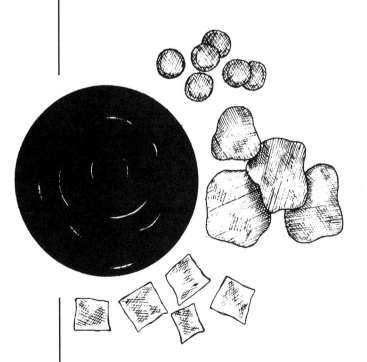

Chapter Five

Toddlers' Pizza Place

Toddlers can expand their baking skills by making and serving pizza to each other by recycling empty pizza boxes and pizza advertisements.

To do

1. Collect empty, reusable pizza boxes and large pictures of pizza from coupons and advertisements. Some restaurants will give you fresh boxes if they know it will be used in a classroom.

2. Cut out large circles from cardboard that will fit into the pizza boxes. Glue pictures of whole pizzas from advertisements on the circles. Pictures of slices of pizza can be glued on to triangular or similar shaped pieces of cardboard. Cover with clear self-adhesive paper for durability.

3. Add the pizzas and boxes to the homeliving area along with the following items:
   ✓ round cake pans and spatulas for making fresh pizza
   ✓ empty Parmesan cheese containers
   ✓ plastic spice containers (especially those from oregano and garlic)
   ✓ hot pad holders and mitts
   ✓ pictures of pizza on the wall

4. Encourage the toddlers to bake fresh pizza and serve each other pieces of pizza. Talk about how tasty the warm, cheesy pizza tastes. Mmm!

To do again

Let the children smell pizza spices like oregano and garlic. Sprinkle a small amount of the spice on a cotton ball. Place the cotton ball in a plastic container or 35mm file canister and make holes in the top by repeatedly hammering a large nail into the cover.

Teaching hints

Encourage parents to save empty pizza boxes and pictures of pizzas to build up a supply.

Home connections

Make pretend pizzas at home with playdough (see the recipe for homemade playdough on page 161). Let your toddler cut you a piece with a plastic knife.

Skills encouraged

imaginative play, social skills, fine motor

Language to use with toddlers

pizza
yummy
taste
warm
cheese
shake
circle
pieces
triangle
share

Materials

pizza to go boxes
pizza advertisements
cardboard circles
clear self-adhesive paper
felt
round cake pans
spatulas
Parmesan cheese containers
empty spice containers

All Right White

Toddlers become familiar with the winter color of white when they explore a variety of white objects and have a "Winter White Day."

Skills encouraged

fine motor, sensory exploration

Language to use with toddlers

white
winter
snow
clouds
paper
cotton
soft

Materials

white objects
basket or small box
computer paper
tissue paper
egg shells
fabric scraps
cotton balls
pillow stuffing
dish pan
children's scissors
hole punchers

To do

1. Collect a variety of white household objects, such as socks, washcloths, plastic cups, ribbons. Place the objects in a basket or small box for the children to explore on their own. Talk with the toddlers about the objects, emphasizing the color white as they explore the items.

2. Place some of the following white items in a sensory table or dish tubs for the toddlers to explore:

✓ pillow stuffing   ✓ scraps of white fabric
✓ white ribbon   ✓ white yarn
✓ white string   ✓ cotton balls
✓ end strips from computer paper

Crushed eggshells can be introduced for older toddlers.

3. Let the toddlers explore the different items. Talk with them about the colors and textures.

4. Save scraps of white paper, tissue paper, computer paper, tissues. Place the paper in a dish tub for the toddlers to tear into smaller pieces. Younger toddlers may crumple the paper into balls more than tearing the paper. Some older toddlers will enjoy the challenge of practicing cutting with children's scissors or using hole punchers. Save the pieces of paper for a white collage (see Winter Weather Collage, page 177).

To do again

Plan a "Winter White Day." Encourage the parents to send their child wearing one article of white clothing. Even white socks will do. Talk with the toddlers about their white clothing. Sing a version of "Mary Wore Her Red (White) Dress" by substituting the child's name and article of clothing. Have a white snack, such as rice, mashed potatoes, ice cream, cheese on crackers. Hang white streamers from the ceiling. Explore white all day (or all week) with any of the following winter or snow activities in this chapter and *Toddlers Together*. Do the above activities with a different focus color. Blue is another ideal color for winter.

Home connections

Explore colors naturally at home with your toddler by talking about the colors of foods, toys and clothing rather than by teaching colors through direct instruction.

Snowball Fun

Toddlers can practice tossing snowballs inside without getting wet and cold by using white socks rolled into balls.

To do

1. Roll old white socks or white knee high stockings into ball shape. Place in a dish tub or small basket for the toddlers to explore on their own.

2. Encourage the toddlers to toss the snowballs to you, each other or into the basket. Have a snowball fight with older toddlers sitting in a circle around you.

3. Introduce other white balls as desired, such as foam balls covered with white stocking or white fabric tied around it, large styrofoam craft balls or even cotton balls.

4. Talk about the sizes and textures of the different white balls with the children.

5. Add other colors of sock balls with the white balls in the basket. Have the toddlers find all the white balls to emphasize this color. Talk about the other colors as well.

To do again

Use the sock balls, foam balls, styrofoam balls for printing using white paint with older toddlers to make snowball pictures.

Home connections

Have your older toddler help you match socks or put socks away in the drawer while doing the laundry. Toddlers can handle simple household tasks when specific directions are given one step at a time. They really do enjoy helping, especially when it's mommy or daddy.

Skills encouraged

fine motor, gross motor

Language to use with toddlers

balls
snowballs
white
squeeze
throw
toss
feel
soft

Materials

old white socks or stockings
dish pan or small basket
cotton balls
foam balls
styrofoam balls

Winter Flurries

Toddlers release some of their built up energy on cold winter days by pretending to be snowflakes or white storm clouds.

Skills encouraged

gross motor, creative movement

Language to use with toddlers

snow
snowflakes
scarf
ribbon
twirl around
blowing
up and down
ground

Materials

white ribbons
old white sheet
instrumental music

To do

1. Cut white ribbon into pieces of about 18" to 24". Gift wrap ribbon, an old white sheet or fabric cut into strips can also be used.

2. Play instrumental music with a slow tempo.

3. Encourage the toddlers to dance with you using the ribbons. Wave the ribbons up high, down low, twirl around.

4. Talk about how the ribbons look like snowflakes blowing in the wind or white clouds on a stormy day.

5. Move and sing the following to the tune of "Are You Sleeping?"

> *Watch the snowflakes, watch the snowflakes*
> *Floating down, floating down (hold arms up high, wiggle fingers downward)*
> *Oh so very slowly, very, very slowly*
> *To the ground, all the way down. (touch floor)*
>
> *See the snowflakes, see the snowflakes*
> *Twirling around, twirling around, (spin around)*
> *Blowing in the wind, just like this,*
> *Twirling all the way down, to the ground.*

Repeat the verses as the toddlers show interest.

To do again

Use different colors of ribbons or strips of fabric throughout the year, such as leaves in the fall, flower blossoms in the spring and butterflies in the summer.

Home connections

Put on any type of music and just dance with your toddler, especially when the weather is bad or after a stressful day. Moving one's body relaxes most toddlers and adults.

Snow Paint

Snowy white detergent makes a thick sensory substance for toddlers to use for some very clean fingerpainting.

Skills encouraged

fine motor, sensory

Language to use with toddlers

snow
soap
white
thick
smear
clean

Materials

white soap powder, such as
   Ivory Snow
water
bowl
flat tray or table top
paper

To do

1. Add water in small amounts to white soap powder in a large bowl and stir until mixture resembles a thin dough.

2. Place two or three large spoonfuls of the "snow" on a flat tray or table top for fingerpainting.

3. Encourage the toddlers to smear the snow around with their hands and to make peaks with the snow by patting it gently. Talk about the color white, the thickness, textures with the children.

4. When the toddlers are finished, place a large piece of construction paper on top of their snow to make a print of their work.

5. The toddlers will have very clean hands after they wash off the soap they used for fingerpainting.

To do again

Add dry tempera or a very small amount of food coloring to make pastel colors, perfect for springtime fun.

Teaching hints

While the white soap powder is gentle to toddlers' sensitive skin, the activity still requires supervision as with any soap or messy substance.

Sensational Muddy Snow

Snow doesn't stay white long so explore the temperature and color changes of snow with chilled shaving cream and tempera paint.

Skills encouraged

sensory exploration, fine motor

Language to use with toddlers

snow
white
cold
hands
feel
black
brown
changes color
muddy

Materials

tray or table top
chilled shaving cream
brown or black powdered tempera paint
white fingerpaint

To do

1. Chill shaving cream or white fingerpaint in the refrigerator overnight.

2. Put a glob of shaving cream or white fingerpaint on a tray or table top for the toddler.

3. Encourage the toddler to feel the chilled shaving cream or fingerpaint and spread it around on the tray with her hands. Talk about the white color and coldness, emphasizing the similarity to snow, especially for toddlers who live in areas where it snows.

4. Sprinkle a tiny amount of brown or black powdered tempera paint on top of the shaving cream or fingerpaint after she has explored the white snow.

5. Encourage the toddler to mix the paint and shaving cream or fingerpaint. Talk about the changes in color and how snow gets muddy too as it melts and people walk in it.

6. Let the toddlers continue to explore the "snow" as long as it maintains her interest.

To do again

Mix other colors of powdered tempera paint in with the shaving cream or white fingerpaint to relate to the topic or season. Also try shaving cream gel for variety since it comes out of the can as a shiny gel but turns to foamy shaving cream as the toddler plays with it.

Teaching hints

As with any soap product, watch that the toddlers do not get the shaving cream in their eyes.

Home connections

Toddlers will love to explore shaving cream in the bathtub for some good clean fun at home.

Chapter Five

Melting Snow

Packing foam that disintegrates when placed in water offers a ideal sensory activity for toddlers that resembles melting snow.

To do

1. Collect the type of packing foam that disintegrates when placed in water. Show parents samples of this packing foam so they can help collect this type.

2. Place some of the packing foam in a dish tub for the toddlers to explore dry.

3. Add a thin layer of water to the bottom of the dish tub.

4. Encourage the toddlers to squish and squeeze the foam in the water. Let them explore the new mixture.

5. Talk about the changes in the foam as it disintegrates or "melts like snow."

6. Replace with fresh foam for the next group of toddlers or just add more packing foam to the mixture.

Teaching hints

Encourage parents to save the packing foam and pieces and send it to school to build up a supply.

Home connections

Styrofoam blocks are also fun for older toddlers to poke or hammer golf tees into to develop their fine motor skills.

Skills encouraged

fine motor, sensory exploration

Language to use with toddlers

packing foam
water
squeeze
squish
bubbly
melts
snow

Materials

packing foam
dish tub
water

Snowflake Designs

Toddlers can make designs as unique as snowflakes by using everyday objects to print with white paint.

Skills encouraged

fine motor, creative
expression

Language to use with toddlers

white snowflakes
pattern
print
design

Materials

spools
corks
circular objects
doughnut cutters
paint
flat trays or dishes
paper

To do

1. Collect a variety of circular objects for printing, especially those that have a pattern. Spools, the circular ends of rolls of butcher paper, doughnut cutters are ideal. Patterns can be made on corks with a knife (by teacher only) to use for printing snowflake designs as well.

2. Pour a small amount of white paint in a flat dish or tray. Place the circular objects on top of the paint.

3. Have the toddler pick out the paper he wants to use.

4. Encourage him to print on the paper with the circular objects with the chant "Paint paper, paint paper."

5. Talk with the child about the designs made with the objects.

To do again

Dishwashing sponge wands and premade bows also make designs like snowflakes when used with white paint for printing. Use sponge balls and styrofoam balls for printing white circles as well.

Teaching hints

Have parents help collect spools and corks to use in the classroom for printing.

Winter Weather Collage

Use cotton balls, tissue paper and doilies with self-adhesive paper for simple collages that resemble snow balls or even a cloudy winter sky.

To do

1. Cut out self-adhesive paper to match the size of construction paper. Staple the self-adhesive paper to the construction paper with the backing facing up.

2. Place cotton balls, tissue paper squares, white circles and cut up doilies in separate bowls.

3. Give the toddler a piece of the self-adhesive paper with construction paper for her collage. Peel off the backing of the self-adhesive paper so the sticky side is exposed.

4. Provide the different collage items for the child to choose from and place on the sticky self-adhesive paper. Encourage her to crumple the tissue paper first if desired.

5. Show the child how the items stick to the paper like magic. Let the child choose as many items as she wants for her collage.

6. Talk with the child about the different items and the color white.

To do again

Use different colors of crumpled tissue paper or paper shapes with the sticky side of self-adhesive paper to make a very colorful collage—perfect for a dreary winter day or with a springtime unit.

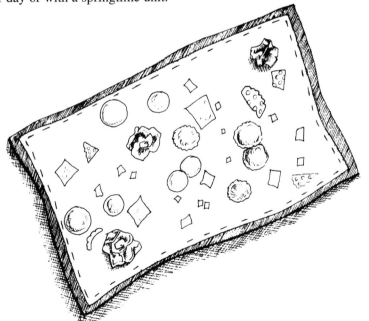

Skills encouraged

fine motor, creative expression

Language to use with toddlers

cotton balls
doily
white
tissue paper
crumple
stick snowballs
cloudy sky

Materials

self-adhesive paper
construction paper
stapler
cotton balls
tissue paper
doilies

Yummy Snowballs

Toddlers enjoy making these no-bake peanut butter cookies with just a few simple steps and ingredients.

Skills encouraged

fine motor, sensory

Language to use with toddlers

mix
smash
stir
roll
peanut butter
honey
sweet
graham crackers
oatmeal
vanilla
raisins
powdered sugar white
snowballs
yummy

Materials

graham cracker
resealable bag
child's hammer
peanut butter
honey
vanilla extract
dry oatmeal
raisins
bowl
large spoon
measuring spoons and cups
powdered sugar
cake pan or metal baking pan

To do

1. Have a small group of toddlers wash their hands with you.

2. Place one or two graham crackers in a resealable bag. Have the toddlers pound on the bag with a child's hammer to make crumbs. Save the crumbs.

3. Have a few toddlers help you measure and mix the following ingredients:
   3/4 cup peanut butter
   1/2 cup honey
   1 teaspoon vanilla extract
   3/4 cup dry oatmeal
   1/4 to 1/2 cup graham cracker crumbs
   1/4 cup raisins (optional)

Mix together with a large spoon until well blended. The toddlers will enjoy helping stir and hold the bowl while you stir.

4. Give each toddler about 1 tablespoon of the mixture to roll into a ball. Show the toddlers how to roll the dough into a ball. Some toddlers may find this challenging and need extra help. Keep in mind that squashed balls are okay too.

5. Pour a thin layer of powdered sugar in a cake pan or metal baking pan. Have one toddler at a time place their ball in the sugar if they desire. Roll the ball around in the sugar to coat it.

6. Eat the snowball immediately or save for snack time.

7. Let the toddlers make more than one ball for their friends not interested in cooking and for the other teachers.

8. Store any left over snowballs in a plastic container with a lid.

To do again

Skip the powdered sugar and rolling the mixture into balls. Let the toddlers form their cookies into any creation, just like a playdough creation that they can eat.

Teaching hints

Give the toddlers numerous opportunities to practice rolling balls with playdough prior to this cooking activity. White playdough is ideal for wintertime (see Dough Play, page 161).

Home connections

Make snowballs at home for an easy-to-do cooking activity with your toddler.

Chapter Five

For Toddlers in Spring

Take Time to Discover

A walk around the school with toddlers inevitably results in special springtime discoveries.

Skills encouraged

sensory exploration, gross motor

Language to use with toddlers

outside
walk
see
hear
grass
leaves
flowers
birds
sky
clouds

Materials

paper bags
self-adhesive paper or
construction paper and glue

To do

1. Take a walk around the school with the toddlers to look for special springtime discoveries.

2. Talk with the children about all the things growing around them, such as flowers, plants, bushes, grass, leaves. Also point out the sky, clouds and birds above them. Don't forget any ants or spiders too. Be sure to take time to smell the flowers.

3. Let older toddlers collect nature items on their walk to take back to the classroom or to take home. They can collect their treasures in paper bags. Expect lots of rocks to come back since toddlers love rocks.

4. If desired, have the children put their nature items on the sticky side of self-adhesive paper or on construction paper with glue to make a collage.

To do again

Have a picnic snack under a tree or by a special place during the walk. Listen for all the sounds of springtime. Encourage the toddlers to feel the grass, even roll in it. Lay down after the snack and look up at the sky with the children.

Home connections

Walks offer an ideal time for parents and toddlers to spend time together and get exercise. So many discoveries of nature can be made just outside the front door. Toddlers are fascinated by even the smallest ant. Try to make this activity a habit in the family, even if just once a week.

Seasonal Scents

Use potpourri to enhance the sensory dimension of the toddler classroom.

To do

1. Add springtime potpourri in baskets (out of reach of the children) in the classroom to add to the classroom scents. Help toddlers smell the potpourri up close now and then.

2. Collect empty plastic soda or sport drink bottles.

3. The teacher carefully pokes ten to twelve tiny holes in the soda bottles with an ice pick.

4. Add potpourri to the soda bottles.

5. Use a glue gun or strong glue to secure the screw top on the bottle so the toddler cannot remove it.

6. Place the potpourri bottles out in a basket or box for the toddlers to explore on their own. Encourage them to smell the scent coming from the bottle.

7. Talk about the name of the scent, the dried potpourri flowers and the colors with the toddler.

To do again

Change the potpourri scent according to the season, such as those associated with the holidays or citrus in the summer.

Home connections

Place potpourri around the home. Let your toddler smell it up close with your help and supervision.

Skills encouraged

sensory exploration

Language to use with toddlers

smell
scent
flowers
nose
dried
cinnamon
peach
lemon

Materials

potpourri
baskets
small soda bottles
ice pick (teachers only)
glue gun (teachers only)

Colorful Flowers

Explore colors with toddlers using plastic and silk flowers.

Skills encouraged

sensory exploration, fine motor

Language to use with toddlers

flowers
colors
petals
soft
silk
plastic
pretty
garden
stem
leaves

Materials

old plastic and silk flowers
florist tape or masking tape
dish tub
styrofoam blocks

To do

1. Collect old silk and plastic flowers, with or without the stems. Some of the wire stems can be removed if desired. Cover sharp ends with florist tape or masking tape. Have parents help collect the flowers as well.

2. Place the flowers out in a dish tub or sensory table for the toddlers to explore on their own.

3. Talk with the children about the colors, textures, types and parts of the flowers.

4. For older toddlers, add small cups or styrofoam blocks for the toddlers to stick the flowers in to make an arrangement.

To do again

Add potting soil and small cups with plastic flowers for the toddlers to plant a garden. This is a fun activity for outside especially since the clean up is easier. (See Planting Fun in *Toddlers Together* for additional uses of potting soil with toddlers.)

Home connections

Take a walk to look at the flowers in the neighborhood. Talk about all the colors you both see.

Blooming MIMs

Toddlers can draw their blossoming "most important marks" (MIMs) on coffee filters with bright colors to resemble blooming flowers.

To do

1. Give the toddler a coffee filter opened up like a flower and markers of different colors.

2. Encourage the toddler to draw on the coffee filter.

3. Talk about the colors and lines the toddler is making on the flower as he draws.

4. Let the toddler add a green strip of construction paper to the flower for a stem if desired. Older toddlers might want to add a few leaves to the stem.

5. Display the Blooming MIMs on the bulletin board, wall or window like flowers in a garden.

To do again

Let older toddlers paint with watercolors on the coffee filters. The filters will absorb the watercolors for an interesting effect. Or, let the toddlers use eyedroppers to drip water colored with food coloring on coffee filters folded into half or fourths. As the water is absorbed, interesting colors and designs are made on the filter. Add the painted coffee filter flowers to the garden of MIMs flowers for an extra special display of toddlers' creations.

Teaching hints

Displaying the toddlers drawings on the bulletin board shows the children and parents that the teacher values the toddlers' scribbles.

Home connections

Toddlers' first scribbles on paper are the most important marks they can make before they write, just as the flower bud must be nurtured before it can bloom into a beautiful flower.

Skills encouraged

creative expression,
prewriting

Language to use with toddlers

draw
write
colors
coffee filter
flower shape
lines
look
flower garden

Materials

disposable coffee filters
markers
green construction paper
scissors
stapler or tape

Simple Gardening

Watering plants and helping with a simple garden nurtures respect for living things and the environment at an early age.

Skills encouraged

sensory

Language to use with toddlers

water
grow
plant
soil
strawberry
herbs
smell

Materials

nonpoisonous indoor plants
outdoor plants
strawberry plants and herbs
potting soil
large pots and flower boxes
watering cans
spray bottles

To do

1. Place a few nonpoisonous plants around the classroom. Hanging plants can be used. Bring them down to the children's level. Place plants in large pots and hanging plants out on the playground, too.

2. Let the toddlers help water the plants periodically. Talk with the toddlers how the water is food so that the plant can grow like them. Provide spray bottles for older toddlers to mist the plants.

3. Plant strawberry plants and herbs, such as mint, on the playground in large pots or flower boxes. Flowering plants can also be used but keep in mind curious toddlers may be tempted to pluck the flowers.

4. As an outdoor activity, let the toddlers help water and mist the plants with small watering cans and spray bottles.

5. Encourage the toddlers to smell the herbs. As the strawberries appear, let the toddlers taste the fruit. Talk with the toddlers about the color, smell and size of the herbs.

To do again

Say the nursery rhyme "Mary, Mary Quite Contrary" using specific children's names as they help care for their garden.

Teaching hints

Make sure all plants used in the classroom and outside are nonpoisonous by checking with a local nursery or information from the state poison control center. Start small with gardening activities and expand the garden as you are comfortable with your own green thumb. Toddlers will respond to the teachers comfort level and excitement about caring for the garden.

Home connections

Survey your home for poisonous plants, which include everyday houseplants, such as poinsettias. A list of poisonous plants can be obtained from your local poison control agency. Include your toddler in gardening activities that involve three of this age's favorite activities: soil, water, and outdoors. Start simple with some of the above ideas if you do not have an interest in plants or a green thumb.

Chapter Six

Found a Flower

Explore colors and parts of flowers with a simple song that can be expanded in many ways.

To do

1. Sing the following verses to the tune of "Found a Peanut."

I found a flower, I found a flower, I found a flower today.

I smelled the flower, I smelled the flower, I smelled the flower with my nose. (point to nose and sniff)

It smelled sweet, it smelled sweet, it smelled so very, very sweet.

I left the flower, I left the flower in the ground to grow some more.

2. Explore colors with the following verses to the tune. Use real or plastic flowers with the verses or cut out flower shapes from construction paper for a visual stimulus. If desired, let each child hold a specific flower and individualize the verse in the following way:

Mae found a flower, Mae found a flower, Mae found a flower today.

It was yellow, it was yellow,
It was a yellow daisy. (change the name, color, type accordingly)

3. With older toddlers, explore the parts and aspects of a flower garden in more detail with more verses, such as:

It had a tall stem, it had a tall stem,
It had a tall stem that held it up. (point to stem on flower)

It had green leaves...on the stem. (point to leaves)

There was a bee...that crawled on top. (move fingers like a bee, show picture of bee)
It blew in the wind...from side to side. (sway side to side)
The flower grew...towards the sun. (stretch up high)

To do again

Use the tune to make up other verses about objects of nature and their properties, such as trees, shells, fruits.

Teaching hints

Using pictures, real or plastic flowers to use with the verses gives the toddlers a concrete stimulus to use when singing about the flowers.

Skills encouraged

language

Language to use with toddlers

flower
garden
colors
smell
sweet

Materials

construction paper
flowers

Carnation Creations

Carnations are sturdy flowers that usually last a while after being cut and can withstand toddlers handling them.

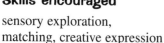

Skills encouraged

sensory exploration, matching, creative expression

Language to use with toddlers

carnations
flowers
colors
stem
same
matching
print

Materials

plastic vase
carnations
scissors
juice cans
construction paper
tape
paint
flat trays

To do

1. Place a plastic vase of carnations out for the toddlers to explore. Talk with them about the flowers and colors.

2. Gather carnations in two or three different colors. Trim the stems if needed to fit inside juice cans.

3. Cover juice cans with construction paper of the same colors as the carnations.

4. Encourage the toddlers to put the carnations in the can of the same color as the flower.

5. For an art activity, let the toddlers paint with the carnations using the same color of paint.

6. Talk with the toddlers about the colors and designs made by the carnations.

To do again

Shorten the stems of the carnations for older toddlers to use with playdough to make flower arrangements. Add plastic or silk flowers if desired. Bring in an assortment of freshly cut flowers (parents with a garden may be willing to contribute flowers). Talk with the children about the colors, names and smells of the flowers. Leave the flowers out in the classroom or on a shelf if desired for all to enjoy.

Home connections

Let your toddler help you put flowers in a vase or make a simple arrangement for the dinner table.

Chapter Six

Growing Up Tall

Pretending to be flowers growing offers an ideal opportunity to emphasize growth and health with a fun creative movement activity.

To do

1. Take a walk to look at the trees, grass and flowers around school. Talk with the children about how plants need rain and sunshine like their bodies need food and rest to grow and stay healthy.

2. Have a nonpoisonous plant out in the classroom or on the playground that the children can help water or mist with spray bottles (see Simple Gardening, page 184).

3. Encourage the toddlers to pretend to be plants growing with the following chant.

> *We're little seeds in the ground. (bend over into ball)*
> *Give us some water and lots of sunshine. (point overhead)*
> *And just watch us grow and grow and grow (raise up bodies with*
> *   hands overhead like flowers blooming)*
> *Into flowers all around. (sway side to side with arms overhead or*
> *   twirl around)*

4. Sing the following to the tune of "Are You Sleeping?" with the children as they grow into flowers.

> *We are seeds, we are seeds*
> *In the ground, in the ground.*
> *Waiting for the sun, to shine up above*
> *And some rain, to come down. (bend over in ball like a seed)*
>
> *We are growing, we are growing*
> *Up so tall, up so tall.*
> *Soon we'll be flowers, sweet smelling flowers*
> *In the garden, in the garden. (pretend to grow and stretch up high)*

Suggested book

Read *The Carrot Seed* by Ruth Krauss.

To do again

Say the nursery rhyme "Mary, Mary, Quite Contrary" with the children (see variations in *Toddlers Together*).

Teaching hints

The topic of flowers and plants growing offers an ideal time to talk with toddlers about how good foods, nutrition, rest and exercise helps them grow big and strong, just like the rain and sun for the plants.

Skills encouraged

language, gross motor

Language to use with toddlers

grow
little seed
ground
water
sun
up tall
stretch
food
rest

Materials

none needed

Home connections

Discuss concrete examples with your toddler of how he has grown, such as looking at baby pictures, comparing his first shoes to the ones he wears now, looking at his old baby clothes and comparing height on a wall chart.

Flower Garden

Toddlers can use a variety of collage materials to make their own flower garden creations.

Skills encouraged

fine motor, creative expression

Language to use with toddlers

flowers
colors
muffin cups
tissue paper
crumple
glue
stick
pretty
green

Materials

egg cartons
paper muffin cups
collage materials
construction paper
scissors
glue
flat tray or dish
self-adhesive paper

To do

1. Cut up egg cartons into individual sections. Gather collage materials: paper muffin cups, tissue paper squares, colored cellophane, plastic or silk flowers. Flower and leaf shapes can also be cut out of construction paper.

2. Cut large sheets of green, blue and white construction paper in half lengthwise to make a strip of paper. Let the toddler choose what color he wants for a backing.

3. Pour glue into a flat dish or tray.

4. Place a sampling of the collage materials out for the toddler to have at least two or three choices. Encourage him to dip the item in the glue and then place it on his paper. Encourage him to crumple the tissue paper and colored cellophane into a flower before dipping it in the glue.

5. Clear self-adhesive paper with the sticky side up can be attached to the paper and used as the adhesive surface instead of using glue if desired. This is sometimes easier for many toddlers.

6. Talk with the toddler about the colors of the collage materials, emphasizing how they resemble a colorful flower garden.

To do again

Provide flower stickers and pictures of flowers from magazines and catalogs for another type of collage.

Teaching hints

Toddlers are not ready for the step of placing stems and leaves with the flowers as this tends to be a teacher-directed activity. Instead let the items be used for a free collage that will still resemble the beauty of a flower garden for the toddler who created it on his own.

Home connections

Flower catalogs that come in the mail offer an ideal way to look at colors with toddlers.

Flower Prints

Provide premade bows in many colors for toddlers to print their own flowers.

To do

1. Collect leftover premade bows in at least three different colors. Different sizes of bows work nicely too.

2. Mix paint to match the specific colors of bows. Pour the paint in flat dishes or trays.

3. Place the bows upside down in the tray (with the sticky side up), putting each color bow in the same color paint.

4. Let the toddler choose the color of paper she wants to print on and which color of paint she wants to use first.

5. Encourage the toddler to print with the bow, saying the chant "Paint paper, paint paper."

6. Talk with the toddler about the colors and how the bow makes prints that look like flowers.

To do again

On another day, collage items resembling flowers can be added to the flower prints for a truly sensational flower garden (see Flower Garden, page 188).

Skills encouraged

fine motor, creative expression

Language to use with toddlers

bows
presents
decorations
colors
print
flowers
garden
colorful

Materials

premade bows
paint
flat dishes or trays
paper

A Tisket, a Tasket

Provide baskets for toddlers to play in one of their favorite games—dump and fill.

Skills encouraged

gross motor, dump and fill

Language to use with toddlers

baskets
colors
sizes
handle
plastic
wicker
inside
carry
empty
full

Materials

baskets
objects
beanbags
plastic eggs

To do

1. Place a variety of baskets with handles out for the toddlers to explore. Fill the baskets with items that have a special focus, such as items of the same color.

2. Or leave the baskets empty and encourage the toddlers to collect items from around the room.

3. Talk about the colors, sizes, types of the baskets and about the objects inside with the toddlers. Count the objects with older toddlers.

4. Sing about the baskets to the tune of "A Tisket, a Tasket."

> *A tisket, a tasket*
> *A red and blue basket.*
> *Austin put some blocks in his basket*
> *And now it's very full.*
>
> *A tisket, a tasket*
> *A red and blue basket.*
> *Austin took the blocks out of his basket*
> *And now it's all empty. (use names of specific objects, colors, children)*

5. Give each child a basket and encourage him to put something special inside, such as a stuffed animal or favorite book. Have a parade of baskets of "Special Things."

To do again

Do similar activities with boxes, gift tins, dish tubs, any container that toddlers can use for dump and fill.

Teaching hints

Use baskets, with or without handles, throughout the room to store classroom toys and materials on the shelves for the children to help reduce clutter and simplify clean up times with the toddlers. Teachers can use baskets to keep their materials for special activities together in one place and have ready as needed.

Home connections

Store your toddler's toys in stacking baskets and boxes to help with clutter and promote early sorting and organization skills rather than using toy boxes, which only teach children to dump. Toddlers will love to dump and fill so provide baskets, boxes, purses and containers to allow for this type of play at home too.

Chapter Six

Basket Case

Toddlers love to get inside small spaces to hide and get away for some quiet time in a busy classroom. Large laundry baskets provide a place for toddlers to relax in before they become a "basket case."

To do

1. Place at least two large laundry baskets out in a quiet area of the classroom or with books nearby. A few small pillows, stuffed animals, blankets can be added for coziness.

2. Let the toddlers get inside the baskets on their own to relax or look at books with the only limit being one child per basket.

3. The toddlers will also enjoy hiding in the baskets by putting another basket or a blanket on top while they are inside the basket. Pretend not to know where the child is and have others help you look for the child. Play peekaboo.

4. Take the baskets and books outside under a tree on the playground.

5. Use the large baskets outside for toddler-style basket ball games outside by tossing balls or beanbags into the basket.

To do again

Small wading pools and appliance boxes for one or two toddlers work well for cozy spaces in the classroom (see Snuggle Up With a Good Book on page 35).

Teaching hints

Toddlers, like adults, need time to be alone. With the busy activity of a classroom full of children, it can be difficult for toddlers to find this alone time. Make quiet spaces a priority in the toddler classroom by providing lots of places where the toddlers can be alone as they feel the need, such as with baskets, boxes, tunnels, corners or even under a table.

Home connections

Toddlers often need some "downtime" with busy days, outings and family gatherings. Young children often communicate through behavior and may not know how to ask for a quiet change of pace any other way than acting fussy or even silly.

Skills encouraged

gross motor, socioemotional

Language to use with toddlers

basket
large
inside
relax
on top
hide
by yourself

Materials

large laundry baskets
small pillows
stuffed animals
blankets
books
balls or beanbags

We're Going on a Picnic

Toddlers can work out some of their boundless energy as they pretend to go on a picnic.

Skills encouraged

language, gross motor

Language to use with toddlers

We're going
picnic
walk
hill
tree
spread
blanket
eat
play
hide and seek

Materials

none needed

Home connections

Toddlers are often timid in unfamiliar settings or with new events. Talking about what will happen, who will be there, what will be done, with the toddlers beforehand often helps alleviate the fears. Parents and teachers can also use the above tune to sing about the details of upcoming events, such as "We're going to the doctor" or "We're going on a airplane."

To do

1. Sing the following to the tune of "The Farmer in the Dell" and do the actions with the toddlers.

> *We're going on a picnic. (clap hands),we're going on a picnic.*
> *Heigh ho Hooray,we're going on a picnic!*

> *We'll walk to the park. (walk around room), we'll walk to the park.*
> *Heigh ho Hooray,we're going on a picnic!*

> *We'll find a perfect spot. (pretend to search with hand to forehead)*
> *We'll find a perfect spot.*
> *Heigh ho Hooray, we're going on a picnic!*

> *We'll spread our blanket out... (rub floor to spread blanket)*

> *We'll sit on the ground... (sit down, rock to the beat)*

> *We'll eat a special lunch... (pretend to eat)*

> *We'll walk back home... (walk around room)*

> *We'll rest after the picnic. (lay down), we'll rest after the picnic.*
> *Heigh ho Hooray, we'll rest after the picnic.*

2. Sing other verses, such as:

> *We'll jump and play in the grass... (jump)*

> *We'll crawl under the trees... (crawl)*

> *We'll roll down the hill... (roll on floor)*

> *We'll dance with our friends... (dance)*

Use your imagination for other activities.

To do again

Have a picnic snack or lunch outside. Sing and act out the verse outside after eating.

Chapter Six

The Perfect Spot

Just a few minor changes to the homeliving area makes it an ideal spot for toddlers to have pretend picnics with their friends and dolls.

1½+

To do

1. Remove some of the homeliving furniture for a few days to make room for a picnic. Place nature pictures on the wall nearby.

2. Spread a blanket or sheet out on the floor.

3. Put out some of the following items for the children to use on their picnic:
   - ✓ picnic basket or other types of baskets
   - ✓ plastic fruit and vegetables
   - ✓ paper plates
   - ✓ napkins
   - ✓ plastic containers and cups
   - ✓ dolls
   - ✓ stuffed animals

4. Encourage the toddlers to have a picnic on the blankets with you and their friends. Talk with them about the foods, serving each other and passing the food. A few dolls or stuffed animals may enjoy joining in too.

5. Leave out some small receiving-size blankets that the toddlers can use for picnics elsewhere in the room or for dolls and stuffed animals.

To do again

Have a picnic outside or have a picnic snack on a rainy day inside the classroom for a change of pace.

Home connections

Have picnics with your toddler, even if it is in your backyard. Being in the fresh air calms many active toddlers and relaxes parents too.

Skills encouraged

pretend play, socialization

Language to use with toddlers

picnic
blanket
basket
food
fruit
eat
share
friend
animals

Materials

pictures of scenes from
   nature
large blanket or sheet
plastic fruit
picnic basket
paper plates
napkins
plastic containers
stuffed animals
small receiving-size blankets

Remember Your Napkin

Napkins can be used in a number of ways with toddlers to practice their self-help and fine motor skills.

Skills encouraged

self-help, fine motor

Language to use with toddlers

wipe face
wipe hands
fold
roll
crumple
throw away
tear
cut
draw

Materials

paper napkins
dish tub
paper, glue and paintbrush or
  self-adhesive paper
scissors
markers

To do

1. Save paper napkins from fast food places and ones left over from parties. Have parents help save napkins too.

2. Place napkins out in the sensory table or dish tub for toddlers to explore. Talk about the different colors and designs on the napkins. Encourage the toddlers to unfold and fold the napkins.

3. Let toddlers tear the napkins into pieces. Younger toddlers will crumple the napkins and enjoy throwing the pieces away. Children's scissors can be placed in the tub for older toddlers to practice their cutting skills on the napkins.

4. Make a collage of the pieces of napkins on another day. Have the toddlers spread glue thinned with water on the paper with a thick paintbrush. Place the napkin pieces on top. Or, attach a piece of self-adhesive paper to construction paper with the sticky side up so that the self-adhesive paper acts as the adhesive.

5. Let toddlers use markers to draw on folded napkins. Unfold the napkin to see how the design ran through the napkin like magic. If desired, attach the unfolded napkin to construction paper for a backing.

To do again

Place three to four pairs of napkins in a basket or box for the older toddlers to match the napkins into sets.

Teaching hints

Provide napkins at snack and mealtimes, even with young toddlers. Encourage the toddlers to wipe their face and hands and throw their napkin away when they are finished. When having to clean a toddlers face, always let them try to do it first, and they will be more agreeable to let you have the last wipe.

Home connections

Allow your toddler to help with their own self-help skills, such as face and hand wiping, as often as possible. Toddlers also enjoy helping out with simple adult tasks, such as putting a napkin or spoon at each place at the table or throwing away the napkins. It is important for adults to let toddlers do things for themselves when possible to encourage their emerging autonomy and to help reduce conflicts over doing things for themselves.

Chapter Six

Basket Games

Use baskets and simple objects to make size and color sorting games for toddlers.

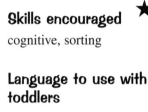

To do

1. Gather two to four plastic storage baskets in different colors.

2. Collect objects of the same colors, such as wooden blocks, felt or fabric squares, bows, plastic eggs. Make sure all of the items pass the choke test for toddlers.

3. Place the items out for the toddler to explore. Talk with the toddler about the different colors and names of the objects.

4. Encourage the toddler to sort the objects into the baskets by color.

To do again

Provide a large and a small basket with little or big objects, such as plastic cups, balls, socks for the toddler to sort. The smaller items may require closer supervision if they do not pass the choke test. Talk with the child about the big and little sizes.

Teaching hints

Use storage baskets and boxes on the classroom shelves to help reduce clutter. Place pictures of the objects that belong in the specific basket or box to help toddlers sort the materials during clean up time.

Home connections

Use baskets and boxes to store toys at home to reduce clutter and to develop early organizational skills.

Skills encouraged

cognitive, sorting

Language to use with toddlers

basket
color
size
big
little
put inside
same
match

Materials

baskets
simple objects

Paw Paw Patch

Older toddlers will enjoy acting out the actions to the traditional song "Paw Paw Patch."

Skills encouraged

gross motor, language

Language to use with toddlers

Where is...?
Come on
Let's go
find
paw paws
picking up
basket
Follow me

Materials

baskets
beanbags, plastic eggs, fabric
scraps

To do

1. Sing the traditional song "Paw Paw Patch" and encourage the toddlers to follow your actions.

> *Where, oh where is dear little Mary? (substitute another names)*
> *Where, oh where is dear little Mary?*
> *Where, oh where is dear little Mary?*
> *Way down yonder in the paw paw patch! (walk around room pretend to search with hand to forehead)*

> *Come on boys, let's go find her.*
> *Come on girls, let's go find her.*
> *Come on friends, let's go find her.*
> *Way down yonder in the paw paw patch! (motion come on with hand and walk around room)*

> *Picking up paw paws and putting them in my basket.*
> *Picking up paw paws and putting them in my basket.*
> *Picking up paw paws and putting them in my basket.*
> *Way down yonder in the paw paw patch! (Pretend to pick up something and put inside pretend basket)*

2. Let the children use real baskets and pick up beanbags, plastic eggs, scraps of fabric with the last verse if desired.

3. Add the following verse to end the activity:

> *Come on boys, let's sit and rest.*
> *Come on girls, let's sit and rest.*
> *Come on children, let's sit and rest.*
> *Way down yonder in the paw paw patch. (sit down and rest with head on hands)*

To do again

Sing the verses and do the actions outside so the children can run as they search for Mary.

Teaching hints

Some toddlers may watch rather than joining in with the movement song. As the children become more familiar with the actions, more of the toddlers will likely join in the fun.

Chapter Six

Bubbles Everywhere

One of the staples of childhood, bubbles provide instant fun for all.

To do

1. Blow bubbles for the toddlers. Let them watch and try to catch them as they blow in the air.

2. Chant:

> *Bubbles, bubbles in the air*
> *Bubbles, bubbles everywhere.*
> *See them, catch them*
> *Before they disappear*
> *Bubbles, bubbles everywhere.*

3. Let older toddlers try to blow bubbles from the wand. Tell them to blow like they blow out birthday candles.

4. Blow a few bubbles from bubble gum for the toddlers. They will be fascinated at your amazing abilities.

To do again

Try the following homemade bubble solution:
> *1 cup water*
> *2 tablespoons dish detergent, such as Dawn*

Some brands may need the addition of glycerin.

Teaching hints

Bubble solution on the classroom floor can be quite slippery so it is best to blow bubbles outside. Always have bubbles handy for an instant playground activity for it captures the interest of all ages.

Home connections

When times get hectic with your toddler at home, go outside and blow bubbles. It will relax you and your child. Blow bubbles even for a few minutes on a cold day.

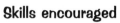

Skills encouraged

sensory exploration

Language to use with toddlers

bubbles
blow
wind
see
catch
air
disappear
everywhere

Materials

bubbles
bubble wands
bubble gum

Tiny Bubbles

Even though it's not the real thing, toddlers can still relax with their hands in the mounds of tiny bubble bath bubbles in a baby bath tub.

Skills encouraged

sensory exploration, fine motor

Language to use with toddlers

bubble
tiny
bath
white
foamy
mounds
squeeze
baby

Materials

bubble bath
baby bath tub
bath sponges

To do

1. Add a small amount of bubble bath to a baby bath tub. Fill with water using high pressure to form bubbles.

2. Pour out some of the water after the bubbles have formed. (The pan should contain mostly bubbles with just a small amount of water.)

3. Place the bath tub on the floor with a few large towels underneath to absorb any spills.

4. Let the toddlers explore the bubbles. Talk with them about the tiny bubbles and the mounds of bubbles. Have them clap with bubbles in their hands to see what happens.

5. Add a few bath sponges to the bubbles. Encourage the toddlers to squeeze the sponges to make more bubbles.

6. Replace the bubbles and water as needed.

To do again

Let the toddlers give baby dolls a bubble bath. Be careful not to get any bubbles in the dolls' eyes.

Home connections

Let your toddler take a bubble bath for a special treat. Have fun with all the tiny bubbles by hunting for floating toys hidden in the bubbles. Encourage your toddler to put bubble mounds on his tummy, his shoulder, his head. Limit the bubble bath to a very special activity as frequent bubble baths can irritate your toddler's sensitive skin.

Bubble Bag

Use resealable freezer bags for lots of nonmessy sensory exploration.

To do

1. Fill a large resealable freezer bag with styling gel.

2. Tape the top portion with clear mailing tape.

3. Put the bags out on the table or tape them to the wall for the toddlers to explore.

4. Talk with them about the bubbles in the gel, the smooth texture, the squishy gel, their squeezing actions.

5. Make a variety of bags by adding some of the following:
✓ food color—let the toddlers mix the colors into the gel by squeezing the bag
✓ glitter, sequins or metal confetti of different shapes—the toddlers watch these objects move around as they squeeze the bag

To do again

Add a variety of sensory material to the bags for the toddlers to explore. Try shaving cream with food coloring, fingerpaint, packing foam peanuts, toothpaste, lotion dish detergent, liquid soap.

Teaching hints

The freezer bags work best as they are thicker than resealable sandwich bags. The sensory bags can be double bagged for extra durability if needed.

Home connections

Make a few sensory bags for long car trips.

Skills encouraged

sensory exploration

Language to use with toddlers

feel
squish
squeeze
bubbles
smooth
colors
shiny

Materials

large resealable freezer bags
styling gel
clear mailing tape
glitter, sequins or metal
  confetti

Pop Music

Challenge toddlers' motor skills with bubble wrap packing material for a truly "pop" musical activity.

Skills encouraged

sensory exploration, fine motor

Language to use with toddlers

bubbles
pop
listen
sound
big
little
squeeze
pound
step
jump

Materials

bubble packing wrap
tape

To do

1. Save bubble wrap from packaging. Have parents help collect the wrap as well.

2. Cut the wrap into large pieces, at least 12" x 12".

3. Encourage the toddlers to feel the bubbles and squeeze or hit the bubbles to make "pop music." Talk about the sounds of the popping.

4. Place the bubble wrap on the floor for the toddlers to feel with their feet. Encourage them to stamp or jump on the bubbles to try to pop them.
Note: On slippery floors, tape the bubble wrap to the floor.

5. Compare wraps with different size bubbles and the different popping sounds made by the big bubbles and the little bubbles.

To do again

Tape a large piece of bubble wrap to a table for the toddlers to use as a surface for fingerpainting. Talk with them about the bumpy texture of the bubbles. Make a print of their fingerpaintings by placing a sheet of paper on top when each toddler is finished painting. Rub on the back of the paper and lift to reveal the design.

Home connections

Let your toddler pop the bubbles and play with the boxes from packages delivered at home.

Eggs-tra Ordinary Sounds

Plastic eggs make ideal shakers for "eggs-tra" ordinary springtime music.
Store the eggs in cartons for a one-to-one correspondence activity.

To do

1. Collect six plastic eggs and a carton from half dozen eggs for younger toddlers, while older toddlers do well with twelve eggs and a carton from a dozen eggs. Cardboard cartons seem to withstand the explorations of toddlers better than the styrofoam variety.

2. Fill each egg with a different dry filler material, such as:
   - ✓ eggshells
   - ✓ rice
   - ✓ aquarium pebbles
   - ✓ small rocks
   - ✓ birdseed
   - ✓ penny
   - ✓ flour

3. Leave one egg empty for a silent shaker.

4. Secure the seam with a hot glue gun or crazy glue. Cover the seam of the egg with colored masking tape for added strength.

5. Place the eggs in the carton.

6. Let the toddlers explore the "eggs-tra" special sounds of the eggs. Talk with them about the different sounds made by the materials.

7. Encourage them to put the eggs back in the egg carton when they are finished for a one-to-one correspondence activity. Count the eggs with older toddlers as they put them away.

8. Shake the eggs to the beat of songs or nursery rhymes.

9. Let older toddlers make their own egg shakers by choosing a colored egg and placing the material inside. The teacher will need to secure the seam for the toddlers.

To do again

Place empty plastic eggs or those made into shakers in a basket for the toddlers to explore and for the dump and fill play so popular with toddlers. Talk with the toddlers about the colors and count the eggs while putting them back in the basket.

Home connections

Leave out the plastic eggs from egg hunts in baskets for continued fun with hiding games and dump and full play—always a toddler favorite.

Skills encouraged

sensory exploration, fine motor, one-to-one correspondence, cognitive

Language to use with toddlers

eggs
colors
inside
sound
Do you hear...?
rice
birdseed
penny
loud
soft
empty
silent
egg carton

Materials

plastic eggs
egg carton
dry filler material
hot glue gun
colored masking tape

Teaching hints

The eggs can crack easily and are not as durable as shakers made from plastic containers. Check their condition often or use them as a teacher-directed activity with a small group of toddlers.

Humpty Dumpty

Toddlers know about falling and can relate to Humpty Dumpty's mishap.

Skills encouraged

language

Language to use with toddlers

egg
sat
wall
fall
crack
broken
Uh oh!
rhyme
pretend
back together

Materials

large plastic egg
permanent marker
shoe box

To do

1. Say the familiar nursery rhyme with the toddlers with the following actions:

> *Humpty Dumpty sat on a wall. (sit up straight, sway side to side)*
> *Humpty Dumpty had a great fall. (hit hands on floor)*
> *All the king's horses and all the king's men, (walk two fingers from each hand on floor)*
> *Couldn't put Humpty together again. Uh oh! (shake head no)*

2. Use a large plastic egg with a face drawn on it and a shoe box for the wall with the rhyme. Crack the egg open when it hits the floor.

3. For fun with older toddlers, put the egg back together, close the seam with a band-aid and say the following additional verse.

> *Humpty Dumpty sat on a wall.*
> *Humpty Dumpty had a great fall.*
> *Blanche and Carrie (teachers' names) and all our friends,*
> *Could put Humpty back together in the end! Yea!*

Suggested book

Read "Humpty Dumpty" from a book of nursery rhymes or the book *Humpty Dumpty* by Tracey Moroney.

To do again

With older toddlers, give each child a large plastic egg with a face drawn on it to use while saying the rhyme. For a special treat, give each one a band-aid to use on their egg. Substitute the child's name in the rhyme if desired.

Teaching hints and Home connections

Often toddlers cry more during the first-aid or ice applications following a fall than they do from the actual mishap. "Humpty Dumpty" is an ideal rhyme to say while comforting a child that has fallen to help get their attention away from the pain or ice on the injury.

Egg-pressions

Use the oval shape like an egg to display the toddlers' "egg-pressions" through their "most important marks" (MIMs).

To do

1. Cut large oval shapes out of light colored construction paper.

2. Let the toddler choose what color of oval shape or egg he wants to color on with crayons or markers.

3. Talk with the toddler about the oval shape, the colors he uses and the lines he makes as he draws his most important marks (MIMs) on the paper.

4. Provide smaller oval shapes for older toddlers to use for variety.

5. Let the toddler color additional eggs as he desires.

6. Display the eggs prominently on a wall or bulletin board of the room with the following heading "Eggs-citing Marks." Green paper can be put underneath the oval shapes or at the bottom to resemble grass if desired.

To do again

Let the toddler decorate the egg shapes with dot stickers or make dots with shoe polish or bingo blotters filled with paint (see All Polished in *Toddlers Together*). Or, let the toddler paint on a large oval shape cut from butcher paper at the easel or at the tabletop.

Teaching hints

Displaying the toddlers' MIMs in the room helps show parents and the children that these early prewriting efforts and "eggs-pressions" should be treasured.

Home connections

Provide markers, crayons and different shapes for your toddler to draw on at home to practice their early efforts at prewriting.

Skills encouraged

creative expression, fine motor

Language to use with toddlers

egg shape
oval shape
colors
draw
paint
lines
designs
decorated
eggs

Materials

paper
scissors
crayons
markers

Eggs-citing Twist

Vary a familiar nursery rhyme to relate to eggs for an "eggs-citing" new twist for older toddlers.

Skills encouraged

language

Language to use with toddlers

eggs
cluck
hen
Yes, ma'am
scrambling
boiling
baking
names

Materials

plastic eggs (optional)

To do

1. Vary "Baa, Baa, Black Sheep" to a verse about eggs with the following changes.

> *Cluck, cluck, Mama Hen*
> *Have you any eggs?*
> *Yes ma'am, yes ma'am*
> *Three dozen I do.*
> *Some for scrambling,*
> *Some for boiling and*
> *Some for baking too.*

2. Sing the verse with an egg-tasting party with scrambled and boiled eggs (see Eggs-quisite Taste on the next page).

3. Vary the verse to include the children's names. Pass out a plastic egg to the specific children when saying their names.

> *Cluck, cluck, Nadine (teacher's name) Hen*
> *Have you any eggs?*
> *Yes, yes, my friends*
> *I surely do.*
> *One for Jessica,*
> *One for Charlie*
> *And one for Ronnie too.*

To do again

Change the "Baa, Baa, Black Sheep" verse in similar ways to refer to other creatures and their products, such as:

> *Buzz, buzz, little bee*
> *Have you any honey?...*

or,

> *Moo, moo, brown cow*
> *Have you any milk?...*

Chapter Six

Eggs-quisite Taste

Explore eggs with toddlers with a "eggs-quisite" tasting samples following a "smashing" good time with the shells.

To do

1. Scramble and hard boil eggs for the toddlers to taste. Save the eggshells.

2. While tasting the eggs, show the toddlers an egg. Talk with them about the shell and the yolk inside. Show the toddlers the leftover eggshells.

3. Place a few egg shells in a resealable plastic bag. Let the toddlers smash the eggshells by hammering them with wooden hammers.

4. Pour the eggshells into a bowl for the toddlers to feel. Talk with them about the sharp and hard textures of the shells.

5. Sing about the eggs with a verse about scrambled and boiled eggs (see Eggs-citing Twist on the previous page).

To do again

Save the smashed eggshells for other sensory activities, such as adding to fingerpaint (see Hand Prints in *Toddlers Together*) and to make shakers (see Eggs-tra Ordinary Sounds on page 201).

Teaching hints

Check for food allergies before any tasting activity.

Skills encouraged

sensory exploration, fine motor

Language to use with toddlers

eggs
egg shells
yolk
scrambled
hard boiled
cooking
cracked
smashed
hard

Materials

eggs
hot plate or stove
resealable bags
wooden hammers

Eggs-ceptional Patterns

Reuse gift wrap and wallpaper samples for an "eggs-ceptional" collage of patterns.

Skills encouraged

creative expression, fine motor

Language to use with toddlers

oval
shape
pattern
design
color
lines
big
little
glue
collage

Materials

old gift wrap
wallpaper samples
construction paper
glue
clear self-adhesive paper

To do

1. Cut a variety of big and little oval shapes out of old gift wrap, wallpaper samples and construction paper.

2. Have the toddler pick out the color he wants to use for his collage.

3. Encourage him to glue the ovals on the paper. Let him glue as many as he desires.

4. Talk with him about the patterns and colors of the ovals on his paper.

5. Instead of gluing the eggs, the toddler can attach his ovals to the sticky side of clear self-adhesive paper.

To do again

Cut other shapes from gift wrap, wallpaper samples for collages of a variety of shapes or all one shape, such as hearts, stars, circles.

Eggs-act Match

Oval shapes cut out of different patterns allows toddlers to practice matching and sorting designs "eggs-actly."

To do

1. Cut old gift wrap or wallpaper samples into 4" x 6" oval shapes, making two of each design. Vary the number of patterns depending on the ability of the specific group of individual toddlers. The shapes can be referred to as decorated eggs.

2. Glue one egg of each pattern on the file folder or poster board.

3. Laminate or cover the remaining oval shapes and file folder with clear self-adhesive paper. Attach a resealable plastic bag on the back to store the shapes.

4. Encourage the toddler to match the eggs with the same designs.

5. Talk with her about the colors and specific patterns.

To do again

Cut three to five oval shapes (eggs) out of two to five different patterns of gift wrap or wallpaper samples. Laminate or cover the shapes with clear self-adhesive paper. Provide small baskets or boxes for the toddler to sort the eggs by patterns. Or, cut two or three different sizes of ovals out of the same pattern for sorting by size into baskets or boxes. Talk with the toddler about the patterns or sizes as they do the activity.

Teaching hints

Vary the complexity of the activity to fit the level of the individual toddler. Some will need the success of sorting or matching just two patterns while others will enjoy the challenge of more patterns.

Skills encouraged ★

matching, sorting, cognitive

Language to use with toddlers

oval shape
egg
pattern
match
sort
color
basket
box
big
medium
little

Materials

old gift wrap
wallpaper samples
poster board or file folder
glue
clear self-adhesive paper
resealable plastic bag

Eggs-actly Right

Plastic eggs can be used for a number of matching games with older toddlers.

Skills encouraged

matching, cognitive, fine motor

Language to use with toddlers

eggs
color
match
same
put together
size
big
medium
little
basket
egg carton
inside

Materials

plastic eggs
basket
colored bowls or small baskets
egg carton

To do

1. Place two to four plastic eggs of two or more different colors in a basket.

2. Provide bowls, boxes covered with construction paper or small storage baskets in colors that match the egg colors.

3. Encourage the toddler to sort the eggs into the container of the same color.

4. For color matching activity with toddlers able to put the plastic eggs back together easily, provide two to six plastic eggs of different colors for an egg carton or a small basket. Encourage the toddler to take the eggs apart and then match them by color as they put them back together.

5. Talk with the toddlers about the colors and the process of matching or sorting the eggs.

To do again

For two activities related to size, provide small, medium and large eggs of the same color. Encourage older toddlers to match the eggs by size when putting the eggs back together. Show the toddler how to nest small eggs inside bigger eggs. Talk with the toddler about the sizes of the eggs.

Teaching hints

Since older toddlers vary widely in their ability to match and sort, tailor the difficulty of this activity to the developmental level of the individual toddler by varying the number of eggs to match by color.

Home connections

Save the plastic eggs from egg hunts for the toddler to explore. Play games with the toddler by encouraging him to match the eggs by color or size. Talk about the colors and sizes. Count the eggs. Store the eggs in a basket. Toddlers, especially younger ones, enjoy the dump and fill play provided by eggs in a basket.

Eggs-plorations

Older toddlers practice their fine motor skills as they explore egg-related sensory materials with plastic eggs for filling, emptying, taking apart and putting back together.

To do

1. Fill a dish pan or sensory bath tub with plastic eggs and one of the following egg-related sensory items.

> ✓ eggshells (use the shells crushed by the toddlers on Eggs-quisite Taste on page 205)
> ✓ birdseed (an ideal activity for outside time to let the birds clean up any spills)
> ✓ confetti (confetti-filled eggs or cascarones are a tradition at Mexican-American parties or fiestas in South Texas)

Note: Supervise the children closely with the eggshells.

2. Allow the toddlers to "eggs-plore" the sensory items. Encourage them to fill or empty the eggs while taking them apart or emptying them.

3. Talk with them about the materials, the colors of the eggs and the sounds made when the filled eggs are shaken.

To do again

For toddlers over two years old, add small, medium or large plastic eggs with the sensory material for toddlers to match by size when putting them back together.

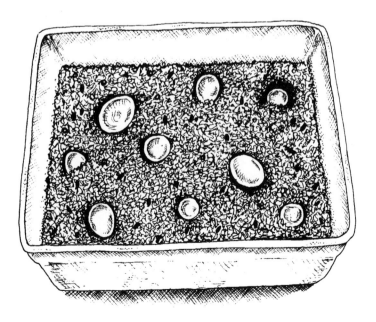

Skills encouraged

fine motor, sensory exploration, cognitive

Language to use with toddlers

egg
colors
fill
empty
take apart
put together
eggshells
birdseed
confetti
paper
soft
hard
shake
sounds

Materials

plastic eggs
crushed eggshells, birdseed
  or confetti
dish pan or sensory tub
plastic containers

Baby Animal Search

Toddlers love hiding games, even one as simple as hiding baby animals in a box while singing a variation of the familiar "A Hunting We Will Go."

Skills encouraged

language, object permanence

Language to use with toddlers

searching
We will go...
Let it go
box
bag
What's inside?
chick
lamb
bunny
duckling
piglet

Materials

pictures of young animals
plastic or stuffed animals
box or gift bag

To do

1. Collect pictures, plastic or stuffed young springtime animals, such as a bunny, chick, lamb, duckling, piglet.

2. Find a box or gift bag in which all will fit.

3. Sing the following variation to "A Hunting We Will Go" using the animals and bag or box.

> *A searching we will go,*
> *A searching we will go.*
> *We'll find a little bunny, (pick up picture or toy bunny)*
> *And put him in a box (bag). (put inside box or bag)*
> *And then we'll let him go. (remove bunny)*

4. If using stuffed or puppet animals, let the toddlers pet the animal or have it pretend to kiss each child.

5. Talk with the toddlers about the young animal in terms of foods it eats, where it lives, how the parents care for it and what they are called (rabbit or bunny, duck or duckling).

6. Repeat the verse with other young springtime animals. Let older toddlers put the animals inside and remove them from the box or bag while saying the verse with them.

7. Leave out a few boxes or gift bags with animals for the toddlers to hide and find animals on their own.

To do again

Use the verse with other animal groups or themes, such as zoo animals or pets. Or provide large boxes for the toddlers to hide inside and sing the verse using their individual names.

Home connections

Play hiding games at home with favorite stuffed animals in gift bags, boxes or even under blankets. Let your toddler hide from you under a blanket as you pretend you can not find him—always a fun part of the good night routine to get him into his room for bed and good night kisses.

Animal Nursery

Combine two of toddlers favorite things—animals and babies—as they pretend to care for baby animals born in the spring in an "Animal Nursery."

To do

1. Gather stuffed animals, puppets or large plastic animals associated with springtime, such as rabbits or bunnies, ducks or ducklings, sheep or lambs, birds. Ask parents for stuffed animals for the class to borrow.

2. Let younger toddlers explore the animals. Talk with them about the names of the animals and the sounds the animals make.

3. For older toddlers, place the animals out for the toddlers to explore in the block area. Encourage the toddlers to build cages, pens or homes for the young animals.

4. Add some of the following for the children to take care of the animals:
   - ✓ boxes or baskets for beds
   - ✓ baby bottles
   - ✓ small blankets
   - ✓ plastic vegetables
   - ✓ green felt cut into irregular shapes for lettuce
   - ✓ carrots made from orange felt
   - ✓ rectangles or large strips cut from yellow felt for hay
   - ✓ dog brush

5. Encourage the toddlers to care for the baby animals by feeding them, putting them in the cage or nest, brushing the animals.

6. Look at pictures of springtime animals. Talk with the toddlers about the names of the animal families (rabbit or bunny, duck or duckling), their features, what they eat, the sound they make.

7. Sing songs about the springtime animals. "Old MacDonald" is an easy one to use with any animal group (see Life At The Pond in *Toddlers Together*). Or try variations of "Baa, Baa, Black Sheep" (see Eggs-citing Twist on page 204).

Suggested books

Read *I Love You as Much* by Laura Krauss Melmed or *Is Your Mama a Llama?* by Deborah Guarino.

To do again

Add stuffed and large plastic animal groups to the block area to make a farm, zoo or a pet store.

Skills encouraged

language, pretend play

Language to use with toddlers

baby animals
young
springtime
born
hatched
gentle
care for
feed
mommy
daddy
duck
duckling
sheep
lamb
rabbit
bunny

Materials

stuffed springtime animals
  or puppets
large plastic farm animals
pictures of young animals
baby bottles
blankets
boxes
baskets
felt
plastic vegetables

Bunny Hutch

Toddlers explore one-to-one correspondence as they place stuffed bunnies back in their cages and feed the animals.

Skills encouraged

cognitive, pretend play

Language to use with toddlers

rabbit
bunny
hutch
cage
inside
count
feed
carrot
lettuce
ears
hop

Materials

two or four boxes of the
   same size
stuffed rabbits
felt
scissors
paper

To do

1. Obtain two to four boxes of the same size and the same number of stuffed rabbits that will fit inside the boxes.

2. Tape the boxes together with the sides touching so that all the openings face the same direction. The boxes can be put together with two on the top and two on the bottom or four in a row.

3. Make four carrots from green and orange felt.

4. Place the one rabbit and one carrot inside each box.

5. Allow the toddler to play with the rabbits. Talk with her about the animals and their special characteristics—long ears, fluffy tails, hopping.

6. Encourage the toddler to put each rabbit back in a cage or hutch. Count the rabbits. Encourage her to give each rabbit one carrot.

7. Use a stuffed bunny with rabbit action songs, such as Little Cottage on page 216 or Sunny Bunny on the next page.

To do again

Have a "Honey Bunny Day." Encourage each toddler to bring a favorite stuffed rabbit from home. Talk about the sizes and colors of all the different bunnies.

Home connections

Use boxes of all sizes at home to make cages for stuffed animals, houses or beds for dolls, garages for cars and trucks or almost anything you or your toddler can imagine.

Sunny Bunny

Toddlers enjoy acting out the fat little bunny in this simple rhyme.

To do

1. Chant the following action rhyme with the toddlers:

> *Sunny Bunny is fat, fat, fat. (pat tummy)*
> *His soft little paws go pat, pat, pat. (pat hands together)*
> *His fluffy little tail goes thump, thump, thump. (pat backside*
> *or pound floor)*
> *And when Sunny Bunny moves*
> *He goes jump, jump, jump. (make hands jump across floor)*

2. Use a stuffed rabbit or rabbit puppet to act out the verse.

Home connections

Visit a pet store with your toddler to see rabbits up close.

Skills encouraged

language, fine motor

Language to use with toddlers

rabbit
fat
paws
pat
fluffy tail
thump
jump

Materials

stuffed rabbit or puppet

Carrot Eater

The traditional verse about a rabbit eating carrots everyday can be varied to be used with toddlers in almost any way.

Skills encouraged

language

Language to use with toddlers

carrot
eat
sweet
crunch
munch
hug
snuggle
vegetables

Materials

stuffed rabbit or puppet
plastic carrot or felt and scissors
carrots
grater

Teaching hints

Use the verse as a transition to hand washing activity for older toddlers by using each child's name (see Step 3 above). After the child pretends to feed or hugs the rabbit, then she goes to wash her hands. Or, use the hugging version to tell each toddler good night before nap time.

To do

1. Chant the following with the toddlers.

> *Rabbit, rabbit, carrot eater.*
> *He says there is nothing sweeter.*
> *Than a carrot everyday,*
> *Munch and crunch and run away.*

2. Use a stuffed rabbit or puppet with a plastic carrot (or one made out of felt) with the verse. Hide the rabbit and carrot with the last line.

3. Use the verse with the children's names. Let that child hold the carrot to feed the bunny. Or, have the bunny give that child a kiss or hug. For example:

> *Jennifer, Jennifer, carrot eater. (or hug getter)*
> *She says there is nothing better*
> *Than a hug every day.*
> *Hug and snuggle and hug this way.*

4. Taste carrots (shredded carrots work best as carrots present a choking risk) or carrot muffins.

5. Substitute other vegetables that rabbits eat, such as lettuce or spinach. Cut an irregular shape out of green felt to resemble lettuce or spinach to use with the verse.

To do again

Make up other versions with the tune, such as Lion Tamer on page 131, or change the verse to other springtime young or farm animals, such as:

> *Lamb, lamb, hay eater...*

> *Pony, pony, apple eater...*

> *Cow, cow, grass eater...*

Home connections

Use the verse at mealtimes to get a finicky toddler to eat or any toddler to try new foods. For example:

> *Thelma, Thelma, egg eater.*
> *She says there is nothing better.*
> *Than a taste of egg once a day.*
> *Yummy, yummy, swallow it away!*

Chapter Six

Little Ducks

Toddlers enjoy the traditional counting song of "Five Little Ducks" with its rhyming words and quacking sounds. As with most repetitive counting songs, most toddlers will do better with fewer animals.

To do

1. Shorten the traditional counting song of "Five Little Ducks" to three for toddlers.

> *Three little ducks went out to play,*
> *Over the hills and far away.*
> *Mother duck said, "Quack, quack, quack,"*
> *And two of the ducks came back.*

2. Repeat the verse with two and then one little duck until "none of the ducks came back."

3. Cut three small and one large duck shape out of felt to use with the song at the flannel board. Or, use rubber duck bathtub toys with the verse.

Suggested book

Sing the song with *Five Little Ducks* illustrated by Jose Aruego and Ariane Dewey.

To do again

Change the verse to chicks, such as:

> *Three little chicks went out to play,*
> *Out of the barn and far away.*
> *Mother hen said, "Cluck, cluck, cluck,"*
> *And two of the chicks came back with luck.*

Repeat for two, then one little chick.

Teaching hints

Adjust the length of counting songs according to the level of the toddlers. Most do best with three repetitions but some groups can handle starting numbers of five.

Skills encouraged

language, counting

Language to use with toddlers

ducks
three
two
one
play
hills
far away
mother
quack

Materials

felt
scissors
flannel board

Little Cottage

The traditional fingerplay of "Little Rabbit" can be changed to a more peaceful version (without a hunter) for toddlers.

Skills encouraged

language, fine motor

Language to use with toddlers

little cottage
house
woods
little man
window
saw
rabbit
hopping
knocking
door
help me
come inside

Materials

none needed

To do

1. Chant the following traditional fingerplay with the toddlers.

> *Little cottage (or house) in the woods. (form triangle with fingers)*
> *Little man by the window stood, (hold up pointer finger)*
> *Saw a rabbit hopping by, (hop two fingers)*
> *Knocking at his door. (pretend to knock)*
> *"Help me! Help me! I am scared." (raise hands up and down)*
> *Come little rabbit, (motion come with hand)*
> *Come inside, safely by my side. (hold arm to chest and rub it as*
> *though were a rabbit)*

Suggested books

Read *Runaway Bunny* or *Home for a Bunny*, both classics by Margaret Wise Brown

Movin' in Spring

Toddlers can release their high energy in appropriate ways as they pretend to be animals playing on a spring day.

To do

1. Look at pictures of animals associated with springtime, such as ducks, rabbits, lambs, chicks, birds with the toddlers. Talk with them about how the animals move.

2. Encourage the toddlers to move like springtime animals as they follow your actions with the following, sung to the tune of "The Farmer in the Dell."

> *The rabbits hop up and down.*
> *The rabbits hop up and down.*
> *Heigh ho. It is springtime,*
> *The rabbits hop up and down. (pretend to hop like rabbits)*

Substitute other animals, such as:

> *The ducks waddle back and forth...(pretend to waddle)*

> *The lambs run in the grass...(crawl quickly)*

> *The chicks scamper around...(walk quickly on tiptoes)*

> *The birds fly in the sky...(pretend to fly)*

3. Let the toddlers suggest other springtime animals.

4. This activity can also be done with the variations to "Mulberry Bush":

> *This is the way the bunnies hop, bunnies hop, bunnies hop.*
> *This is the way the bunnies hop on a fine spring day. (hop)*

Vary the verse with other animals.

To do again

Use the verses to move like other animal groups or themes, such as zoo animals, pets, farm animals.

Teaching hints

Use the activity as a transition to focus the toddlers' movements when the group must move together from one place to another, such as out to the playground or to another classroom.

Skills encouraged

gross motor, creative expression

Language to use with toddlers

move like
follow
waddle
ducks
rabbits
hop
jump
lambs
run
crawl
chicks
tiptoe
birds
fly

Materials

pictures of animals

Home connections

Move like animals on a rainy day in spring when you and your toddler both have pent up energy that needs to be released.

Animal Play

Toddlers thrive and relax with opportunities for sensory play. Add plastic animals to the sensory tub with any number of materials for lots of hands-on play.

Skills encouraged

sensory exploration, fine motor

Language to use with toddlers

feel
dirt
rocks
hay
grass
shells
seed
water
animals
box
truck

Materials

sensory table or dish tub
large plastic animals
berry baskets or small boxes
plastic grass or real grass
hay or potting soil
birdseed or eggshells
rocks
plastic eggs

To do

1. Gather plastic animals associated with springtime—farm animals, rabbits.

2. Over a period of days add the following to the sensory tub or a dish tub for the toddlers to explore:
   ✓ plastic farm animals in potting soil or hay with a few large rocks
   ✓ small dump trucks, berry baskets or small boxes
   ✓ ducks and rabbits in plastic or real grass
   ✓ rubber ducks in water
   ✓ chickens or birds with plastic eggs in crushed eggshells or birdseed, especially for an outside activity

3. Let the toddlers explore the animals in the sensory material on their own.

4. Talk with the children about the animals, the sounds they make, the feel of the sensory material and so on.

To do again

Let the toddlers wash the plastic animals in a small amount of water with small cloths and old toothbrushes.

Teaching hints

Small plastic animals do not pass the choke test for children under three. It is best not to use them even with children over two as the pieces would still require close supervision.

Home connections

Water relaxes almost every age group, especially active toddlers. Let your toddler play with plastic farm or other types of animals in the bathtub. Older toddlers enjoy relaxing with plastic animals at a sink filled with water when baths are not feasible.

Bunny Tails

It's not a tall tale that toddlers can paint with bunny tails when they are made from pillow stuffing or cotton balls.

To do

1. Tear off small chunks of pillow stuffing or spread open large cotton balls to resemble bunny tails. Let the toddlers feel the pretend fluffy tails. Talk with them about the soft texture.

2. Mix two or three different colors of paint, preferably in white, light brown, brown or black, similar to the colors of rabbits. Pour each color into a pie tin or flat container.

3. Attach the cotton balls or chunks of stuffing to clothespins and place a few in each color of paint.

4. Let the toddler choose the color of paper he wants to paint on and the color of paint he wants to use first.

5. Encourage the toddler to paint with the bunny tail making spots by patting it on the paper and swishing it side to side.

6. Talk with him about the colors and actions he is using.

7. If desired, glue can be added to the paint so the toddler can leave the bunny tail on the paper after he is finished painting.

To do again

Place large chunks of pillow stuffing in a dish tub for the toddlers to explore. Talk with them about the soft texture and encourage them to pull apart the stuffing to make bunny tails. Provide tongs for the toddlers to pick up the stuffing and small containers with lids for them to stuff the cotton inside. Let the toddlers make a collage of bunny tails on paper with glue or on the sticky side of self-adhesive paper when finished with the sensory activity.

Skills encouraged

fine motor, creative expression

Language to use with toddlers

bunny tails
fluffy
soft
cotton
swish
pat
spots
spread apart
stuff inside

Materials

large cotton balls or pillow
  stuffing
paint
pie tins or flat containers
clothespins
paper
glue

Put the Tail Game

Have toddlers match fluffy tails to a bunny for a toddler version of the classic pin the tail games.

Skills encouraged

cognitive, matching, fine motor

Language to use with toddlers

rabbit
bunny
tail
pompom
match
same
color

Materials

large craft pompoms
paper
scissors
felt
box
milk jug tops or craft fur

To do

1. Gather two to four different colors of large craft pompoms. Milk jug tops, circles cut out of paper or craft fur for bunny tails can be used instead if needed.

2. Cut out two to four rabbit silhouettes from felt without tails in colors that match the pompoms or the other items.

3. Glue the rabbits to the inside of a shirt-size gift box.

4. Draw a circle the size of a quarter where the tail should be.

5. Encourage the toddler to put the pompom tail on the bunny of the same color. Talk with her about the colors and the soft texture of the tail.

6. Store the bunny tails inside the box.

To do again

Cut carrots and rabbits out of felt in two to three different sizes for the toddlers to feed the bunnies a carrot of the same size (small, medium or large).

Teaching hints

The large craft pompoms work best as they pass the choke test while the smaller ones do not and require constant supervision.

For Toddlers in Summer

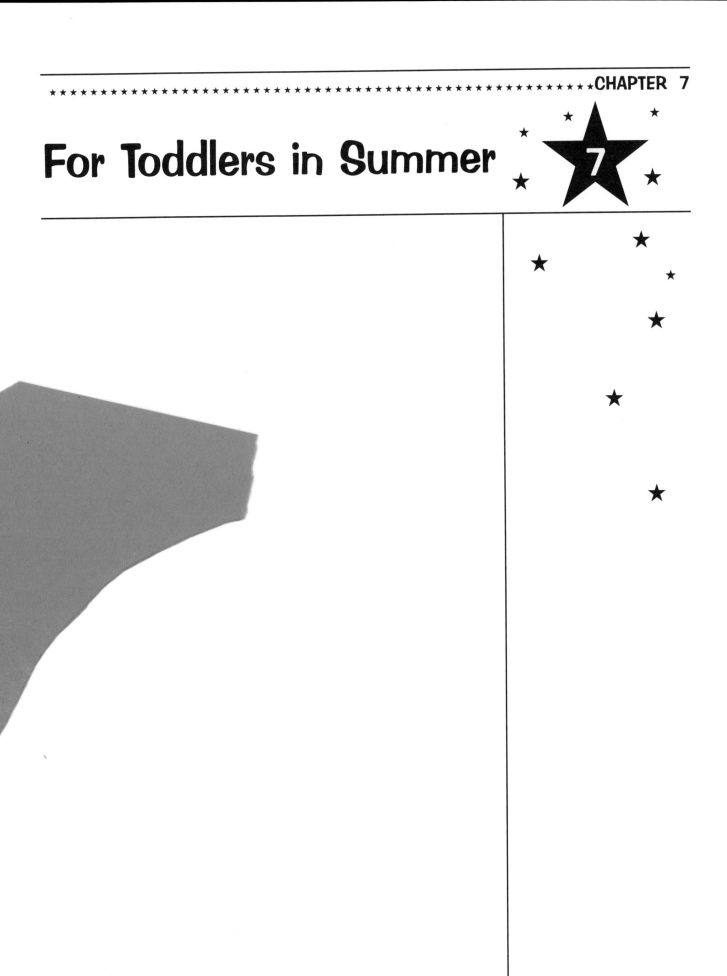

Snail's Pace

Slow down with toddlers to look for snails, ants and other tiny creatures.

Skills encouraged

language, fine motor

Language to use with toddlers

look
see
go slow
tiny
crawling ants
doodle bugs
worms
snails

Materials

plastic jar

To do

1. Take a walk around the school. Look for tiny creatures on the ground, such as ants, bugs, snails, worms, spiders.

2. Let older toddlers collect bugs in a plastic jar.
Note: Keep bugs only for a short period of time. Release them where they were found.

3. Look for little creatures on the playground too.

4. Spend time watching the bugs. Talk with the toddlers about the insects and spiders.

To do again

If the school has a garden, look for snails, worms or other insects near the plants. Adopt a few of the snails for a day as a new class pet. Ask a parent with a garden to bring in a few snails or worms for the toddlers to see.

Teaching hints

Toddlers learn from our reactions, so it is important to put any negative feelings about insects and spiders aside. While the bug doesn't need to crawl on you, it is important to show interest in the creature. Encourage the toddlers to respect nature and not step on the bugs.

Home connections

Spend time looking for bugs and other creatures in the backyard or around the neighborhood. Collect bugs, watch ants crawling and take time to even enjoy a snail.

All Kinds of Spiders

Explore colors, sizes and emotions with toddlers with variations on the all-time popular "Eeensy Weensy Spider."

To do

1. Sing the traditional song "The Eensy Weensy Spider" with the toddlers.

> *The eensy weensy spider went up the water spout. (pretend to climb like a spider using fingers)*
> *Down came the rain and washed the spider out. (wiggle fingers in downward motion)*
> *Out came the sun and dried up all the rain. (raise hands overhead)*
> *And the eensy weensy spider went up the spout again. (climb with finger again)*

2. Change the "eensy weensy" part to any of the following types of spiders.
   "big" or "super huge" (sing in loud voice and slowly)
   "teeny weeny" spider (sing in quiet voice and quickly)
   "silly willy" spider (sing in squeaky/silly voice)
   "happy snappy" spider (sing quickly)
   "angry" spider (sing in angry voice)
   "whining" or "crying" (sing with a whine)

3. Sing about different colors using spiders cut out of construction paper. Use the paper spiders like a puppet to emphasize the color while singing the verse.

4. Let older toddlers suggest what type of spider they want to sing about with the verse. Be prepared for some "hamburger spiders" or "Raggedy Ann spiders."

Suggested book

Read *The Itsy Bitsy Spider* by Iza Trapani.

To do again

Look at a few pictures of spiders with the toddlers. Talk about the features of the spider and that their house is a web.

Skills encouraged

language, fine motor

Language to use with toddlers

spider
eensy weensy
small
big
huge
hairy
black
brown
silly
crying
happy
angry

Materials

construction paper
scissors

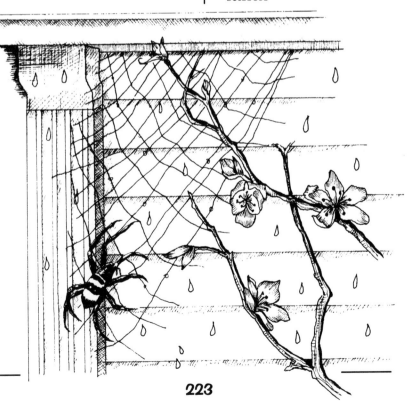

Little Muffet

Little Miss Muffet can do more than fall off her tuffet. Use the familiar nursery rhyme to explore insects, parts of the body and names.

Skills encouraged

language

Language to use with toddlers

names
sat
tuffet
curds and whey
spider
mosquito
bee
tickled
chin
knee
head
leg
foot

Materials

spider puppet (optional)

To do

1. Say "Little Miss Muffet" with the toddlers. Add actions to the rhyme in the following ways:

> *Little Miss Muffet (show little size with hands)*
> *Sat on her tuffet (touch floor)*
> *Eating her curds and whey. (pretend to eat)*
> *Along came a spider (wiggle fingers like spider)*
> *And sat down beside her, (put extended fingers on floor like a spider)*
> *And frightened Miss Muffet away. (run two fingers along floor)*

2. Vary the rhyme with the children's names and parts of the body using fingers like a crawling spider, such as:

> *Little April Muffet*
> *Sat on her tuffet*
> *Eating her curds and whey. (or substitute in child's favorite food)*
> *Along came a spider (wiggle fingers)*
> *That crawled over beside her, (crawl fingers towards child)*
> *All the way up to her head. (touch child's head)*

Substitute individual names, foods and parts of the body.

3. For a more playful version, have spider tickle the child with the following ending to the verse as an example:
> *...That crawled over beside her*
> *And tickled her under the chin.*

4. If possible, use a spider puppet with the verse too.

To do again

Change the verse to other insects, such as mosquito, bee, ladybug.

Home connections

Name parts of the body while your toddler bathes with the following bath time variation:
> *Little (or big if your toddler insists) Erin Babe (child's name)*
> *Sat in the bathtub*
> *Getting her body all clean.*
> *Along came a soap bug (or water bug) (make bar of soap "swim" in the water)*
> *That swam over to her and washed her shoulder clean. (rub bar of soap on child's shoulder)*

Mary's Creatures

Explore all sorts of bugs, spiders and creatures with the very adaptable verse of "Mary Had a Little Lamb."

To do

1. Cut small butterfly shapes out of different colors of felt.

2. Allow each toddler to pick out one to hold. Sing the following to the tune of "Mary Had a Little Lamb" with each child's name and color of butterfly.

> *Ann and Ray have green butterflies,*
> *Green butterflies, green butterflies.*
> *Ann and Ray have green butterflies*
> *In their hands.*

3. Repeat the verse with the other names and colors.

4. Show the toddlers pictures of different insects and spiders. Talk with them about the creatures.

5. Let each child pick out a picture to hold. Vary the song according to the child's name and insect in the picture.

To do again

Sing the song with pictures of other types of animals. Use pictures, stuffed animals and puppets when possible.

Home connections

Use the variations of "Mary Had a Little Lamb" at home to sing about family members and their clothing, favorite toys or even physical features, such as:

> *Cassie has curly blonde hair*
> *Curly blonde hair, curly blonde hair.*
> *Cassie has curly blonde hair*
> *On her head.*

Skills encouraged

language

Language to use with toddlers

names
colors
butterfly
ladybug
bumblebee
spider
little

Materials

felt
scissors
pictures of insects and
   spiders

Here's the Buzz

Toddlers can explore bees and their characteristics through simple songs and chants.

Skills encouraged

language, fine motor

Language to use with toddlers

bees
honey
buzz
fly
beehive
knee
toes
nose

Materials

pictures of bees
bread and honey
felt and scissors (optional)
bee puppet (optional)

To do

1. Look at pictures of bees with the toddlers. Talk about how they make honey, fly around and buzz. Put honey on a small piece of bread for toddlers to taste.

2. Say the following chant about bees.

> *Here is the beehive. (cup hands together)*
> *Where are the bees?*
> *Soon they'll come out of their hive.*
> *1, 2, 3, 4, 5 (hold up fingers one at a time)*
> *BUZZZZ! (wiggle fingers like bees)*

3. Cut a beehive and five bees (black ovals work fine for bees) out of felt to use at the flannel board with the chant if desired.

4. Sing the following variation of "Baa, Baa Black Sheep" to refer to bees and honey.

> *Buzz, buzz Mr. Bee*
> *Have you any honey?*
> *Yes ma'am, yes ma'am*
> *I sure do.*
> *Some for your bread, some for your cookies,*
> *And some to taste just on your finger!*

5. Say the following verse about a bee.

> *A bumblebee came to visit me,*
> *First she landed on my knee. (touch knee)*
> *Then she tried to land on my toes. (touch toes)*
> *Now she's sitting on my nose! (touch nose)*

This is a fun chant to use with a bee puppet if possible, touching the parts of the child's body.

To do again

Explore other creatures through books and songs throughout the year, especially those that the toddlers seem to have a special interest in or talk about.

Chapter Seven

Here Comes the Bumblebee!

The thrilling anticipation of a playful bumblebee game elicits rounds of giggles and requests to do it again with many toddlers.

To do

1. Say the following while pretending that your index finger is a bumblebee.

> *Hereeeeee comes the (use index finger to pretend to be a flying bee) (PAUSE) Bumblebee! (gently tickle toddler under the arm or chin)*

2. Repeat as the child shows interest by tickling the child in different places and lengthen the pause for increased anticipation.

3. With older toddlers, have a small group pretend to be flowers by laying on the floor or sitting in a circle around you. Talk with them about what color of flowers they each want to be. Remind them how bees love to land on flowers.

4. Say the verse while pretending to be a bee (with index finger) that flies over the flowers and then lands on a flower. Use a long pause as the bee flies slowly over each child.

5. Let the bee land by gently tickling a child. Talk about the color of flower he landed on (the child's choice of color or what he is wearing).

6. Repeat as the toddlers show interest. Say "I wonder what color of flower the bee will find next?" to spark their interest.

To do again

Have the children hold large felt or paper shapes of flowers of different colors and use a bumblebee puppet to do the tickling.

Teaching hints

The bumblebee tickle game works well during diaper changes for a playful one-on-one interaction. With all tickle games, remember to keep the tickles gentle and to be respectful of toddlers that do not want to be tickled.

Home connections

Use the bumblebee as a way to redirect a toddler's attention away from a conflict in a playful way.

Skills encouraged

social interaction, language

Language to use with toddlers

bumblebee
flowers
colors
land
tickle

Materials

none needed

Honeybee Yellow

This is an ideal time to explore the color yellow with toddlers.

Skills encouraged

fine motor, sensory exploration, creative expression

Language to use with toddlers

honey
sticky
yellow
bright
color
paint
sun
bananas

Materials

honey
yellow fingerpaint
yellow paint
paintbrush
paper
yellow markers and crayons
yellow collage materials
yellow objects
yellow ribbons
yellow foods
yellow food coloring
basket or dish tub

To do

1. Taste honey with the toddlers. Talk about the sweetness and the color of the honey.

2. Over a period of days, let the toddlers explore the color yellow just like the honeybees with the following:
   ✓ yellow fingerpaint
   ✓ shades of yellow paint at the easel or tabletop
   ✓ yellow markers and crayons
   ✓ a collage of scraps of yellow paper, ribbon, yarn.

3. Add a variety of yellow objects to a basket or dish tub for the toddlers to explore on their own, such as yellow ribbons, yellow fabric scraps, yellow toys, yellow margarine containers. Talk with the toddlers about the items, the color yellow and so on.

4. Dance or parade around the room with yellow ribbons like bees.

5. Add yellow food color to the water at the sensory tub. Use yellow margarine tubs with the colored water. Or, add a few drops of yellow food color to shaving cream.

6. Have a Yellow Day where everyone wears yellow for a bright day that is "sweet as honey." Serve a yellow snack, such as bananas and lemonade.

To do again

Explore other colors with just a change of color to the above activities.

Spider Webs

Yarn glued to poster board in the design of spider webs makes a unique texture board for toddlers.

To do

1. Read *The Very Busy Spider* by Eric Carle with the toddlers. Encourage them to feel the web as it emerges on each page.

2. Cut a dark colored piece of poster board into fourths.

3. Paint a thin layer of glue on the poster board.

4. Place white yarn, rickrack or string on the glue in a web-pattern on the poster board. Make a different pattern on each poster board.

5. Encourage the toddlers to feel the spider webs.

6. Talk with the toddlers about the bumpy textures of the yarn webs. Look at pictures of spiders as well.

7. Attach the poster boards to the wall for the toddlers to feel the spider webs on their own.

To do again

Put white masking tape on the table in web patterns for the toddlers to feel and pull up the tape for a fine motor challenge.

Home connections

Try to find some real spider webs around the house or yard with your toddler.

Skills encouraged

sensory exploration, fine motor

Language to use with toddlers

spider webs
spiders
home
string
yarn
feel
design
bumpy

Materials

The Very Busy Spider by Eric Carle
poster board
glue
paintbrush
scissors
white yarn, string or rickrack

Toddler Webs

Spider webs are often hard to find and easily break when touched. Instead, use white yarn or string with the toddlers for sensory and art activities to explore spiders and their homes.

Skills encouraged

fine motor, creative expression

Language to use with toddlers

string
yarn
spider web
feel
soft
long
short
colors
stick

Materials

white string or yarn
scissors
dish pan or sensory table
tongs (optional)
large plastic spiders or spider
   puppets (optional)
self-adhesive paper or glue
   and paper
paint
clothespins

To do

1. Cut white yarn or string into various lengths from 3"-10". Place the yarn or string in a dish tub or sensory table for the toddlers to feel.

2. Provide tongs for them to use to try to pick up the strings if desired. Add large plastic spiders or spider puppets to the strings.

3. Talk with them about the feel of the string and the long and short lengths of the string.

4. Provide pieces of white yarn or string for the toddlers to make a collage on paper with glue or on the sticky side of self-adhesive paper.

5. A few circles for spiders cut out of black or brown paper can be added to the collage if desired.

6. Let older toddlers paint with string on dark paper. Attach the string to a clothespin. Dip the string in white paint and then encourage the toddler to swish it back and forth on the paper or fold the paper and pull the string out for a magical effect.

To do again

Fill the sensory tub with a variety of colors of yarn. Encourage older toddlers to pick out specific colors and fill a cup of the same color. Make a collage of yarn of all the colors in the rainbow or of colors related to the season.

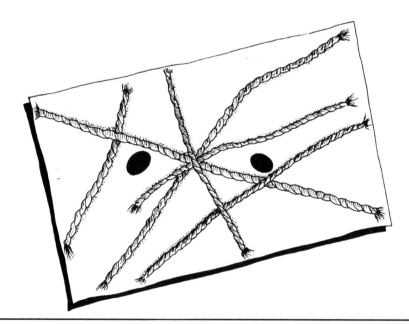

Very Busy Creatures

Small things, such as spiders and ants, fascinate toddlers. Toddlers can explore the world of these tiny creatures through nature walks and creative movement.

To do

1. Look at a few pictures of spider and ants with toddlers. Take a walk to look for spiders and ants or have a spider and ant search on the playground.

2. Encourage toddlers to crawl and be spiders and ants with the following chant.

> *Crawl like an ant,*
> *Crawl like an ant,*
> *Fast and quiet. (crawl quickly around room)*
>
> *Move like ants,*
> *Move like ants,*
> *All in a line. (encourage toddlers to crawl behind each other)*
>
> *Creep like a spider,*
> *Creep like a spider,*
> *Just like this. (crawl with legs straight)*
>
> *Spin like a spider,*
> *Spin like a spider,*
> *To make your web. (spin standing up or while crawling)*
>
> *Rest like a spider,*
> *Rest like a spider,*
> *In your web. (curl up in a ball)*

3. Encourage the toddlers to move like spiders or ants with the following variation to the tune of "Here We Go 'Round the Mulberry Bush."

> *This is the way the spiders crawl*
> *The spiders crawl, the spiders crawl.*
> *This is the way the spiders crawl*
> *Up to their web. (crawl like spiders)*

Substitute other actions related to spiders, such as spin, rest, catch a fly, eat. The verse can also be used with ants.

To do again

Pretend to be other small creatures, such as snails, butterflies, bees with the above chants and variation to "Here We Go 'Round the Mulberry Bush."

Home connections

Collect bugs in a bug jar with an older toddler (for a short period of time). Take the time to observe and really look at spiders, ants and other insects that are outside. Toddlers are not necessarily frightened by these creatures until they experience our reactions to them. Join in your toddler's natural curiosity and enjoy the wonders of nature.

Skills encouraged

language, gross motor

Language to use with toddlers

walk
look
crawl
spider
creep
spin
rest
web
ant

Materials

pictures of spiders and ants

Teaching hints

Toddlers do not necessarily fear or despise spiders and insects. They learn this from our reactions. It is important to put aside our own inhibitions or repulsion and show interest when finding spiders and insects with the children nearby. Show amazement and interest about any tiny creatures found during the day. Look at them with the toddlers, even from a distance.

Ants on a Log

Toddlers love to help make this easy and quite tasty snack.

Skills encouraged

sensory exploration, fine motor

Language to use with toddlers

celery
peanut butter
raisins
ants
log
sticky
crunchy
chewy
taste
eat
wash

Materials

celery
peanut butter
plastic knife
raisins

To do

1. Wash hands.

2. Give the toddler a stalk of celery to wash. Dry.

3. Have him help you spread peanut butter inside the stalk of celery with a plastic knife.

4. Give him raisins to put on the celery like ants walking on a log. Count the ants as he puts them on the log.

5. Talk with him about the crunchy celery, the sticky peanut butter, the chewy raisins, the colors and the tastes.

6. Save the log to eat for snack.

To do again

Fill celery with cream cheese or pimento cheese, or have celery with dip.

Home connections

Make Ants on a Log at home for a picnic snack to eat outside after looking for ants.

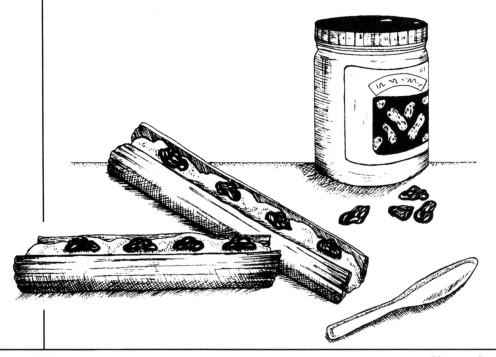

Busy, Busy Bees

Toddlers by nature are as busy as bees and can release some of their never-ending energy by pretending to be bees.

To do

1. Encourage the toddlers to move like busy bees by singing the following to the tune of "The Farmer in the Dell."

> *The bees fly all around,*
> *The bees fly all around.*
> *Buzz, buzz the busy bees*
> *The bees fly all around. (pretend to fly around room on tiptoes)*
>
> *The bees spin in circles,*
> *The bees spin in circles.*
> *Buzz, buzz the busy bees*
> *The bees spin in circles. (spin in circles)*
>
> *The bees crawl on flowers... (crawl)*
>
> *The bees sleep in their hive... (the group pretends to sleep together)*

2. Listen to a recording of fast paced instrumental music, such as "The Flight of the Bumblebee." Encourage the toddlers to dance like bees to the music, moving around the room as the music plays. Add yellow ribbons if desired.

To do again

Pretend to be other flying insects, such as butterflies or ladybugs with variations to the above verse.

Teaching hints

Pretending to fly like bees works well as a transition when going to a different room or the playground. It will help focus the toddlers' attention and reduce running or other random behaviors.

Skills encouraged

gross motor, creative movement

Language to use with toddlers

bees
honey
spin
fly
buzz
land
flower
hive

Materials

instrumental music
yellow ribbons (optional)

Bee-utiful Flowers

Toddlers practicing matching colors as they "land" colorful bees on some "bee-utiful" flowers.

Skills encouraged

matching, cognitive

Language to use with toddlers

bee
flower
colors
match
same
land
fly
spider
web

Materials

paper
scissors
self-adhesive paper
poster board or file folder
envelope or resealable plastic
   bag
velcro pieces

To do

1. Cut two to five daisy flower shapes out of different colors of construction paper. Cut a small bee shape (oval with two wings for a simple version of a bee) out of the same colors.

2. Attach the flower shapes to a file folder or poster board. Vary the number of colors from two to five depending on the level of the class or individual children.

3. Cover the bees and poster board or file folder with clear self-adhesive paper or laminate the items for durability.

4. Attach an envelope or resealable freezer bag on the back to store the bee pieces.

5. Attach a small piece of velcro to each bee (hook side) and flower (fuzzy side) so the bee can stick to the flowers.

6. Encourage the toddler to match the bee to the flower by landing (placing) the bee on the same color.

7. Talk with the child about the colors and how bees land on flowers.

To do again

Cut out small and large bees and flowers for the toddlers to match by size. Or match spider shapes to webs made from different colors of yarn.

Teaching hints

Toddlers often recognize colors before they can name them. Ask the toddler to show you or point to a specific color before asking them, "What color is this?" Toddlers will differ widely in their ability to recognize colors. Adjust the matching game to the level of the individual toddler by varying the number of colors. Some toddlers do best with only two options while some need the challenge of more colors.

Home connections

Watch bees working around flowers with your toddler.

Zoobilation

Create a zoo in the classroom with two all-time toddler favorites—stuffed animals and boxes.

To do

1. Collect stuffed animals and puppets of animals associated with the zoo, such as elephants, lions, bears, monkeys. Large plastic animals can also be used.

2. Gather boxes of different sizes that the animals can fit into for cages. Place the boxes on their side and cover the opening with strips of fabric or large ribbons.

3. Encourage the toddlers to put one animal in each box for a one-to-one correspondence activity.

4. Talk with the toddlers about the animals, their sounds, how they are cared for at the zoo, what they eat.

5. Provide additional props for older toddlers to play zoo keeper, such as:
   ✓ small boxes covered with brown paper for hay
   ✓ felt cut into fish shapes and fruit shapes
   ✓ plastic fruit
   ✓ dump trucks
   ✓ blocks for building more cages
   ✓ dog brush for brushing the animals

6. Encourage the toddlers to care for the animals like a zoo keeper.

7. Provide one or two large appliance boxes for the toddlers to pretend to be zoo animals in their cages or caves as well.

8. Have a picnic at the zoo for a special "zoobilation." Lay a sheet or blanket on the floor by the zoo animals and eat animal crackers for snack. Let each child hold one of the zoo animals. Or have a special "Animal Crackers Picnic" where everyone dresses in something with animals on it and brings a stuffed animal from home (see *Toddlers Together* activity).

Suggested book

Read books about zoo animals; *A Children's Zoo* by Tana Hoban has excellent pictures for toddlers.

To do again

Put large plastic zoo animals in a dish tub with a small amount of water and cloths for the toddlers to wash the animals. Other sensory materials can be used with the zoo animals, such as sand, hay or potting soil. Or, let the toddlers print with the plastic zoo animals (see Animal Prints on page 130).

Skills encouraged

pretend play

Language to use with toddlers

zoo
cages
zoo keepers
take care
feed
wash
animals
elephants
lions
monkeys
bears

Materials

stuffed animals or large
   plastic animals
boxes
strips of fabric or large
   ribbons
glue or tape
dump trucks
felt
blocks
large sheet or blanket
animal crackers

Home connections

Make cages for your child's stuffed animals from boxes or blocks, or construct a large cage under a table or between chairs with a blanket or sheet over the furniture.

Have You Ever...?

Introduce toddlers to a wide variety of animals and their movements with pictures and a few changes to "Have You Ever Seen a Lassie?"

Skills encouraged

language, gross motor

Language to use with toddlers

Have you ever seen...?
monkey
lion
seal
elephant
zoo
Move this way

Materials

pictures of or books about
  zoo animals

Teaching hints

End the movement activity with a sleeping animal to help refocus the toddlers' energy.

Home connections

Visit the zoo with your toddler. Talk with him about the foods and movements of the animals. Encourage your toddler to move like the animals at each cage or back at home. Sing the above verse with them. Bring animal crackers for a snack.

To do

1. Provide pictures of and books about zoo animals for the toddlers to look at. Talk with them about the different animals found at the zoo.

2. Hold up a picture of a zoo animal while singing the following to the tune of "Have You Ever Seen a Lassie?"

> *Have you ever seen an elephant, an elephant, an elephant*
> *Have you ever seen an elephant at the zoo.*

Sing about other animals found at the zoo.

3. Let older toddlers pick out their favorite zoo animal and hold up the picture while singing the verse. Vary the ending to include the child's name if desired.

> *Have you ever seen an ostrich...*
> *That is Marc's favorite.*

4. With older toddlers, add additional verses for a gross motor activity.

> *Have you ever seen a monkey, a monkey, a monkey*
> *Have you ever seen a monkey jump up and down this way. (jump)*

Other suggestions include:

> *...lion...prowl around this way (crawl slowly)*
> *...elephant...swing his trunk this way (swing arm like trunk)*
> *...gorilla...stamp his feet this way (stamp feet)*
> *...giraffe...stand up tall this way (stand on tiptoes)*
> *...flamingo...on one leg this way (stand on one leg)*
> *...bear...sleep quietly this way (curl up on floor)*

Use your imagination, and also let the toddlers make suggestions for animals.

Suggested book

Read *1, 2, 3 to the Zoo* by Eric Carle to the toddlers. Talk with them about the animals in the book.

To do again

Use the variation to "Have You Ever Seen a Lassie?" with other animal groups, such as farm animals or pets.

Walking Through the Zoo

Enter the world of animals at the zoo with a traditional rhyme about seeing all sorts of animals.

To do

1. Look at pictures of different animals found in the zoo.

2. Say the following traditional rhyme. Use the pictures, stuffed animals or puppets as a visual stimulus.

> *Walking through the zoo,*
> *What did I see, see, see?*
> *A huge lion roaring*
> *At me, me, me! (point to self)*
>
> *Walking through the zoo,*
> *What did I see, see, see?*
> *A baby seal waving*
> *At me, me, me!*
>
> *Walking through the zoo,*
> *What did I see, see, see?*
> *A silly monkey laughing*
> *At me, me, me!*

Repeat with other animals.

3. With older toddlers, move like the different animals while saying the rhyme. For example, crawl like a bear, stand tall like a giraffe, fly like an eagle.

Suggested book

Read *Polar Bear, Polar Bear* by Bill Martin.

To do again

Say the rhyme with other animal habitats, such as forest or farm.

Home connections

Say the rhyme while walking through the zoo, especially when an exhibit is crowded and your toddler might have to wait.

Skills encouraged

language, creative movement

Language to use with toddlers

zoo
animals
move
looking
me
lion
monkey
seal

Materials

pictures of zoo animals
stuffed animals or puppets of
 zoo animals (optional)

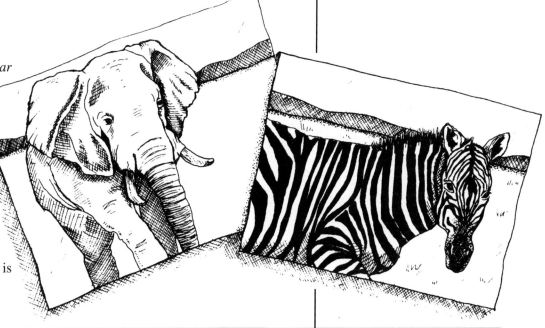

It's More Than Just Black & White

Go beyond the basic primary colors to explore black and white with a number of sensory activities.

Skills encouraged

creative expression, sensory exploration, fine motor

Language to use with toddlers

zebra
black
white
lines
draw
paint
olives
cheese

Materials

black markers and crayons
white paper
charcoal, chalk (optional)
black and white paint
black and white yarn, fabric or other materials
black olives
white cheese
black and white ribbons and scarves
black and white tape

To do

1. Provide black markers and crayons for the toddlers to color on white paper. For older toddlers, provide black and white markers, crayons, charcoal and chalk to use on light colored paper.

2. Provide black and white paint for the toddlers to use at the easel or tabletop.

3. Talk with them about their actions, the black and white lines and how black and white looks like the colors on a zebra.

4. Let older toddlers make a collage of black and white yarn, ribbon, fabric pieces and felt on the sticky side of self-adhesive paper or on any color of construction paper. Talk with the toddlers about the colors and textures.

5. Taste black olives (cut in half) and white cheese.

6. Dance with black and white ribbons and scarves. A number of black and white pieces of curling ribbon can be tied to a canning ring or small hoop for a dancing prop.

7. Let the toddlers play with black and white fabric, felt and scarves. Older toddlers can explore black and white strips of paper, streamers and tissue paper in a dish tub or sensory table.

8. Look for black or white things around the room. Borrow black and white baby toys from the parents for the toddlers to examine.

9. Put black electrical tape and white tape on the table in different patterns for the toddlers to explore. Allow them to pull up the tape as they desire.

10. End the focus with a Black and White Day where everyone dresses in "zebra colors."

To do again

Focus on other specific colors with the above activities over a period of a week or so.

Leo the Lion

Children enjoy expressing their power with loud sounds. A verse about powerful lions ending in a loud roar is sure to be a hit with toddlers, while it also introduces the concept of loud and soft.

To do

1. Show the toddlers a picture of a lion. Talk with them about the lion, the loud roar it makes, its size, big teeth.

2. Chant the following slowly and softly, except for the roar at the end.

> *Leo the lion*
> *Is the king outside,*
> *And his mouth is big and wide.*
> *ROAR! (loudly)*

3. If desired, use a lion puppet or stuffed animal with the verse.

4. Encourage the toddlers to crawl around slowly like a lion.

5. Show older toddlers a picture of a pride of lions. Talk with the toddlers about the mama (lioness) and the baby (lion cubs).

6. Repeat the above verse with changes to refer to "Lala the mama lioness" or "Lucky the lion cub." Sing the verse loud for Leo, medium for Lala and softly for Lucky.

To do again

Add this second verse for older toddlers:

> *Leo the lion*
> *When he stalks (crawl or walk hands on floor)*
> *How we wish we were inside.*
> *So we better run away and hide! (cover face)*
> *ROAR!*

Teaching hints

Use the verse to channel toddlers' loud, playful sounds into an acceptable form while also exploring the concept of loud and soft.

Skills encouraged

language, creative movement

Language to use with toddlers

lion
king
jungle
lioness
lion cub
outside
mouth
wide
roar
stalk
run away
hide

Materials

pictures of lions
lion puppet or stuffed animal
(optional)

The Mane Color

A collage of lion colors is a roaring fun way to explore textures, colors and lion sounds with toddlers.

Skills encouraged

fine motor, creative expression

Language to use with toddlers

lion
fur
mane
daddy lions
face
feel
fuzzy
yellow
brown
tan
gold

Materials

yellow, brown and tan yarn, craft fur, curling ribbon or felt
scissors
paper plates
glue

To do

1. Gather some or all of the following for a texture collage:
    ✓ yellow, brown and tan yarn
    ✓ pieces or strips of yellow, brown and tan craft fur
    ✓ pieces or strips of yellow, brown and tan felt
    ✓ yellow or gold curling ribbon

2. Cut out the inside of paper plates.

3. Place the collage items and paper plate ring out with glue. Encourage the toddlers to glue some of the items to the ring.

4. Talk with the toddlers about the colors and textures of the items they are gluing. Emphasize how the colors resemble lion's fur and the mane on a daddy lion.

5. When the collages are dry, encourage the toddlers to put it up to their face like a lion's mane and look at themselves in the mirror. Encourage them to growl like a lion or say "Leo the Lion" with their names in place of Leo (see Leo the Lion on page 239).

6. Have a parade of lions with the collages.

To do again

Provide a variety of colors for a "Rainbow Lion" or items of all one color on a piece of paper for a "Color Collage" related to the season or topic.

Teaching hints

For an easy collage without the mess of glue, have the toddlers attach the items to the sticky side of clear self-adhesive paper.

Monkey Tails

Monkey tails made from rope and yarn lead to lots of playful fun for toddlers.

To do

1. Cut up pieces of brown or black yarn, rope, macramé string. Put in a sensory tub or a dish tub for the toddlers to explore. If desired, add in small boxes, cups and tongs.

2. Talk with the toddlers about the colors, textures, long and short lengths and how the pieces look like monkey tails.

3. Let the toddlers make a collage of pieces of yarn and rope on construction paper with glue or on the sticky side of self-adhesive paper.

4. Older toddlers can paint with the pieces of string and rope. Hold the string or rope with a clothespin and dip the end in paint of the same color. Encourage the toddler to swish the monkey tail back and forth on a piece of paper.

5. Provide spools or large beads that pass the choke test and macramé rope or shoelaces for older toddlers to practice threading fancy monkey tails.

6. Provide pieces of string or yarn with round cereal or pretzels for the older toddlers to make their own "Monkey Tail Snack." These can also be hung on trees for bird feeders.

To do again

Tape an 8" piece of rope or macramé string to the backs of toddlers. Encourage them to dance like monkeys to upbeat music or to move like monkeys (see Monkey Business on the next page).

Skills encouraged

sensory exploration, creative expression, cognitive

Language to use with toddlers

monkey tails
long
short
colors
rope
yarn
string
swing

Materials

black or brown yarn, rope or macramé string
dish tub or sensory table
paper and glue or self-adhesive paper
paint
clothespins
spools or large beads
round cereal or pretzels

Monkey Business

Like monkeys, toddlers have boundless energy. Let them pretend to be monkeys with a chant about "monkey business" to help keep their physical play within bounds.

Skills encouraged

gross motor, creative movement

Language to use with toddlers

monkey
like to do
jump
dance
spin
clap
wiggle
shake

Materials

none needed

To do

1. Encourage the toddlers to move like monkeys with the following chant. Emphasize the beat.

> *The monkeys like to dance.*
> *Yes, they really like to dance.*
> *Monkey business keeps them busy.*
> *The monkeys like to dance. (dance)*

Additional suggestions include:
> *The monkeys like to...*
> > *...swing (swing arms)*
> > *...spin (spin around)*
> > *...jump (jump)*
> > *...wiggle (wiggle body)*
> > *...shake their heads (shake head)*

2. End the activity with the following to help calm the toddlers after being monkeys.

> *The monkeys like to rest... (lay down)*

To do again

Let the toddlers make suggestions of activities. Substitute the individual children's names in place of the monkeys, such as:

> *Greg likes to run.*
> *Yes, he really likes to run.*
> *Running running keeps him really busy.*
> *Greg likes to run. (run outside or let toddlers "run" on their knees inside)*

Teaching hints

Keep in mind that toddlers have a tremendous need to move their bodies. Use this chant at any time to help them focus their energy in positive ways.

Home connections

Use the chant to exercise with your toddler to keep both of you in good health.

Zoo Today

Give toddlers an opportunity to move their bodies and release all their energy in appropriate ways as they pretend to go to the zoo and join the animals.

To do

1. Read books and look at pictures of zoo animals with the toddlers. Talk with them about the different animals and special features and movements.

2. Encourage toddlers to be some of the zoo animals with you. Pretend to be the animal sleeping, moving around, playing, eating and then sleeping again. Follow the toddlers' lead in their interpretation of the animal's moving.

3. Chant or sing the following verses in a sing-song style about going to the zoo. Move like the animal to the beat of the chant.

> *We're going to the zoo today, zoo today, zoo today.*
> *We're going to the zoo today to see the animals. (march around room)*
>
> *We'll see the elephants, the elephants, the elephants.*
> *We'll see the elephants with the long trunks going up and down.*
>   *(put arm to nose like a trunk, move it up and down)*
>
> *We'll see the seals, the seals, the seals.*
> *We'll see the seals with the heads swaying side to side.*
>   *(sway head side to side)*
>
> *We'll see the kangaroos...jumping all around. (jump)*
>
> *We'll see the hippos...hiding in the water. (bend down, hide face)*

End with:

> *We're very tired and sleepy, tired and sleepy, tired and sleepy.*
> *We're very tired and sleepy after our trip to the zoo.*
>   *(lay down and rest head)*

4. Substitute other animals and actions. Let the toddlers make suggestions.

To do again

Change the chant to refer to other animal groups, such as going to the farm, to the forest.

Home connections

Visit the zoo with your toddler. Say the chant on the way to and from the zoo.

Skills encouraged

language, gross motor, creative movement

Language to use with toddlers

zoo
going
today
see
monkeys
jumping
elephant
long trunks
swinging
seals
heads
swaying
side to side

Materials

books about and pictures of
  zoo animals

Chugga Chugga Choo Choo

Toddlers still enjoy lap bouncing games. Take them on a train ride on your lap with a chugga chugga choo choo rhyme or a horse ride with a few gidayups.

Skills encouraged

gross motor

Language to use with toddlers

train
chugga chugga choo choo
horse
bounce
giddayup

Materials

none needed

To do

1. Sit on the floor with legs out straight. Have the toddler sit on your lap facing you.

2. Tell the toddler that the two of you will be going for a train ride. Ask her where she wants to go.

3. Hold the toddler's hands. Move your arms back and forth to the beat of the following chant.

> *Chugga chugga choo choo*
> *Chugga chugga choo choo*
> *Chugga chugga*
> *Chugga chugga*
> *Choooooo Choooooo.*

4. Vary the tempo of the chant, always ending with a slow choooooo choooooo like a train coming into the station.

To do again

Sitting the same way, take a horse ride with the toddler by bouncing your leg to the following chant.

> *Giddayup, giddayup, giddayup, up up*
> *Giddayup, giddayup, giddayup, up up*
> *Giddayup, giddayup, giddayup, up up*
> *Giddayup, (stop, with legs slightly up)*
> *Giddayup, up up!*

Home connections

Let your toddler take a different kind of horse ride on your legs. Lay down on your back with legs up in the air and bent at the knee. Have your child lay on your lower legs, holding her in place with your feet. Hold hands and bounce her gently with your legs moving slightly up and down to the giddayup beat.

Chapter Seven

Far Away, Up and Down

Toddlers travel to town and up and down together with the following variation to a traditional rhyme.

To do

1. Chant the following rhyme.

> *Seesaw, far away (rock back and forth to beat)*
> *This is the way*
> *We go to town.*
> *First go up, (arms up)*
> *Then go down, (arms down)*
> *This is the way we go to town. (rock back and forth)*

2. Have a toddler sit facing you with both legs outstretched. Hold his hands and rock back and forth to the beat.

3. Older toddlers can seesaw together in pairs.

4. Say the chant slowly then quickly.

To do again

Chant about other places, such as Grandpa's town, downtown even zoo town.

Home connections

Hold your toddler standing or sitting down. Rock back and forth to the beat. Lift your child up and down in the air with the "first go up, then go down" line in the chant.

Skills encouraged

language, gross motor, social interaction

Language to use with toddlers

seesaw
up and down
back and forth
way
town
downtown
together

Materials

none needed

London Bridge

Take cars and boats over and under a bridge with variations to the traditional nursery rhyme of "London Bridge."

Skills encouraged

language

Language to use with toddlers

bridge
down
build
wood
clay
cars
over
boats
under

Materials

none needed

To do

1. Sing the traditional nursery rhyme of London Bridge with the following actions to the beat of the tune:

> *London Bridge is falling down,*
> *Falling down, falling down. (hit floor with hands)*
> *London Bridge is falling down,*
> *My fair lady.*
>
> *Build it up with wood and clay,*
> *Wood and clay, wood and clay. (pound fists together)*
> *Build it up with wood and clay,*
> *My fair lady.*

2. Add the following verses as the toddlers show interest:

> *The cars go over the bridge,*
> *Over the bridge, over the bridge. (make over movement with hand)*
> *The cars go over the bridge,*
> *My fair lady. (or, on their trip)*
>
> *The boats go under the bridge*
> *Under the bridge, under the bridge. (make under movement*
>   *with hand)*
> *The cars go under the bridge,*
> *My fair lady. (or, on the water)*

Chapter Seven

Treasure Hunt

Take a walk with the toddlers to hunt for special things around the school. They will surely find their own treasures.

To do

1. Show toddlers pictures of things they might see on a walk around the school grounds, such as cars, truck, wheels, tree, clouds, bird, bugs, ants. Talk with them about the items.

2. Take a walk to look for the items. Take the pictures along as a guide.

3. Say the following chant while hunting for the items.

> *We're searching, we're searching*
> *We're searching for a... (state an item)*
>
> *We found it, we found it*
> *We found a ... (state item) right here.*

4. Talk about the cars, trucks, wheels, trees, clouds, insects that they see on their treasure hunt. Emphasize the colors and sizes of the items. Spend time to examine the objects as long as the toddlers remain interested.

5. Write down what the toddlers saw on their treasure hunt to make a "On our walk today, we saw" chart for the parents to see. List each child's name with the object that truly caught his interest. This will help parents in talking with their child about the walk.

To do again

Do a treasure hunt on the playground or in the classroom with pictures. School supply catalogs works as an excellent guide.

Teaching hints

Follow the toddlers' interest while on the walk because it is their own treasures that will capture their interest.

Home connections

Take a treasure hunt walk at home looking for specific items, such as a red car, blue truck, mail box. Look at all the different kinds and colors of vehicles and houses around the neighborhood.

Skills encouraged

language, cognitive, gross motor

Language to use with toddlers

look for
search
find
see
outside
colors
cars
truck
wheels
trees
bird
bugs
ants

Materials

pictures
paper and marker

Toddler's Set of Wheels

Toddlers love a parade. Let them show off the favorite set of wheels with a parade of toddler wheel toys.

Skills encouraged

gross motor

Language to use with toddlers

parade
wheels
ride
pull
push
follow
decorate
favorite

Materials

toddler riding toys, push toys, pull toys
boxes and rope
bows
ribbons
marching music

To do

1. Provide a variety of toddler riding and push/pull toys for the toddlers. Simple pull toys can be made from boxes and rope (see Pull Toy Boxes in *Toddlers Together*).

2. Have each toddler pick out a "set of wheels" she wants to use in a parade. Cars, trucks, trains and other vehicles can also be carried in the parade if the toddler prefers.

3. Older toddlers can help decorate some of the riding toys, if desired.

4. Put on lively or marching music. Encourage the toddlers to follow you in a "parade of wheels" around the classroom or playground.

To do again

Have a parade of cars and trucks around the classroom. Have the toddlers crawl behind you as they push their car or truck along on the ground.

Home connections

Have your toddlers help you decorate their stroller, wagon or riding toy for a parade around the neighborhood. Add a favorite doll or stuffed animal to the "float." Invite a neighbor or two along for a very special stroll.

We'll Be Comin'

"She" has been comin' round the mountain forever. Now it's time for toddlers to show how they can come and move!

To do

1. Look at pictures of and talk about different forms of transportation with the toddlers.

2. Sing about ways to travel with variations to the tune of "She'll Be Coming 'Round the Mountain."

>   *We'll be walking down the sidewalk when we come.*
>   *(walk around room)*
>   *Hi, guys! (wave hand)*
>   *We'll be walking down the sidewalk when we come.*
>   *Hi, guys!*
>   *We'll be walking down the sidewalk, we'll be walking down*
>   *the sidewalk,*
>   *We'll be walking down the sidewalk when we come.*
>   *Hi, guys!*
>
>   *We'll be riding on the train when we come. (walk on knees with arms*
>   *moving like wheels on the train)*
>   *Choo, choo! (pretend to blow whistle)*
>
>   *We'll be rowing the boat when we come. (sit and pretend to row boat)*
>   *Splash, splash!*
>
>   *We'll be flying on the airplane when we come. (walk around room*
>   *with arms stretched out to the side)*
>   *Zoom, zoom! (point up to sky)*

3. Substitute children's names in place of "we'll" and the toy vehicles they are using, such as:

>   *Jimmy will be driving the truck when he comes...*

Suggested book

Read *Train Ride* by June Crebbin with older toddlers.

To do again

Explore other ways of moving in the room or on the playground.

>   *We'll be crawling around the room (playground) when we*
>   *come...(crawl)*
>   *We'll be jumping...(jump)*
>   *We'll be marching...(march)*

Skills encouraged

language, gross motor

Language to use with toddlers

we
come
walking
sidewalk
riding
train
choo choo
rowing
boat
splash
flying
plane
zoom
jumping
crawling

Materials

pictures of types of
  transportation

Teaching hints

Use the song as a transition when toddlers have to travel together to the playground or another room. The verses will focus their energy into "going" rather than running or pushing.

Home connections

Take a walk. Do the activities while singing the verses as you both go down the sidewalk. Think of new ways to "travel" around the neighborhood.

Up in the Clouds

Toddlers relax with a unique sensory experience of flying up in the clouds.

Skills encouraged

sensory exploration

Language to use with toddlers

clouds
white
fluffy
soft
airplanes
fly
sky
shaving cream

Materials

shaving cream
table or flat tray
plastic airplanes

To do

1. Put shaving cream out on a table or a flat tray.

2. Place plastic airplanes in the shaving cream.

3. Encourage the toddlers to fly the airplanes through the shaving cream clouds.

4. Talk with them about the airplanes and how the shaving cream looks like white fluffy clouds.

To do again

Cut airplane shapes out of plastic milk jugs or lightweight boxes if small planes are not available. Color the planes with permanent markers to have them show up in the shaving cream.

Teaching hints

Gel shaving cream provides a different experience as the toddlers can make the shaving cream clouds appear as they play with the gel.

Home connections

Let your toddler play with shaving cream in the bathtub with airplanes, boats or just by itself.

Chapter Seven

On the Airplane

Sing about the special features of airplanes with variations to the all-time favorite of "Wheels on the Bus."

To do

1. Look at pictures of airplanes. Talk about them with the toddlers.

2. Sing about airplanes with variations to the very familiar tune of "Wheels on the Bus":

> *The wings on the plane fly through the clouds, through the clouds,*
>   *through the clouds,*
> *The wings on the plane fly through the clouds*
> *Up in the sky. (hold arms out to the side)*
>
> *The propellers on the plane go 'round and 'round, 'round and*
>   *'round, 'round and 'round.*
> *The propellers on the plane go 'round and 'round*
> *Up in the sky. (roll hands)*
>
> *The people on the plane look out the window, look out the*
>   *window, look out the window.*
> *The people on the plane look out the window*
> *Up in the sky. (hold hands up to eyes)*
>
> *The pilot of the plane says fasten your seatbelt, fasten your seatbelt,*
>   *fasten your seatbelt.*
> *The pilot of the plane says fasten your seatbelt*
> *Up in the sky. (pretend to fasten seatbelt)*

3. Additional suggestions include:

> *The wipers on the plane go swish, swish, swish...*
> *The lights inside the plane go on and off...*
> *The shade on the window goes up and down...*
> *The children on the plane take a nap...*

Home connections

Watch airplanes arriving and departing with your toddler when picking up people at the airport or visit the airport for a special outing. Sing the verses about airplanes while waiting. When the planes taxi, include verses for planes on the ground, such as:

> *Wheels go 'round and 'round...*
> *The ground crew says come this way...*
> *Suitcases on the belt go up and down...*
> *The people get on and off...*
> *The families hug and kiss...*

Skills encouraged

language, fine motor

Language to use with toddlers

airplane
up in the sky
wings
flies through the clouds
propellers
round and around
people
window
pilot
fasten seatbelt

Materials

pictures of airplanes

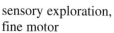

Under Construction

Add cars and trucks with gravel or sand to the sensory tub for toddlers to make roads under construction.

Skills encouraged

sensory exploration,
fine motor

Language to use with toddlers

cars
trucks
dump trucks
gravel
sand
move
fill
dump

Materials

brown wet sand or aquarium
    gravel
small vehicles
dish tub or sensory table

To do

1. Put brown aquarium gravel or wet sand in a dish tub or sensory table with cars, trucks, dump trucks, front end loaders.

2. Let the toddlers explore the vehicles and gravel or sand.

3. Talk with them about the items, their actions and how they can build a road.

4. Take the construction site outside too. This works especially well in the wet sand after it rains.

To do again

Let the toddlers wash the vehicles with a small amount of water and old toothbrushes.

Teaching hints

Use cars and trucks that pass the choke test with toddlers. While the smaller cars and trucks really interest the older toddlers, they do require close supervision and should only be used when a teacher can be present the entire time.

Home connections

Wet the sand in your child's sand box and build roads with the cars, trucks and construction vehicles. Use sticks and pieces of wood if desired.

Chapter Seven

Sail Away

Drift away into a world of adventure with a sailboat made from your lap and a traditional sailing song.

To do

1. Have the toddler sit in your lap. Tell her you are her pretend sailboat that rocks side to side.

2. Sing the following to the tune of "Drunken Sailor." Use the child's name. Rock side to side to the beat.

> *I'm sailing a boat with a girl named Tessie.*
> *I'm sailing a boat with a girl named Tessie.*
> *Early in the morning (or, all day long). (rock side to side)*
>
> *Aye, aye, and up she rises.*
> *Aye, aye, and up she rises.*
> *Early in the morning. (hold child's hands up and rock side to side)*

3. Repeat the verse as the child shows interest.

Suggested book

Read *Sail Away* by Donald Crews.

To do again

Sing about a row boat. Have younger toddlers sit in your lap and move back and forth to the beat. Older toddlers can sit facing you, moving back and forth as you both hold hands. Sing the following:

> *I'm rowing a boat with a boy named Kenny...*

Teaching hints

Both touch and the rocking motion calms upset or overly active toddlers. Use this verse as a way to help toddlers relax or when they need a few minutes of extra attention.

Home connections

A perfect good morning activity to sing to your sleepy toddler before "sailing off" into another day.

Skills encouraged

language

Language to use with toddlers

boat
sailing
name
boy
girl
rocking
rowing
morning
day

Materials

none needed

Seashell

Open up the world of the ocean to toddlers with a chant about seashells and sea life.

Skills encouraged

language

Language to use with toddlers

seashell
story
tell me
ocean
sea
fish
whales
sharks

Materials

shells
basket

To do

1. Look at different kinds of shells with the toddlers. Talk with them about the rough and smooth textures, the colors, sizes.

2. Place some out in a basket for them to examine on their own. See the activities for shells in *Toddlers Together* for more ways to explore shells with the toddlers.

3. Show the toddlers how to hold up a conch shell to their ear to hear the "ocean."

4. Encourage them to hold a shell (any type of shell will do) up to their ear with the following chant.

> *Seashell, seashell*
> *Tell a story to me.*
> *Tell me about the ocean*
> *And all about the sea.*

5. Add another verse if desired:

> *Seashell, seashell*
> *Tell a story to me.*
> *Tell me about the fish*
> *With you in the sea.*

Suggested book

Read *The Owl and The Pussy Cat* illustrated by Jan Brett. Point out the seashells in the illustrations.

To do again

For older toddlers, look at pictures of and sing about specific types of sea life on the third line, such as a whales, sharks, sea horses. Hold a picture up of the creature if possible from books, such as *The Owl and the Pussy Cat* or *Sea Animals* by Amy Erickson.

Home connections

Collect shells at the beach with your toddler. Bring some home for your toddler to wash with old toothbrushes in the sink or in a baby bath tub outside for some relaxing water play.

Ocean Treasures

As precious as any ocean treasure, a toddler's scribbles are their "most important marks." Display the toddlers drawings prominently on the bulletin board as a display of ocean treasures.

To do

1. Cut fish shapes out of paper. Make big, little, different types and colors so the toddlers can have a choice.

2. Have the toddler pick out what kind of fish she wants to color.

3. Provide markers or crayons for the toddlers to make her "most important marks" with on her fish.

4. Talk with the toddlers about the colors she is using and the marks on the paper.

5. Put blue paper or fabric on the bulletin board or a section of the wall for water. Let the toddler show you where she wants her fish in the water.

6. Let the toddler color another fish shape is she desires.

7. When all the fish have their "most important marks," cover them and the water with blue cellophane or plastic for a class aquarium.

8. Label the display "Ocean Treasures" or "A Most Important Aquarium." Encourage the toddlers to show their parents their "most important marks" on their fish.

To do again

Use watercolors or paint on the fish shapes. Also, add a few shell shapes for the toddlers to color or paint.

Teaching hints

Emphasize to the parents how their toddler's scribbles are just as precious as any treasures found in the ocean.

Home connections

Prominently display your toddlers "most important marks" at home to show that you do value her early writing attempts. Have blank paper for your toddler to use at home with markers or crayons rather than coloring books.

Skills encouraged

fine motor, creative expression

Language to use with toddlers

fish
draw
paint
colors
aquarium
swimming
water

Materials

paper
scissors
markers or crayons
blue paper or fabric
tape
blue cellophane

Beach Bottles

Aquarium gravel and shells make an ideal filling to make colorful beach bottle shakers.

Skills encouraged

sensory exploration

Language to use with toddlers

colors
shake
sounds
gravel
rocks
water
empty
light
heavy

Materials

clear plastic soda bottles
hot glue gun
aquarium gravel
basket or small box

To do

1. Collect plastic soda, water or sport drink bottles, preferably clear ones.

2. Fill the bottles about 1/4 full with aquarium gravel. Fill each bottle with a different color if possible.

3. Secure the top tightly with a hot glue gun.

4. Place the bottles in a basket or small box on the shelf for the toddlers to explore on their own.

5. Talk with them about the colors and the sounds made as they shake and play with the bottles.

6. For older toddlers, fill three bottles with different amounts (empty, 1/4 and 1/2 full) of gravel. Talk with them about the empty, light and heavy bottles.

To do again

Fill bottles with small shells, sand and water for more ways to make beach bottles.

Home connections

Let your toddler practice pouring by letting him experiment with plastic bottles and cups in the bathtub or wading pool.

Beach Ball

Beach balls are more than just a toy for the beach. They are also ideal for motor skills fun in the classroom.

To do

1. Provide a few beach balls in the classroom or on the playground for the toddlers to use. Talk with them about the colors and sizes of the balls.

2. Let them watch you blow up the ball and watch it deflate. This fascinates many toddlers. Have them pretend to blow up their own beach ball by blowing into their hands.

3. The valves of the balls can be covered with tape if needed.

4. Encourage them to roll, toss, catch, kick the beach balls with you.

5. See additional activities with balls in *Toddlers Together*.

To do again

Add a few blow up swim toys to a small wading pool for the toddlers to explore without water in the classroom. Try a few large swim rings or floats in the cozy library area for the toddlers to sit in while looking at books.

Teaching hints

Since they are extremely light, beach balls are ideal to use inside with toddlers. Redirect a toddler who is throwing toys to throwing the beach balls. When helping older toddlers learn how to catch, beach balls work best because of their large size,

Home connections

Get your beach ball out of the family's beach bag! At home your toddler can use it for lots of fun without it blowing away like they often do at the beach.

Skills encouraged

gross motor

Language to use with toddlers

beach ball
light
colors
big
little
roll
toss
hit
catch
blow
air

Materials

beach balls
tape (optional)

Kick the Bucket

Don't be too quick to "kick the bucket." Sand buckets can be used with toddlers in a number of ways.

Skills encouraged

fine motor, cognitive

Language to use with toddlers

bucket
shovel
sand
colors
same
inside
smallest
biggest
full
empty

Materials

plastic sand buckets
plastic shovels or paper and
    scissors
shells

To do

1. Provide plastic buckets in the classroom for toddlers' dump and fill play. See what they do with the buckets on their own.

2. Have two or three buckets of different colors with shovels of the same color. Encourage the toddlers to match the colors by putting the shovel in the bucket of the same color. Cut shovels out of colored paper if plastic ones of the same color are not available. Talk with them about the colors.

3. Use two or three buckets of different sizes as a nesting activity. Encourage the toddlers to put the little buckets inside the larger ones. Talk with them about the sizes.

4. Have small and large shells for older toddlers to sort into small and large buckets.

5. Use the bucket with the following variation to "Jack Be Nimble" with older toddlers:

> *Flora be nimble, (child's name)*
> *Flora be quick,*
> *Flora jumped (stepped) over the bucket. (place bucket on the floor for*
>   *child to jump or step over)*

6. Use your imagination with the buckets. They can be used in a number of ways with toddlers.

To do again

Provide tennis or ping-pong balls (with older toddlers) with the buckets for loads of fun.

Home connections

Use buckets around the house to store and sort your toddler's toys with multiple pieces. Have a bucket of special toys for special times (see Saving for a Rainy Day on page 50). Let your toddler eat snack or lunch outside with his food in a bucket. Buckets also are handy in the car to hold food or special car toys.

Such a Rough Time

Sand added to fingerpaint makes for "such a rough time."

To do

1. Let the toddlers choose the color of fingerpaint he wants to use. Place a spoonful on a tray or piece of fingerpaint paper.

2. Sprinkle some sand on top of the paint.

3. Encourage the toddler to smear the paint and sand with his hands.

4. Talk with him about the color, the rough textures of the sand, his actions.

5. For comparison, let an older toddler paint with the fingerpaint without sand first. Talk about how smooth it is. Then, sprinkle some sand on top of the paper and talk with him about how it now feels (rough or bumpy) as he paints.

To do again

Pour glue thinned with water into a small dish. Provide a paintbrush for older toddlers to paint the glue on the paper. Fill a seasoning or spice container with holes in the top with some sand. Encourage the toddlers to shake the sand on the paper. Let them feel the rough texture when the glue has dried.

Skills encouraged

sensory exploration, fine motor, creative expression

Language to use with toddlers

sand
feel
rough
bumpy
paint
hands
shake

Materials

fingerpaint
tray or fingerpaint paper
sand

For Toddlers in Summer

Starfish

Toddlers practice counting to five with a chant about the legs on a starfish in the sea.

Skills encouraged

language

Language to use with toddlers

starfish
sea
me
1, 2, 3, 4, 5
counting
big
little

Materials

starfish, if possible
scissors
felt

To do

1. If possible, show the toddlers a starfish. Let them feel the bumpy textures. Count the legs. If more than one is available, compare the sizes.

2. Say the following chant about a starfish with the toddlers:

> *I'm a starfish in the sea. (hold hand with fingers stretched out*
> *   like a starfish)*
> *Take a close look at me*
> *And you will see*
> *Five legs on me.*
> *1, 2, 3, 4, 5 (count each finger with other hand)*

3. Cut big and little starfish (star shapes with bumpy edges) out of yellow felt for the toddlers to play with at the felt board and to use with the rhyme.

To do again

Cut big and little starfish out of yellow paper. Let the toddlers glue the starfish on blue or tan paper. Talk with them about the sizes, colors, shape.

Home connections

Visit a shell shop to see all kinds of starfish and other shells.

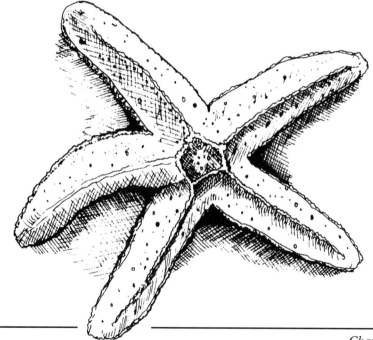

Chapter Seven

All Kinds of Boats

Introduce older toddlers to the many types of boats and their features with a simple chant and actions.

To do

1. Look at pictures of different kinds of boats. Talk with the toddlers about the special features of each boat.

2. Move like boats with the following simple chant:

> *Motorboat, motorboat*
> *Going fast in the water*
> *Motorboat, motorboat*
> *Bbbbbbb, bbbbbbbb (make engine noise and move hand*
>   *quickly along ground)*
>
> *Sailboat, sailboat*
> *Moving with the wind*
> *Sailboat, sailboat*
> *Whooooo, whooooo (blow air and sway side to side)*
>
> *Rowboat, rowboat*
> *Floating in the water*
> *Rowboat, rowboat*
> *Rowing backing and forth (pretend to row)*
>
> *Paddleboat, paddleboat*
> *Splashing in the water*
> *Paddleboat, paddleboat*
> *Paddle with your feet (move legs back and forth in pedaling fashion)*

To do again

Explore sizes of boats with the following two verses:

> *Big ship, big ship*
> *Out at sea*
> *Big ship, big ship*
> *Toot, toot (say loudly and slowly; hold hands far apart)*
>
> *Toy boat, toy boat*
> *In my bathtub*
> *Toy boat, toy boat*
> *Toot, toot (say softly and quickly; hold hands close together)*

Home connections

A fun chant to use at home with boats in the bathtub. Make up verses about the colors, sizes and types of toy boats.

Skills encouraged

language, gross motor

Language to use with toddlers

boats
motorboat
sailboat
rowboat
paddleboat
sounds
wind
water

Materials

pictures of boats

Hands-on Aquarium

Watching fish in the aquarium is relaxing for all ages. Yet, toddlers also want to feel the fish and plants in the aquarium. Let them do so with this special hands-on aquarium sensory activity.

Skills encouraged

sensory exploration

Language to use with toddlers

aquarium
fish
swim
shells
rocks
water
plants
feel
look

Materials

dish tub or sensory table
aquarium gravel
plastic fish, plastic aquarium
    plants
shells

To do

1. Place a thin layer of aquarium gravel in the bottom of a dish tub or sensory table with water.

2. Add in a few plastic fish, plastic aquarium plants and shells.

3. Let the toddlers explore the fish, plants and gravel. Talk with them about the textures, colors, the floating fish, how the fish like to hide in the plant.

4. If possible, let the toddlers look at the fish in a real aquarium.

To do again

Let the toddlers explore the gravel with cups, scoops, small strainers.

Home connections

Visit a pet store with your toddler. Spend time watching all the different fish in the aquariums.

Chapter Seven

Day at the Beach

Explore all the fun that can be had during a day at the beach with variations to the traditional "This is the Way" verse.

To do

1. Look at pictures of and read books about beach activities.

2. Sing the following to the tune of "Here We Go 'Round the Mulberry Bush."

> *This is the way we walk on the sand, walk on the sand, walk on the sand.*
> *This is the way we walk on the sand*
> *For a day at the beach. (walk around room)*
>
> *This is the way we swim in the water... (pretend to swim with arms)*
>
> *This is the way we jump in the waves... (jump)*
>
> *This is the way we pick up shells... (pretend to pick up shells)*
>
> *This is the way we lay on our towel... (lay down)*

3. Add other verses as desired:

> *This is the way we rub on sunscreen... (rub arms and legs)*
>
> *This is the way we catch some fish... (pretend to hold fishing pole)*
>
> *This is the way we feed the seagulls... (pretend to throw food in air)*

Use your imagination or let the toddlers make suggestions of other beach activities.

Skills encouraged

creative movement, gross motor

Language to use with toddlers

beach
swim
jump
waves
pick up
shells
lay
sand
rub
sunscreen
fish
seagulls

Materials

pictures of and books about beach activities

By the Sea

Spend a day at the seashore with the toddlers without the worry of sunburn by bringing the shells, sand and buckets to the classroom in a wading pool.

Skills encouraged

sensory exploration, fine motor, pretend play

Language to use with toddlers

sea shore
shells
sand
shovel
bucket
fill
empty
touch
rough
smooth
inside

Materials

small wading pool
shells, buckets, shovels
ocean environmental music
plastic tablecloth or shower
  curtain
goldfish crackers
oyster soup crackers

To do

1. Place a small wading pool in the classroom.

2. Add shells, buckets and shovels to the pool.

3. Let the toddlers explore the shells. They can get inside the pool if they desire.

4. Encourage to empty and fill the buckets with shells. Sort the shells into different buckets or even count the shells as they fill them.

5. Talk with them about the shells, the rough and smooth textures, colors.

6. Play ocean environmental music.

7. Have a "Day at the Seashore" with everyone wearing a swimsuit or beachwear and sandals. Have a picnic near or even in the "seashore" pool with goldfish and oyster soup crackers.

8. Look at pictures of and read books about the beach. Sing songs about shells and fish (see Seashell on page 254).

To do again

Add a small amount of sand with the shells to use with the buckets and shovels. Put a plastic tablecloth or shower curtain under the wading pool to help contain the sand. Or, take the pool of shells outside and add a small amount of water with sand for a sensory experience.

Teaching hints

Keep in mind that dump and fill is a favorite activity of all toddlers. The youngest ones will enjoy dump and fill play with the shells and buckets while the older toddlers will enjoy the fantasy of pretending to play at the seashore.

Skills Index

Terms Index